POLITICAL BEHAVIOR

Choices and Perspectives

Dean Jaros

Lawrence V. Grant

POLITICAL BEHAVIOR

Choices and Perspectives

Basil Blackwell • Oxford

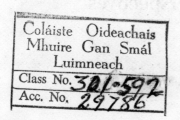

For Cindy, Lisa, Aaron, and Elizabeth

PREFACE

The "behavioral" approach to the study of politics is nothing more than some straightforward procedures for getting information, and it has a great deal to offer people who are curious about the way the political world functions. Often, however, the literature of political behaviorism has fallen at one of two extremes: the research article, which presents an array of facts or statistics with little interpretation, and the theoretical monograph, which attempts to explain political behavior by means of a single, all-encompassing abstraction. Both of these types of literature are undeniably valuable, but to a student new to the field they may seem opaque, technical, and difficult to approach. There is a need, we believe, for an introductory textbook that falls between the extremes, one that will acquaint students with a variety of theories, concepts, models, and research results while demonstrating alternate ways of coherent interpretation. This book attempts to serve that purpose.

Of course it has not been our intent to ignore or bypass the existing behavioral literature; indeed, our purpose has been to incorporate in this volume a generous sampling of the best work in the field. Many research results, for instance, are reproduced here nearly as they appeared in the original publications; in each case, however, we analyze the findings in some detail, asking such questions as: What problem confronted the author? Why did he choose his particular methods? And precisely what do the findings tell us? Similarly, we discuss a number of the dominant theoretical approaches in the field, such as role theory and attitude theory, in order to show the student the implications of choosing one rather than another.

We consider the idea of *choosing* important, and we have made it one of the main organizing principles of the book. Each of the first three parts begins with a Prologue in which we examine the choices that confront the student or practitioner of political behaviorism. Some of these choices are what make one a political behaviorist in the first place: one decides to approach politics in a certain way. Others are alternatives within the discipline, choices of substance or conceptualization.

Our hope is that the discussion of choices will show the student what it means to be a political behaviorist, while the frequent examples of research and theory give him or her a solid foundation for further reading on the subject. Needless to say, we have not been able to include everything of interest in this one volume. Since we have designed the book primarily for students, we have had to omit some professionally interesting nuances and qualifications. For example, we delve into neither the philosophical problems of causation and explanation nor the epistemology that leads to distinctions between fact and value. We treat such matters in a straightforward, "conventionally" scientific manner, on the assumption that students need to understand basic propositions before they can appreciate the subtleties.

Admittedly, then, our aims in this book are modest ones. In the concluding chapter, we examine the inevitable limitations of a textbook of this sort, as well as the incomplete nature of the behavioral approach itself. We trust that our treatment of political behaviorism is accurate, so far as it goes, and that the student will emerge from the book at least headed in the right direction. If that is indeed the case, we will feel that our time and effort have been well spent.

Many of the ideas in this book were initially presented to our undergraduate students. Their responses were invaluable in the process of evaluation and revision. To them, our sincere thanks. In addition, we would like to acknowledge the assistance of Gregory Caudill, presently a student at the University of Kentucky.

DEAN JAROS
LAWRENCE V. GRANT

CONTENTS

PART III   Purpose and Direction
Among the Behaviorists:
The Imposition of Order on Eclecticism

POLITICAL BEHAVIOR

Choices
and Perspectives

PART I

The
Discipline of
Political
Behaviorism:
Goals
and
Procedures

PROLOGUE

Disciplinary
Choices

Essentially, there are two questions affirmative answers to which make one a political behaviorist: "Is systematic, general information about political events desirable?" and "Is such information obtainable?" In this section we examine why behaviorists think the answer in both cases is yes.

In Chapters 1 and 2 we describe the basic logic of behavioral research. The thinking of behaviorists and the procedures they follow, as well as their goals and methods, are laid out in a way that leads one to the most basic choice of all: "Do I want to accept the discipline of political behaviorism? Do I want to become a political behaviorist?"

1

The
Logic of
Political
Behaviorism

The term "political behaviorism" identifies a particular way of studying political events. It is at the same time an unfortunate and a wise name. First, it is obvious with a little thought that all of what we commonly call political is dependent upon the *behavior* of human beings, either individually or as members of a class or group. Laws—often thought to be among the chief objects of political studies—clearly owe their existence to the fact that some human beings somewhere thought them desirable and succeeded in getting them passed. Moreover, the effect of laws does not proceed mystically from their formal existence, but is dependent upon the behavior of the citizens or subjects to whom the laws are addressed. Are they obeyed or are they not? If not, they are hardly important. And the question of whether laws are obeyed is patently a behavioral question. Similar observations may be made about other political constructs. For example, we may want to consider the functions of the U.S. Supreme Court. We read of this body's laying down desegregation guidelines or determining the rights of accused persons. Though it may seem that we are considering the activities and powers of a political institution, we are in fact dealing with assertions about human behavior. To say that the Supreme Court interprets statutes and the Constitution by deciding legal cases is really quite a complicated statement, involving assumptions about the behavior of Supreme Court Justices and persons who bring cases to be tried and having implications for the reactions (behaviors) of legislators, executives, lower court judges, attorneys, prosecutors, the police, and, indeed, citizens at large.

We often speak of the *power* of countries when discussing international affairs. But to say that a nation has power necessarily implies that some people (usually in important positions) behave in a way that causes certain things to occur. Decisions are made to build arms, to seek allies, or to obtain strategic military bases. These actions, which may create power, are a consequence of someone's behavior. Today's passionate partisan of the New Left may decry repression and manipulation of the news while advocating liberation and revolution. Though such notions may be discussed in a highly charged atmosphere that seems remote indeed from the study of political behavior, they all refer to kinds of political behavior. Our passionate partisan will not consider himself a behaviorist; but he is likely to discuss not only these behaviors, but people who perform (or will perform) them: the "establishment," the older generation, students, workers, or "the people." All these groups are important to the political behaviorist, and their actions are clearly within the province of political behaviorism.

Political philosophers, commentators, and practitioners of all kinds have made behavioral statements through the ages. Plato said that if we educate citizens properly they will be docile and predictable. Hitler said that if we repeat political propaganda often enough people will begin to believe it. Today's activists and reformers assert that if blacks are accorded inferior status they will engage in politically directed violence. All these statements are behavioral assertions.

Thus it appears that the term "political behaviorism" is redundant. That which is political, from ancient philosophy to contemporary activism, is necessarily behavioral. Politics cannot even exist without inputs of human behavior, and it cannot be studied without considering human behavior. Such a curious name for a discipline, it might be argued, should be dropped, for it does not seem to distinguish one political scientist from the other. All students of politics are political

6

behaviorists. But of course no one subscribes to such a literal interpretation of the term. Students know that if a course is billed as "behavioral" it is likely to involve quantitative analyses and "math and statistics." If they have had difficulty with math or statistics in the past, they are likely to avoid behavioral courses in favor of those with a different approach. Registration time is likely to find students contrasting behavioral courses with "traditional," "practical," or "relevant" courses. It is clear, then, that "behavioral" has acquired some special meaning. The nature and implications of that meaning are the subject of this chapter. The definition of the political behavior approach is rather complex and requires considerable discussion. We can say at this point, however, that it is an approach which emphasizes and makes explicit the fact that all political phenomena depend on human acts. In studying any political event, the behaviorist is likely to ask, explicitly, "What behavior performed by whom produced this event?" and "How can we explain that particular behavior?" Nonbehaviorists, though they cannot deny the existence of the basic human behavior in question, may choose to emphasize literary, historical, institutional, or moral aspects of the event. In short, "political behaviorism" has come to refer to a particular component of the political. It suggests, as a mode of study, the putting aside of literary, historical, or moral considerations for the sake of clarity. Of course this is not possible for everyone. These kinds of considerations are so important to some people that they cannot be put aside even for the purpose of research. "Political behaviorism," then, represents one way of dealing with political events.

An investigator who is explicitly concerned with the causes and effects of human political acts is a *behaviorist*, while those who focus on secondary, derivative, or instrumental concerns go by other names. Distinguishing between the various kinds of political investigators will help us to appreciate the goal, intent, and value of the study of political behavior.

Polsby, Dentler, and Smith[1] suggest a simplified way of classifying political scientists—as political theologians, political historians, political engineers, political anecdotalists, and political behaviorists. If we are to comprehend the behaviorists' work, we must understand how they are different from the other four. This can best be accomplished by noting five basic considerations in the acquisition of knowledge. These considerations are (1) the fact-value question, (2) the dichotomy between generalizations and specifics, (3) the relative merit of explanation and description, (4) the value of adding to what is known versus learning what is already known, and (5) the dichotomy between analysis and substance.

The Fact-Value Question

Political theology, observe the above-mentioned authors, "is concerned with such questions as, 'How should men live together?', 'What is a good man?', and 'What is a good society?' Theologians formulate and defend answers to questions such as these. . . . [The theologian] does not necessarily seek ways and means of bringing about the good society; he is rather, concerned to justify his values as the 'correct' ones."[2] The political behaviorist differs radically from the theologian in that he is not primarily concerned with values; in fact, in his effort to be scientific, he may attempt to avoid making value judgments altogether.

There appear to be two great traditions in the study of politics, each claiming that different classes of things should be the currency of the discipline. Some—political theologians among them—insist that it is the job of the political investigator to find out what decisions, institutions, people, or ideologies are morally superior to others, and then to teach, justify, and otherwise further those which he approves. The scholar, in other words, is to be a specialist in making moral judgments.

On the other hand, there is a tradition which emphasizes the realm of fact, the accumulation of knowledge as to what *is*. The job of the scholar is to discover this and to describe what he finds. The behaviorist is of this tradition in that he discovers and describes relevant human behavior. Of course, there are times when this tradition seems weak and sterile, and decidedly less exciting than an analysis of moral values. In many courses students are required to accumulate, without interpretation, large quantities of facts for no apparent purpose except to regurgitate them on the final exam. This deadening experience lends credence to the political evaluator's charge that facts are meaningless unless one draws inferences from them. Indeed, it may seem true—as some progressive educators insist—that an undue emphasis on facts actually inhibits any useful form of thinking. Though the behaviorist is decidedly a specialist in fact rather than in value judgments, he would agree that one must draw inferences from and interpret whatever facts are discov-

8

ered. He differs from the political evaluator in that he does not believe that this drawing of inferences or interpretation must—or even should —involve value judgments. As we shall see, the behaviorist is not a purveyor of a dull bag of facts collected for their own sake. He is as interested in thinking about and building upon his observations as is a moralist, but in a different way—the way of scientists and empirical theorists.

Just as there are two traditions regarding the object of political inquiry, so are there two schools of thought regarding the *methods* to be used in studying politics. One emphasizes going out and looking at the things that interest you. If you want to know the impact of the Watergate scandal, go and ask people how they feel about Watergate. Though this seems a sensible way to proceed, and though this technique has been used in political research at least since the time of Aristotle, it has not been universally accepted. Indeed, in modern political science, it has a relatively short history. Modern *empiricists*—as we shall call scholars who acquire their knowledge through the use of their physical senses—were preceded by large numbers of investigators who based their assertions on other kinds of observations. And, of course, empiricists have contemporaries who do not always favor their methods. Those who stand opposed to empiricism we shall call *intuitionists*. These people feel that the important philosophical question "How do you know?" can be answered by contemplation, logical reasoning, introspection, revelation, or other means. These mental processes—like evaluation in relation to factualism—are sometimes thought to represent a higher order of philosophical procedure than "crude" empiricism. It is said that Aristotle was considered somewhat gauche for suggesting to a group of speculative philosophers that they resolve their discussion of the number of teeth in a horse's mouth by going to the barn and looking. The behaviorist, however, would reply that in those areas where empiricism has long been emphasized, the so-called physical sciences, the increase in knowledge has been spectacular and infinitely useful. The method has been proved.

Generally, political investigators who deal with facts proceed by empirical means, while those who are concerned with moral judgments claim to perceive something more than mere facts and to use some sort of intuition to do so. Though the congruence of empiricism to factualism and of intuition to valuation is by no means perfect, these remarks serve to emphasize the difference between behaviorists and political theologians. They differ not only in their subject but in their basic method.

Of course, the chasm between behaviorists and moralists may appear artificial and overdrawn to some of the other kinds of investigators mentioned above. Political engineers—a category in which we might include reformers and activists of all types—are generally committed to a value position, and yet many of them seek as many facts as possible about the objects of their interest in order to know how to implement their desires more effectively. Common Cause, a highly value-motivated organization if there ever was one, also has a high degree of confidence in fact. For example, it collects data on the political tactics of powerful and wealthy groups. Once these tactics are known, effective countermeasures can be undertaken and, it is hoped, their political aspirations can be frustrated.

Any kind of intelligent activity—whether it be advocating a political cause or a less directly value-related action—requires factual knowledge. How can one support some political alternatives and condemn others in any sensible way unless he knows what each one entails? He cannot. One cannot evaluate that which one does not know. Facts aid one in pursuing one's goals. Thus, it is quite possible to mix considerations of fact and value, but facts are so basic that someone must be charged with their collection if human concerns are to proceed. This alone should justify the posture of behaviorists.

Since fact and value clearly mix, one might ask why behaviorists (or at least the purists among them) eschew excursions into political evaluation. Indeed, for not so doing they have been charged with lacking the courage of their convictions, or worse yet, having no convictions. From a scholarly point of view, it is accurate to say that behaviorists have no moralistic convictions. But this is not due to weakness or intellectual flabbiness. There are sound, knowledge-related reasons for such a position. Value judgments ultimately rest on human *preferences*. Though one must possess at least some facts to make an evaluation, the accumulation of facts alone is insufficient to produce a value judgment. No matter how much factual information one acquires, the "right" policy alternatives will not automatically emerge; somewhere along the line, the evaluator must say, unsupported by data (but perhaps supported by some kind of intuition), "I prefer this." Many behaviorists fear that strong preferences may interfere with one's ability to determine what the facts actually are. Since political facts are often difficult to discover, it is possible for an observer to distort what he sees into what he *wants* to see. Preferences may bias a person's observational abilities. Unlike the political engineer or reformer, the behaviorist does not feel that this risk is justified. To him, as a scholar, knowledge is more important than moral position.

In summary, the behaviorist is distinguished from political theologians and from political engineers or reformers by his position on the fact-value question. He would agree with the theologian and engineer that political value judgments are important. Indeed, as citizens we are all, behaviorists included, called upon to make hundreds of political value judgments during our lives. But factual knowledge is fantastically useful. It is basic to any kind of intelligent human activity, including the implementation and even the making of value judgments. The behaviorist is unwilling, as a scholar, to risk this valuable commodity by adopting points of view that may compromise his observational ability; hence, he avoids the realm of value in his investigations.

Generalizations and Specifics

Though we are now getting some idea of what the political behaviorist does and why he does it, many questions are yet unresolved and behaviorists have still not been differentiated from some other types of political investigators. Some consideration of what they do with the facts they collect should help clarify the picture. As we have already noted, the behaviorist does not advocate the accumulation of encyclopedic collections of discrete bits of information; the ultimate scholarly achievement is not to commit to memory millions of facts or to become an information specialist, but to render knowledge into its most useful form through the application of the canons of science. The basic operation involved in this process is *generalization*.

It is generalization that distinguishes behaviorists from political historians and political anecdotalists. These two groups, like behaviorists, are usually interested in questions of fact rather than value. But they tend to appreciate each individual political event for its unique characteristics. They wish to describe phenomena of the past (the his-

11

torians) or of the present (the anecdotalists), often in detail. Historians may trace "the fortunes of nations through wars, treaties, alliances" or may follow various incarnations of similar ideas through the centuries. Anecdotalists may record events much in the fashion of journalists or perform detailed case studies of some political occurrence. They are motivated by the entirely proper belief that it is good to have the most elaborate knowledge possible of political events. Contemplating many and varied events results in an understanding of the nuances of politics. Often it is the *unique* character of the events described that receives the greatest amount of the historian's or anecdotalist's emphasis; interest and perhaps even the justification for continued investigation inhere in the unique. A new unique event—of which there are an infinite number—requires detailed investigation.

Behaviorists do not question the utility of the facts these scholars collect. Such operations are undoubtedly necessary to the continuing progress of humankind. But the behaviorist treats collected facts differently. Rather than emphasizing the *uniqueness* of each, he prefers to synthesize those that are similar into *general* statements. That is to say, the behaviorist emphasizes what political facts have in *common*. In this way, inferences can be drawn, lessons can be learned, and *useful* knowledge can be gained. That general statements sometimes have greater utility than descriptions of unique events is quite clear. If one knows that on April 10, 1785, a British soldier placed a lighted candle in a barrel of gunpowder and that a violent explosion occurred, killing the soldier and damaging surrounding objects, one has a fact. But unless one generalizes from this fact, and others like it, it is certainly trivial. Taken of and by itself, it offers no useful advice to those of us presently in the proximity of gunpowder. It was a unique event that took place long ago. What, after all, does the action of a long-dead soldier with respect to an obsolete form of lighting have to do with choices in the present? We might as well toss our lighted cigarette into the gunpowder.

On the other hand, we may try to learn a lesson from the experience of the unfortunate Briton. But then we are no longer treating the event as unique. We have begun the process of generalization. We are saying, "There are aspects of this situation that are repeated in others." We may speculate that there were elements in the situation that caused the explosion. We may further contemplate that recurrences of these elements will be followed by recurrences of explosions, events we wish to avoid. Several *general propositions* suggest themselves—for example (1) gunpowder explodes in the presence of the British, (2) gunpowder explodes in the presence of soldiers, (3) gunpowder explodes on April 10, (4) gunpowder explodes when heated, (5) gunpowder explodes when in barrels. Clearly, if we can determine the truth or falsity of these and similar generalizations, we will be in excellent position to behave prudently in gunpowder magazines. Obviously, our situation would be vastly safer than if we knew only of the unique explosion of 1785.

Of course, starting only with the description of that single event, it takes some work to discover which general propositions are true and which are false. Only by repeated observations of other situations in which gunpowder explodes can this be accomplished. However, if enough explosions are observed, and their common elements noted, it will soon be evident that some of the elements of the 1785 incident were not important to the explosion (e.g., the nationality of the soldier or the date), while others were. Observations will show that all the explosions were associated with the heating of gunpowder. Thus we will have arrived at a generalization (that gunpowder explodes when heated) that is highly useful; not only will it save our lives, but we need not embarrass our British friends by shunning them and we may work in the magazine on April 10 without fear. We would much rather have this general knowledge than be aware of the unique and, to us, trivial event of April 10, 1785.

This caricature illustrates a process—called *induction*—that is commonly used in the *physical* sciences. The physical scientist operates in a world of generalizations. We are not concerned about the researches of Newton because they are unique or possess some quaint features; rather, they are important because they led to important *generalizations* about the way in which physical objects behave. University students do not perform experiments in chemistry laboratories in order to produce something unique; rather, they are seeking iterations of important generalizations about the behavior of certain reagents. Few would challenge the assertion that generalizations are more useful than observations of unique facts in the physical branches of scientific inquiry. But what about in the *social* sciences, and *political science* in particular?

The behaviorist believes that scientific principles of inquiry can be applied to the behavior of human beings just as they can to the action of physical particles, chemical reagents, plants, animals, planets, clouds,

13

rocks, and other phenomena commonly thought of as within the purview of science. Until rather recently, the "science" half of the term
"political science" has not had much literal meaning. It is the intent of
the behaviorist to give it some. He tries to be rigorously scientific, to
some extent emulating the procedures that have proven so successful in
the natural sciences. He goes at the task of discovery in ways that are
logically, if not obviously, identical to those used in apparatus-filled
laboratories.

The assertion that human beings can be treated like other scientific
subjects, that human behavior can be equated with that of lifeless
chemicals, may seem startling. Indeed, it is a suggestion some find
offensive. Objections to a scientific study of human behavior are made
on several grounds, but they usually center about the idea that such a
study is either impossible or immoral or both. Indeed, the idea that one
can make valid generalizations about human behavior may take a little
getting used to. It is based on the assumption that human behavior
follows *regular patterns*, and that these patterns can be known (just as
gunpowder's behavior follows regular patterns that can be known). That
is, each isolated human action is not unique any more than each explosion of gunpowder is unique or any more than each chemical reaction in
each individual test tube is unique. Nearly everyone will admit that the
latter two classes of phenomena are not groups of unique events. Why
should the first not be accorded the same characteristics? Perhaps one
reason is that if it is possible to make generalizations about human
behavior, it is possible to *predict* human behavior. If the generalization
"education is associated with interest in politics" is true, then we can
predict that persons with little education will have little interest in
politics. This is of course directly parallel to taking the generalization
"gunpowder explodes when heated" to be true and predicting that if we
toss our cigarette into some nearby gunpowder we will be in trouble.
Similarly, it is directly parallel to taking Boyle's law (certain
generalizations about physical substances—in this case, gasses) to be
true and predicting the successful operation of an air compressor. But
although we readily predict the behavior of gunpowder or of gasses, we
somehow believe that human behavior is not subject to the same rules.
One can easily say, "My behavior cannot be predicted. I make up my
own mind what to do, regardless of the generalizations made by social
scientists." We may argue that our behavior is controlled by our indi-

vidual *human will*, which is independent of anything outside ourselves, that it is fundamentally different from the will-less action of physical matter and cannot be predicted. This argument is often supplemented by moral considerations. Will is described as a God-given attribute, as part of what makes man the unique creature he is. To say that his behavior can be predicted like that of any other scientific object is viewed as depriving him of characteristics God intended him to have. Not only is the scientific study of human behavior impossible, but to attempt it is to deny a moral reality.

Though these arguments seem weighty, the behaviorist believes they can be refuted, and, moreover, without overturning anyone's religious beliefs. First, the question of whether it is *possible* to make empirical generalizations about humans can be answered only by trying. All manner of generalizations about human behavior have been suggested. Does human behavior really conform to them? The answer is clearly yes. Milbrath has suggested hundreds of generalizations about political participation.[3] It is, for example, associated with income and with age. A large number of generalizations about many types of human behavior have been collected by Berelson and Steiner.[4] They note, for example, that marriage rates increase in times of prosperity and decrease in times of depression. Is the decision to marry an act of free will, or is it behavior one can predict from a knowledge of economic conditions? These generalizations are noteworthy precisely because a great many studies of what people actually do show that their behavior does *in fact* fall into patterns. These patterns are, moreover, known to social scientists and used by them as a basis for predictions.

These assertions seem less exceptional when one reflects on everyday life. One does not need to engage scholarly research to see general patterns of behavior. Hundreds of times a day we *predict* what people will do and govern our behavior accordingly. For example, in driving to school or work we assume that other drivers operate their cars on the right side of the road. We do this on the basis of our knowledge of the general patterns into which human behavior falls. On the basis of the generalization "professors meet their classes," we expect, when we arrive for a lecture, that we will hear one. And in most cases, we are right. In political affairs, the most mundane institutional statements really rest upon predictions (based in generalization) of human behavior. Consider, for example, the assertion "Congress passes laws." Is this a behavioral statement? Most assuredly. Its truth rests on very complex patterns of behavior on the part of Congressmen, aides, service personnel, communications specialists, and others. We predict, at the beginning of every session of Congress, that these complex behavior patterns will occur. And they do.

We make predictions about behavior all the time—and usually correct ones. Experience confirms that human actions, despite human will, follow regular patterns. Of course, most of the "predictions" described above are only common sense. But their similarity to the generalizations made in the scientific study of human behavior—or any science for that matter—is considerable. Science is merely the formalization and extension of sensible, everyday observational procedures. As for the theological objections to a science of human behavior, perhaps they can be met by suggesting that if God gave humans will, He also provided that it should be used to enact patterns of behavior.

Explanation and Description

Even though it is possible to make generalizations that account for *some* human behavior, it is still true that for every such generalization there are *exceptions*. These exceptions cause some observers to reject behavioral science altogether, for they believe that a generalization not 100 % true is no better than a casual commentary on events. Usually, this posture is accompanied by an unfavorable comparison of the exceptions encountered in social science to the invariant laws of natural science. Others, though they admit that partially true generalizations are useful, attribute the exceptions to the "human factor," something which is very much akin to *will* and, they assert, often beyond the purview of science.

These observations can best be dealt with by considering another cardinal feature of political behaviorism: its attempt to be *explanatory* rather than only *descriptive*. Most of the generalizations with which behaviorists try to deal tell not only *what* people do, but also *why* they do it. In fact, many strictly descriptive generalizations tend to be trivial. Statements such as "63 percent of the American public consider themselves to be Democrats" and "American children learn to idealize the President" may be interesting, but the question of why these things are

16

so immediately comes to the curious mind. It is much more interesting and much more useful, when observations are explained as well as reported. Scientific explanations often take the form of *cause-and-effect statements*, like some of the generalizations we have already considered: for example, "gunpowder explodes when heated" (or, heat causes gunpowder to explode).

Let us consider the generalization "education is associated with interest in politics." It is explanatory; it tells us that education causes people to participate. As we have noted, on the basis of this statement we would predict a lower degree of participation among less educated persons and a higher degree of participation among the better educated. Suppose, however, that we find a Ph.D. in chemistry who has never voted and never reads anything about politics. What happens to our generalization? Has it been falsified? And should it then be relegated to the scrap heap? This generalization (like generalizations in all the sciences) is only partially true. But this does not mean that it should be abandoned. There are, after all, causes of political participation other than education. And these causes too can be represented by generalizations. For example, the statements "social class background is associated with (causes) political participation" and "age is associated with (causes) political participation" are also partially true. Perhaps our Ph.D. is from a family of modest means where political participation was not stressed. Perhaps he was a child prodigy and is only twenty years old. Perhaps these factors were so powerful, in this instance, that they offset effect of education on participation. Or perhaps some other cause of nonparticipation—a cause that has not yet been discovered—was operative. The latter is a decided possibility, since we are extremely far from knowing everything there is to know about the political behavior of human beings. There are many, many generalizations still unknown.

One may accept these explanations as reasonable and yet feel that their implications make political science a very weak discipline compared to the physical sciences. Indeed, in light of this "weakness," some would deny the name "science" to the study of human behavior. This, of course, is unfair, for investigators in the natural sciences also encounter multiple or unknown causes. Consider the science meteorology. Meteorologists know several partially true generalizations about, for example, the movements of storms. On the basis of them, they make predictions and issue storm warnings for threatened locales. Some-

17

times, however, they do not predict the paths of storms accurately. How can this occur? Storms are affected by a variety of factors. In a given instance, prevailing wind patterns may be thought to be the dominating factor. However, ocean currents also cause storms to move, and they may unexpectedly play a larger role than wind. Thus we have an erroneous weather forecast. Of course, the fact that the meteorologist did not know which factor would be dominant means that his knowledge about the movement of storms is incomplete. Some generalizations remain unknown. Presumably, as these generalizations are discovered, better weather predictions will become possible. In the meantime, meteorologists do the best they can with their imperfect knowledge. No one suggests that their services are useless because their forecasts are inexact, and no one denies that they are scientists proceeding by methods altogether appropriate to scientific inquiry.

Even the most "exact" sciences are subject to the constraints that trouble political science and meteorology. They are fortunate, however, in that they can often *control* causes other than those in which they are interested at the moment. In making predictions about political participation on the basis of education, we cannot control the intrusion of factors like class and age and other possible but unknown variables. An analogous situation might arise in the science of chemistry if an investigator had to work with impure reagents. The impurities would definitely cause results that were exceptions to what the chemist would predict on the basis of known chemical generalizations. If he were able to find out what substance had contaminated his reagents, he might be able to explain why the exceptional reaction was produced. If he could not, it would remain a mystery. As it happens, chemists now know a great deal about reagents, and the chance of contamination or the occurrence of unknown substances is quite remote, unless, of course we are talking about undergraduate neophytes toiling in a university chemistry laboratory. But these kinds of conditions were quite common in the days when chemistry was a young science. Centuries ago the baffling exceptions produced by chemical impurities were legion. Perhaps early chemists working under these conditions were urged by cynics to give up, and told that chemistry, because of the unpredictability of chemical reactions, could never be made into an exact science. Of course, chemists worked through the years to resolve the apparent exceptions to chemical generalizations they encountered, and chemistry today is an undeniably useful science that encompasses a very large number of highly reliable generalizations.

Political behaviorism today is at a stage of development comparable to that of seventeenth-century chemistry. The political behaviorist's generalizations are crude and have many exceptions. But is he to be denied scientific status because his results are inexact? This would be as unjust as denigrating the early chemists as nonscientific, when in reality they were courageous scientific pioneers. It is unfair to compare "inexact" political science with "exact" natural science. The natural scientist, having been at his task several centuries more than the political behaviorist, naturally has more explanatory statements at his command. The degree of exactness of a discipline merely reflects the amount of knowledge possessed by its practitioners; it has nothing whatever to do with the degree of scientificness of the studies involved.

Moreover, when an exception to a scientific generalization occurs, it is not to be regarded as a tragedy. One of the goals of science is to *explain* events, as well as to *describe* them. Generalizations are typically statements of cause and effect. To the extent that they are true, the effect they describe is successfully explained. When an exception occurs, it means that the effect is not totally explained by the cause noted and that additional causes must be sought. Exceptions are not signs that scientific enterprise has failed; indeed, they are an impetus to additional discoveries. It is through the resolution of exceptions that a body of knowledge grows. They are the phenomena that typically excite curiosity. Why does this observation not conform to the generalization? There must be other generalizations about the effect I expected, and I must search for them. A series of generalizations to which there were never any exceptions would represent a body of total knowledge. There would be nothing more to find out. It is hard to imagine this condition obtaining in any field. There always seems to be something more to find out. But if it could occur, the result would surely be a form of stagnation. There would be no researchers in the field, no attempts at advancement, no progress. Clearly, this is not the case in any of the dynamic, growing areas of study that we call sciences—whether physical or social, natural or behavioral.

This argument can be demonstrated dramatically by looking at advanced research in the most "exact" of our sciences, physics. Physical generalizations, such as Newton's laws of motion, Boyle's law, and

Ohm's law, seem to the layman or beginning student to be universally true. Indeed, the name "law" given to them suggests that there is something immutable about the cause-and-effect relationships they describe. However, consider the research physicist exploring the structure of matter (about which a great deal is not known). In recent years, much has been learned about the building blocks of the Universe. It has long been known that matter consists of various kinds of particles, often subdivisible into other particles. We are all familiar with molecules, atoms, protons, neutrons, and electrons and the general way in which they fit into atomic conceptions of matter. But recently the list of subatomic particles has grown considerably. It has been discovered that the Universe is composed of additional particles as well—anti-protons and neutrinos, for example. A few years ago, no one had heard of such things. How were they discovered? Through the process of exploring observations that were exceptions to the best generalizations of the moment. For example, cloud chamber experiments revealed a good deal. The movements of subatomic particles in such chambers can be traced by the visible "cloud" trail they leave as they travel. Experiments were set up in which particles fired through such chambers were expected to travel in straight lines. Occasionally, however, the paths of some particles would deviate from the predicted pattern. This could only mean that there were gaps in physical knowledge. Physicists did not know why the deviations took place. The search for causes led to the discovery of previously unknown particles. The deviant paths were due to collisions with the new particles. Clearly, it was only the discovery that some of the laws of physics were inexact that made these new discoveries possible.

Inexactness, then, is hardly a mark of scientific failure. Indeed, it is often through the resolution of inexactness that scientific knowledge is increased. The fact that there is a great deal more inexactness in the social sciences than in the physical sciences should not, therefore, cause discouragement or the abandonment of scientific enterprise. Rather, it should be a signal that there is a great deal to be done, that there are many observations to be resolved. It indicates that the field is wide open for the excitement of new discovery. The search for better explanations of observed events—common to political science and all other sciences—means the discovery of additional causes for these events. The discovery of these additional causes can occur only if inexactness in generalizations is investigated. Far from precluding scientific endeavor or revealing an inexplicable "human factor," the exceptions of social science merely indicate that there are yet unknown causes, or explanations, of events. As in other sciences faced with identical kinds of exceptions, the proper response is to seek the unknown causes, to construct increasingly better explanations of what we see.

Learning vs. Discovery

Probably any kind of scholarship in any field can be divided, roughly, into two kinds of inquiry: learning what is already known, on the one hand, and adding to what is known, or discovery, on the other hand. By far the greater part of undergraduate study is of the former type. Most of a student's labors are devoted to finding out what others have said, written, and discovered. Textbooks, lecture materials, and the other paraphernalia of learning are designed primarily to make one aware of the accumulated wisdom of the ages, of the contributions others have made to knowledge. To the undergraduate, the word "discovery," which supposedly denotes the purpose of a good part of higher education, usually means *personal* discovery rather than discovery in the sense of uncovering something previously unknown to all of mankind. The other avowed purposes of college training, such as developing critical faculties or honing the thinking process in general, are also oriented toward personal development. The emphasis is on absorbing and weighing information rather than on locating it. One is generally provided with the facts to be learned, the objects to be criticized or to be thought about. Scholarship is achieved through assimilation.

This of course is as things should be. All disciplines must proceed in this way if knowledge is to be communicated. Political behaviorism is no exception. Students are asked to learn generalizations put forth by others. They are asked to examine data collected by other people. But the political behavior approach has, in addition, a particular concern with *adding to what is known.* An undergraduate oriented toward personal discoveries may look rather uncritically at bodies of knowledge, taking them as given. How they came to be may seem nowhere near as important as how to get them into his head. This is unfortunate for two reasons. First, bodies of knowledge are dynamic. They are

21

constantly expanding; they are constantly being modified as a result of new information that qualifies existing generalizations. Evidence of the continuing expansion of knowledge in all fields is all around us. Examples of progress are everywhere; perhaps the most spectacular are in the treatment of disease or in space exploration. It has been said (though admittedly this would be a very difficult proposition to test) that more has been discovered since the turn of the century than in all the previous history of man. In an era of such rapid discovery, taking a body of knowledge as given is extremely dangerous. One must look upon knowledge as tentative and subject to modification. New discoveries may make what once was very important information quite insignificant. Obviously, a thorough understanding of the working of steam locomotives is of considerably less value today than it was forty years ago. A person without a keen awareness of the continuous process of adding to what is known runs the risk of becoming trapped by his own body of personal knowledge and of becoming obsolete. The political behaviorist, being very much discovery oriented and very tentative in his view of knowledge, ought to be able to avoid this kind of misfortune.

Second, an orientation toward personal development can encourage an attitude of passive acceptance. If a person knows nothing of the discovery process, then he must depend on someone else's assessment of what is. He has no criteria to judge whether something is worth learning. He cannot tell whether something is true; he can only learn what he is told. This is especially critical when we consider that knowledge is not easy to discover. What the facts are, what generalizations are true, is far from obvious. A person who claims to say the truth, therefore, cannot easily be checked by anyone who might wish to do so. In speaking the alleged truth, he may make mistakes, or he may lie. He can be held to defend his remarks only by persons who are familiar with the process of discovery and who can therefore assess the means by which the supposed truth was discovered. The superior position of such a person is obvious.

Avoidance of a posture of passive acceptance not only enables one to evaluate what others offer as truth, but it also allows one to discover truth oneself. This is not as unusual an act as it may seem; it certainly is not behavior confined to the rarified atmosphere of academic research. Suppose a man is in charge of advertising for a firm. He wonders whether a particular kind of appeal will sell bubble gum. But does he know enough about the process of discovery to set up an apparatus for finding out, or must he hire another firm (at a greater cost) to make the necessary discoveries and transmit the information (possibly in distorted form) to him? Suppose a group of women desperately want new legislation to prohibit discrimination by sex in hiring or education. How can they make the most effective use of their resources? If they are oriented toward discovery, they may be able to answer this question for themselves; if not, they will probably have to pay someone to answer it for them.

Finally, the person who is geared toward passive acceptance is unable to experience the gratification of the discovery process itself. Finding out something totally new can be exhilarating in and of itself; unearthing information, previously unknown, that will benefit others may be even more gratifying.

In short, the person who is entirely oriented toward personal development and has no interest at all in adding to what is known runs several kinds of risks. He may be unable to keep pace in a developing world, he may be unable to act for himself when new information is needed, and he cuts himself off from very real sources of gratification. It is with the intention of avoiding this unfortunate state that the political behaviorist focuses not only on personal development, but on discovery as well.

Analysis and Substance

The emphasis on learning what is known is probably partly responsible for the essentially substantive differentiation of academic disciplines and subdisciplines. Perhaps the most sensible and intuitively appealing way of organizing what is known is to chop it up and create little compartments full of different kinds of substantive knowledge. Such a compartmentalized curriculum characterizes the overwhelming majority of universities and colleges. In order to major in a given subject, or even to graduate at all, one is required to become at least minimally familiar with some of these compartments arranged in different combinations. Generally, though not always, the compartments do not overlap. A given item of knowledge can usually be unambiguously pigeonholed in a compartment with a particular name. The same course is not typically offered in more than one department or in more than one field within a department. Political science, for example, usually consists of a series of courses that fit into generally exclusive and more or less exhaustive fields. These fields describe a group of complementary areas of investigation. There may be major breakdowns into American politics, international relations, and comparative politics, with further breakdowns, perhaps by institution (legislative, executive or whatever) in the first case and by country in the last. The subject matter of each field is generally quite different from that of others.

This scheme, on which student majors, departmental recruitment patterns, and teaching assignments are based, is quite orderly and rational. But political behaviorism does not fit into it. There is no specific subject matter which is the special province of political behaviorism. Though the study of French politics may unambiguously belong to the field of comparative government, and though the investigation of the governor's office is without doubt the responsibility of those in the field of state government, no similar set of specifications can be delimited for political behaviorism. Why is this the case? The answer is simple. The term "political behaviorism" denotes an *approach* to the study of politics rather than a particular batch of stuff to be studied. At the beginning of this chapter, we suggested that all things political depend on the behavior of human beings. Regardless of where that behavior takes place—in a legislature, on a court, among the French citizenry, at an antiwar demonstration, or at an international peace conference, it may be approached in the way we have outlined here. Analyses of the antecedents of Supreme Court Justices' opinions on civil liberties, studies of the effect of parties on Congressmen's votes, comparative examinations of the factors underlying American and Norwegian voting patterns, and inquiries into the vagaries of international communications are all equally likely to occupy the attention of the behaviorist.

One might ask why, if it is possible to use the political behaviorist approach in studying constitutional law, legislative processes, comparative politics, and international relations, political behaviorism is treated in a special course. Why can't it be practiced within each of the substantive fields of political science? The answer is that it can be; indeed, to a large extent, it is. A separate course is useful precisely because it focuses on ways of thinking that may be necessary in a great variety of political inquiries. In this respect, political behaviorism is like political philosophy, or "political theology," as it was termed above. Both offer ways of approaching political observations. Both are devoted to the validity of *generalizations* about politics, though a behaviorist focuses on *empirical* generalizations whereas a political philosopher seeks *normative* generalizations. Both involve an attempt to make statements that are valid beyond any set of particular circumstances. The behaviorist, as we have seen, desires factual statements that comprehend large numbers of individual events; the political theologian desires ethical principles that, for example, prescribe *general* standards for evaluating societies or tell how *all* men ought to behave. Obviously, neither the process of science nor the process of political evaluation stops at the boundaries of the subfields of political science. All objects may be studied scientifically, and all objects may be subjected to normative scrutiny. Appropriately, there are courses in both scientific study and normative scrutiny. Both may be useful in the subsequent appraisal of a great variety of political phenomena. It is not surprising that both kinds of endeavor are sometimes lumped together under the heading of political theory. The word "theory," after all, comes from the Greek verb *theorein*, to look at. Political behaviorism courses (and those in political philosophy) are courses in ways of looking at politics.

The political behaviorist's way, it should be quite clear, is anything but casual. Concentration on facts rather than values, on generalizations instead of specifics, on explanation as opposed to description, and on adding to knowledge in addition to learning what is known requires some pretty definite procedures. It is to a consideration of these procedures—that is, what the political behaviorist actually does—that we now turn.

Notes

1. Nelson W. Polsby, Robert A. Dentler, and Paul A. Smith (eds.), *Politics and Social Life* (Boston: Houghton Mifflin, 1963), pp. 1-14.
2. *Ibid.*, p. 2.
3. Lester W. Milbrath, *Political Participation* (Chicago: Rand McNally, 1965).
4. Bernard Berelson and Gary A. Steiner, *Human Behavior: An Inventory of Scientific Findings* (New York: Harcourt, Brace, and World, 1964).

2

The Procedures
of Political
Behaviorism

Measurement

In the previous chapter, we saw that the study of political behavior is not really very ominous or frightening. It is merely a way of looking at and studying the political events that have always interested man. If political behaviorism refers to anything, it refers to ways of organizing what one sees in the world of politics. These ways of organizing things bear a remarkable similarity to the everyday, commonsense ways of organizing human activities. We are really talking about an extension and formalization of those commonsense procedures.

This picture of simplicity and similarity to traditional methods may seem to be belied by what most undergraduates already know about the study of political behavior. They may have heard from friends that political behavior studies involve statistical presentations, mathematical models, and other seemingly complicated quantitative devices. An advance look at some of the primary source material and research reports that one might be asked to read in a political behavior course (or for that matter, later chapters of this book) may confirm this impression. Many political science articles alleged to be behavioral are resplendent with tables, graphs, charts, mysterious notations, and references to techniques that seem to be the preserve of only the most advanced scholars. In persons without a quantitative orientation, these initial encounters may arouse considerable anxiety. Two caveats are needed at this point. First, despite their apparent complexity, these accoutrements of the discipline *are* but extensions of common sense, and their functions can be appreciated without esoteric mathematical knowledge. One need not be an accomplished statistician to grasp political behavior studies, but one does need to develop an appreciation of quantitative data. Second, the "intimidating" paraphernalia of political behaviorism are absolutely necessary to the accomplishment of its task. Authors do not use such devices to impress uninitiated readers or to demonstrate a facility with difficult procedures. They use them to communicate a message, an understandable and sensible message.

Basically, the presence of such phenomena in the literature of political behaviorism is a consequence of scholars' attempts to perform a basic operation critical to the conduct of science—the operation of *measurement*. Interesting political generalizations (and remember, the discovery of true generalizations is a chief pursuit of the political behaviorist) can be meaningfully assessed only if some sort of measurements are made. Often, this entails nothing more than the assignment of quantitative values to common observations, but sometimes more complex procedures are involved. In any event, it is the simple desire for unambiguous classification that accounts for the numbers.

Unfortunately, there is no strong tradition of the measurement of political phenomena. This is true for several reasons. First, the moral-value approach discussed in Chapter 1 is a popular one; many investigators wish to deal with moral concerns that are not amenable to measurement or any other kind of empirical treatment. To them, objects of real political interest (or at least the most important of them) must be dealt with by other means—through insight, for example. Second, there is a viable democratic tradition which holds that political data are self-evident and thereby suggests that measurement is unnecessary. As citizens, we are asked to evaluate a large number of political objects and to make decisions about them by voting. Since all may participate in the political process, all must be able to make meaningful observations of political life. The task of acquiring political information is thus assumed to be easy—a job that anyone, no matter how insignificant, may perform. In the true sense of Jacksonian democracy, one man's observations are as good as the next; certainly measurement—which implies systematic processes to discover something not immediately evident—is inappropriate. It is easy to carry over this notion from one's role as a democratic citizen to one's role as a scholar, and as a result some political scientists may not feel the necessity of measurement. Third, even if one wishes to proceed in the realm of empirical fact and sees the value of measurement, and even if one believes that all empirical facts are not self-evident, impediments to measurement may still appear formidable. The very fact that there are often no commonly accepted standards in terms of which political phenomena can be measured is a tremendous problem.

Consider the following situation: Controversy has raged over what kinds of public policies should be adopted to deal with poor people in this country. Advocates and opponents of various welfare plans have argued merits and demerits nearly, it seems, to the point of exhaustion. Which of the alternatives will be the most successful? Unfortunately, there is no ready answer to this question, because different people have different criteria of success. To some, substantial subsidies for those with low incomes would be success; others, despising the idea of subsidies, would be happier with low cost educational programs for all. Controversy can legitimately continue. Similar controversies about such important political concepts as "fascism," "representation," "liberalism," and "conservatism" are easy to envision.

Could an analogous problem develop with respect to a civil engineering project? Suppose two engineers approach a river to plan the building of a dam. One says, "This is a shallow river, so we can use lightweight structures that don't have to endure much stress." The other, disagreeing, replies, "You're wrong. This river is on the deep side, and we'll need heavy materials capable of bearing substantial loads." A heated argument ensues, similar in tone and ferocity to that between the proponents of different antipoverty policies. Of course, such a dispute is not very likely to occur, chiefly because the variables involved in building a dam are easily measured. Rather than argue about the depth of the river, the engineers would measure it in feet or meters. Both would accept feet or meters as legitimate standards of measurement; there would be no basis for disagreement. Since the pressure produced by water of various depths is also measurable by commonly accepted standards, our engineers would eventually have to agree as to how much stress would be placed on the dam. This parable is not meant to suggest that fields like engineering are free of controversy. Moral issues intrude there as well (should a bomb which everyone knows *could* be built actually be constructed?) and disagreements about unknowns are rife. Yet the engineer's ability to measure physical phenomena undoubtedly enables him to avoid a great many disputes of the kind that trouble political observers.

The political behaviorist must persevere in the face of these difficulties; if he is to succeed in the scientific study of political behavior he must devise standards for assessing phenomena. Only in this way can the problem of multiple interpretations of political events be overcome. Just as dams cannot be built on the basis of individual engineers' subjective assessments of whether rivers are "shallow" or "deep," accurate generalizations about, for example, the nature of government in different nations cannot be based on individual assessments of whether political systems are "democratic" or not. What depth is as well as what democracy is can be subject to any number of individual interpretations. A person may entertain a particular interpretation because of some emotional commitment. He may see what he wants to see, subconsciously making what he observes consistent with his own preferences. But assessing phenomena on the basis of subjective preferences does not help in the acquisition of scientific knowledge. Instead, one must assess phenomena against commonly accepted standards. That is, one must measure.

WHAT IS MEASURED?

Clearly, the task of measuring human phenomena that surround political behavior is not identical to the job of an engineer who measures the depth of water with a marked lead or a natural scientist who measures properties of physical bodies with balances and graduated cylinders. Yet, though what must be done is not quite so obvious as placing the object of one's interest up against a yardstick, the procedures are logically the same. It is the instruments that must be used that are different.

Some aspects of political behavior are quite easy to measure. If one is interested in voting behavior, one can go to the county courthouse —or perhaps to the local newspaper the day after an election—and find precinct-by-precinct returns for all relevant electoral contests. The proportion of voters in each precinct who voted Democratic, or the proportion of eligible voters who actually went to the polls, can be measured simply by counting up the votes. Race, which is thought to be a prominent factor in contemporary political behavior in the United States, is easily determinable by simple observation. Public opinion pollsters, for example, would have no difficulty in classifying respondents by race. Many measurements, be they of individuals whose behavior is directly under investigation or of collectivities of people such as precincts or states or countries, are just that easy to make.

The Behavior of People. Most often, perhaps, political behaviorists wish to understand the behavior of people directly. We see individuals perform acts and we wish to understand them. Several generalizations about people have already been mentioned. For example, in Chapter 1 we mentioned the proposition that education (which people possess) is associated with interest in politics. It is also asserted that young people's political views are related to those of their parents. Historically, the behavior of many kinds of people has been a matter of political interest. As one would discover from the readings assigned in any political behavior course, not only citizens but legislators, judges, bureaucrats, policemen, civic leaders, and many others have performed actions of great interest to political scientists.

Why do populations support (or fail to support) dictators? Who do ghetto residents riot (or fail to riot)? How can one explain student antiwar demonstrations? Do Congressmen respond to interest groups? In what circumstances will judges decide in favor of defendants? What makes a civil servant deny (or approve) a request for welfare payments? What motivates policemen to treat suspects harshly (or respectfully)? Why do local party leaders commit themselves to particular Presidential candidates? The number of important questions is endless, for the behavior of these various kinds of people affects our political lives in a multitude of ways. And the answers to these questions are scarcely known.

Probably the most common method of approaching these kinds of questions about the political behavior of people is the *sample survey*. A sample survey is very much like a public opinion poll, but its purpose is generally to provide data on a scholarly problem rather than to determine the popular consensus on an issue. Moreover, surveys may be designed to elicit information about any kind of people, not only "publics." Always, they involve asking people questions. The answers to these questions constitute the measurements political behaviorists seek. The questions need not deal with simple statements of preference such as polls report in the newspapers, but can and should approach the important kinds of problems noted above.

Often, it is impossible to question the entire group of persons with whom one is concerned. For example, one may be interested in American trial judges. There are too many such people and they are too dispersed geographically to make it practical to survey them all. We therefore draw a *sample*, some smaller number that we have reason to believe is *representative* of the whole. Obviously, generalizations based on data from an unrepresentative sample can have little validity. But though survey research is sometimes criticized on the ground that samples are biased, there are techniques for minimizing this danger.

Let us consider how we might approach a problem of explaining individual behavior through the use of a survey. In order to understand representation in democracies, one must understand the antecedents of legislative representatives' voting behavior. To whom (or what) do they respond: the dictates of their own principles, the wishes of party leaders, offers of money, the desires of their constituency? Suppose we want to assess the proposition that state representatives' votes are a consequence of what they perceive their constituencies as desiring. Assessment of the generalization "representatives votes are related to their perception of constituency desires" requires two measurements.[1] First, we must measure how the representatives vote. Fortunately, this is simple, since the necessary roll-call information can be obtained from official state records. Second, we must assess the representatives' perceptions of their constituencies' feelings. This is more problematical. The best way to obtain this information is probably to survey a sample of the representatives—to go to these men and ask them what one wants to know. But what should the measuring instrument (the survey question or questions) be like in order to extract such information? It is in matters like these that political measurement is neither self-evident nor easy. There are no obvious standards of constituency perception. The solution

31

lies in defining the property to be measured in terms of the operations one wishes to perform. The term *operational definition* is one frequently heard in the social sciences. It means simply this: One selects some sort of indicator and declares that certain types of observations have a particular meaning, whereas other possible observations have alternate meanings. In the example cited above, one would declare that certain subjects' responses constitute a perception of constituents as being anti policy X. Perhaps the indicator may be nothing more than a single question: "Do your constituents generally favor policy X, are they neutral toward it, or would you say that they generally are opposed?" Perception of constituents' wishes is thus measured in terms of positive, neutral, or negative, depending on the answers to this question. At times the choice of indicators may seem arbitrary. Although a great deal of controversy rages over the appropriateness of various scholars' measures, there is generally some rhyme and reason to their selection. In a recent study of citizens' attraction to demagogic appeals, for example, indicators were developed by consulting a panel of experts and selecting items on which they agreed.[2]

Another technique for developing survey instruments in some favor, because it cuts arbitrariness to a minimum, is the construction of scales. A *scale* is nothing more than a series of items, or questions, which one presents to one's subjects. The answers to such questions, however, consistently show a considerable relationship to one another. This relationship indicates that there is a *dimension* being measured, that one is not measuring an incidental and spurious set of responses that may happen to be rendered to a single item. An example is the "Political Efficacy Scale."[3] The extent to which citizens feel that their actions or beliefs with respect to government are efficacious (that is, have an impact on political events) has been shown to be related to many kinds of citizen behavior in democracies. Indeed, it is possible that people who feel efficacious are patriotic, while those who feel inefficacious are not. It is thus of great importance to test hypotheses about efficacy and, it follows, there must be some way of measuring it. One might do so by simply asking a sample, "Do you feel that you are able to influence political decisions in America today, or do you think that events will follow their course regardless of what you do?" This might be acceptable, but it is possible that many respondents will not see these alternatives as mutually exclusive. Perhaps they feel able to exert some influence but also believe that some events are really governed by an outside force. If so, responses may be made on a random basis, and the investigator has measured nothing at all. In short, no objective standards against which responses can be placed are at hand. The four items of the Political Efficacy Scale, however, all appear to elicit responses only along the desired dimension. This has been determined by actual tests on groups of people that have revealed the necessary degree of relationship among the answers. The four items are:

1. I don't think public officials care much about what people like me think.
2. Voting is the only way that people like me can have any say about how the government runs things.
3. People like me don't have any say about what the government does.
4. Sometimes politics and government seems so complicated that a person like me can't really understand what's going on.

Subjects are asked whether they agree or disagree in each case. They are then given a score on the scale that is a measurement of the degree to which they feel efficacious. One compiles the score simply by adding the number of "agree" answers a respondent gives. Clearly, it can range from 0 through 4. The lower the score, the more efficacious the subject feels; the higher the score, the less efficacious he feels. A scale is very similar to a test. Consider, for example, a political behaviorism exam with 100 multiple-choice questions. Everyone is given a score of from 0 to 100 depending on the number of questions answered correctly. A student's score determines his grade. Such a test is really a 100-item scale that measures a student's proficiency in political behaviorism. All undergraduate exams are measuring instruments that purport to assess student abilities. The typical social science scale is also a measuring instrument, but it purports to measure qualities other than academic abilities.

Of course, it is not always possible to use a scale. Scales have not been developed for all the politically relevant properties of human beings, and developing one's own is not easy. It is likely to require more than one study, since some testing is normally necessary. If an investigator has resources for only one survey, he may have to rely on *single-item measurement*, as in the survey of the state legislators discussed above, or upon *indices*, less formal combinations of questions. However, these instruments are not as trustworthy as a scale, and measurements based on them must be viewed with a greater degree of reservation.

Some interesting questions about political behavior may require the direct measurement of people's properties but be best approached by a method other than the survey. The survey, regardless of the kind of instrument used (scales, etc.), generally depends upon responses which subjects make to stimuli (questions) put by the investigator. Typically, one is asking for information. We saw how a researcher attempting to understand legislative behavior might logically proceed by asking legislators for information on their own acts. If an investigator were interested in judges, however, it might be preferable for him to visit courtrooms and actually observe judicial behavior being performed, as well as, perhaps, explanatory factors.[4] One might observe, for example, the amount of fines imposed by judges, as well as the demeanor of the defendants. This process, of course, is analogous to gathering information on behavior from official records, as is possible in the case of some courts, legislatures, bureaucratic agencies, and the like. One would resort to observation only when the desired data were not available from records. It might also be possible to observe systematically some aspects of citizen behavior, for example, obedience to traffic laws, by standing on a street corner with a ledger.

Though direct observation can be employed only in certain circumstances (it could hardly be used in a study of voting by secret ballot, for example), it does have certain advantages. It is surely an asset to secure measurements of *behavior* directly. In survey work, one must rely on what the subjects *say* they have done or will do. This is not, strictly speaking, a measurement of behavior at all. There is presumably a very explicit connection between the verbalization made in response to a survey instrument and the behavior of the subject, but it is probably not perfect. At least some subjects will lie to interviewers, and bad questions can elicit very faulty information. Some cynics even charge that survey research is not a valid method of inquiry because of the proxy nature of the verbal responses. Though this is an extreme position, it is well to be aware of the limitations of surveys. Direct observation, when it is possible, may help one to avoid some of these limitations.[5]

34

Individual behavior may also be amenable to another kind of observational design—the experiment. Of course, this procedure is familiar to all contemporary students of psychology. Experimental research is quite different from surveys and from observation in that there is deliberate manipulation of the explanatory factors. An investigator may be curious as to how people react to condition "A." So he imposes condition "A" upon a number of subjects (called the *experimental group*) in his laboratory and compares their reaction with that of another unit (known as the *control group*), whose members have been specifically shielded from condition "A." Any differences in the behavior of the two groups can logically be attributed to the causal action of condition "A." Reactions to physical stimuli such as lights or to social situations in small groups are typical subjects of experiments. Clearly, it is generally impossible to manipulate whole populations in order to watch their behavioral response to political stimuli. But it is possible to manipulate small groups in a laboratory and observe their response in terms of a verbalization (as in survey research) or of some other surrogate for actual political behavior. For example, the formation of coalitions for the attainment of some collective goal is thought by some to be a basic political act. Military alliances, legislative logrolling, and "political deals" all involve some sort of coalition to achieve power. It is possible to create laboratory situations in which the formation of coalitions is necessary to achieve some surrogate of political power. Different conditions, such as the degree of knowledge or the concentration of resources in individual hands, can be manipulated. The subjects' responses may tell us something about how the basic political act of forming coalitions occurs. Though not widespread in political behavior studies, experimentation and allied procedures are increasingly common in studies of international relations and various kinds of citizen behavior.[6]

The Behavior of Collectivities. Sometimes an investigator wishes to study the behavior of aggregations of people: of precincts, states, cities, nations. The behavior of such units is patently composed of the behavior of individuals; logically, then, they can be explained by a sufficient number of true generalizations about individual behavior. But sometimes the behavior of a collectivity is of importance in and of itself; its investigation and explanation can then proceed directly. For example, we may be interested in whether nations are ruled by democratic forms

of government. Clearly, form of government is a property of collectivities of people. What makes nations democratic? Though seeking an
answer to this question may lead us to a consideration of the *political
culture* citizens manifest—that is, to the distribution of socially relevant
attitudes in the population—it is clear that we are talking about something which attaches to nations and not to people. *Nations,* not their
citizens, are democratic or undemocratic. [7]

Similarly, we may be interested in state governments' positions on
various public issues. How can one explain whether a state is generous
or frugal in spending for public welfare, or roads, or education? These
are not questions about the behavior of individuals but about the behavior of collectivities made up of individuals. The examples could be
multiplied. If one is concerned about international affairs, the *policies* of
nations may be a crucial object of study. How do you explain which
policies nations pursue? Clearly, policies are the result of the behaviors
of a great many people—probably more than can be identified in any one
study. But focusing attention on these individual behaviors alone, and
even satisfactorily explaining them, does not necessarily complete our
task. We may not know the processes by which these behaviors are
translated into policy. We still need to focus on policy output as an
aggregate, for that is the ultimate object of our interest. [8]

Sometimes there are clear parallels between individual behavior
and aggregate behavior, so that the difference is not clear. For example,
we could attempt to explain voting patterns by conducting a survey of
individuals. Suppose we hypothesized that being black and voting for
Democratic aldermen were associated. Each person interviewed could
be asked how he voted in the aldermanic election and his race could be
observed (that is, every respondent would be measured twice, once for
vote and once for race). If, by and large, the people who were black were
the same people who voted for the Democrats, the hypothesis would be
confirmed. We could also approach the problem by gathering data on
collectivities. We could go to the local courthouse and measure the
proportion of voters in each precinct that voted Democratic. We could
then go to the U.S. Census reports and find data which we could
translate into a measure of the proportion of "nonwhites" in the population of each precinct. If, by and large, the precincts that had a high
nonwhite population were the same as those that had a high proportion
of Democratic voters, we would regard the hypothesis as confirmed.

Both approaches are legitimate. However, though the basic problem is the same, the findings are addressed toward different kinds of objects. In the survey study, one is making statements about *people*. In the aggregate data analysis, one is making statements about *precincts*. It is important to know about both people and precincts, but one should not be confused about what one is studying. There could, possibly, be a relationship between race and Democratic voting at the precinct level, but *not* at the individual level.[9] This state of affairs would have quite different implications from a situation where the findings were directly parallel. Being clear about what one is measuring is a good way to avoid making false inferences from one's data.

Generally, measurements of aggregate behavior are simpler to make than those of individual behavior. Often, as in the example above, one need only determine proportions or means from statistics already available. Of course, if one has to collect the information on which these proportions or means are based, the process of measurement can become very difficult indeed.

It follows from these remarks that the absence of generally recognized standards for evaluating observations may not be as great a problem in the analysis of collective behavior as it is in the analysis of individual behavior. If the population of a precinct is shown to be 25% nonwhite, there is little arguing with this fact. However, the problem of standards raises its head even in research on collectivities, and especially as one moves into some of the more interesting areas of research. For example, suppose, as in the example above, one is interested in the causes of democracy. Not only must the causes be measured, but so must the presence or absence of democracy in various nations. There is no self-evident way of classifying nations in this regard. What seems democratic to one man may seem oppressively totalitarian to another. Argument is to be expected. Again, we can see how difficult measurement can become, but at the same time we can see how necessary it is that it be performed so that we can assess the validity of generalizations.

The distinction between individuals and collectivities is not unique to the social sciences. An engineer may be concerned with the properties of steel, such as tensile strength or ductility. Clearly it is important to know about these things and the factors that affect them. The heating of steel is associated with an increase in its strength. To an engineer, this is a legitimate generalization of some importance. However, steel may be considered a collectivity of constituent particles. Various elements must be joined in such a way as to make steel. The physicist deals with generalizations about iron, carbon, and other ingredients. To pursue this line of thinking further, the study of the atomic makeup of matter leads to studies of the behavior of quite minute particles such as electrons and neutrons—which compose elements like carbon and iron. None would deny that we need to know about the behavior of these subatomic particles, as well as about the behavior of elements and of steel. But knowledge of one does not automatically translate into knowledge of the others. Scientists must choose a level on which to focus their efforts.

KINDS OF MEASUREMENT

If we are to use convenient labels in our discussion, we must first agree on some terminology. The properties of people, collectivities, or whatever political behaviorists happen to be measuring are called *variables*. This is appropriate enough, for interesting things are those that conceivably could change, that might be different from time to time, place to place, or person to person. Race is interesting because some people are white and some are black. It *varies* from person to person. Party identification is interesting because people may be Democrats or Republicans or Independents, or something else. Party identification is a *variable*. Thus, variables are properties of objects that may assume different values. Political behaviorists are generally involved in asking why objects assume the values they do on a variable rather than some other possible value. We are interested, for example, in why countries (objects) are more or less democratic or totalitarian (assume different values) on the variable "form of government."

The alternative to a property's being a variable is its being a constant. Constant features are the same for all the objects one is interested in. Constants are definitional. They are the criteria by which we classify things for study. All the behavior we study in a political behavior course is political. Being political is a constant feature of the objects of our interest. But once we have so defined the objects of our interest, the constants become quite uninteresting. To be sure, the question of whether something is political or not might interest some scholars—but "politicalness" would then become a variable. Clearly, variables are what generate scientific interest. We shall return to this very point shortly in the next section.

Interval Measurement. As we have already indicated, variables may be measured in a variety of ways, or by a variety of *scales*. The word *scale* is used here in a different sense than when it was used to describe a series of questions designed to measure individual responses along a dimension. In this case, we are discussing the levels, or the refinement, of measurement. The most precise kind of measurement used in the social sciences is the *interval scale*. This kind of scale is characterized by *units* of equal size, analogous to the inches or centimeters of a ruler. Thus any object can be assigned an absolute value, and any two measured objects can be compared in terms of the absolute difference in their magnitudes. For example, we may measure the height of books according to an interval scale, using inches as units. One book may be unambiguously determined to be 8-7/8 inches high. A second book may be unambiguously determined to be 6-1/2 inches high. By comparing the two, we know which is larger and, moreover, exactly *how much* larger it is. This degree of precision is often achieved in the so-called natural sciences —indeed, virtually all such fields depend heavily on this kind of measurement. Given the difficulty of obtaining ready measurement standards, it should come as no surprise that interval measurement is not always possible in political science. But there are some circumstances in which it is feasible. For example, personal income may be measured in a sample survey. If exact income figures on each of the subjects are obtained, one may discover that A has an income of $9,654 and B has an income of $12,978. B's is larger and by exactly $3,324. Fines meted out by judges may be measured by interval scales, as may age or years of formal education. Interval scales are frequently used to measure properties of collectivities. For example, we can easily determine precisely how Democratic any precinct is compared to other precincts by noting the proportion voting Democratic in a given election. Government appropriations can be handled in the same way, as can most of the means and proportions that often characterize aggregate data on collectivities.

Ordinal Measurement. Interval measurement is clearly desirable for the amount of information it communicates. Unfortunately, in the social sciences, it is often impossible to measure the properties of objects by ascribing to them absolute values in terms of some units. It is often possible only to ascribe *ranks*. That is, the value assigned to an object locates it in one of a series of categories that have an ordered relationship to one another. This is called *ordinal measurement*. The notion of ordinality is common. For example, in horse racing the performance of competing steeds is measured by the order in which they finish. At least as far as the payoffs to bettors are concerned, the absolute margins that separate the horses are unimportant. The important thing is whether a horse finishes first, second, or third. Ordinal measurement is what counts. Many other kinds of commonly used rankings come to mind.

Perhaps most political science measurements are of this type. Many single-item instruments elicit responses measurable on an ordinal scale. Earlier in this chapter we considered the possibility of measuring Congressmen's perceptions of the degree of favorability of their constituencies toward a given policy. We suggested a single question to be asked of the legislators: "Do your constituents generally favor policy X, are they neutral toward it, or would you say that they generally are opposed?" Perception was to be measured in terms of pro-, neutral, or anti-, depending on the answer to this question. The three possible responses can be thought of as constituting an ordinal scale for measuring perceived support. Those who answer "pro-" perceive the most support, those who answer "neutral" see the next most support, and those who answer "anti-" see the least. The three possible answers are clearly arranged in a rank order and thus constitute an ordinal scale. The political efficacy scale discussed above is also an ordinal variable. The five possible scores, 0 through 4, indicate the degree of felt efficacy in individuals. But though a score of 3 indicates less perceived efficacy than a score of 1, it is impossible to say in any real sense how much less. The interval between the scores is not determinable. The scores differ by two, but two what? The statements composing this scale are interrelated, but not in the same way as interval units. Thus the measurements taken must be treated as ordinal measurements, and the respondents' scores are ranks rather than absolute values.

Nominal Measurement. Finally, there are many interesting political phenomena that cannot be measured even with ordinal scales. Race and religious affiliation, for example, are not properties people possess in varying degrees. One is usually thought of as Caucasian, Mongoloid, or Negroid, as a member of one of a set mutually exclusive and exhaustive categories. Similarly, one is or is not a member of a specific denomination. Membership in such groups is not a matter of degree, nor is the difference between groups a matter of degree. The same is true of the sex of persons. Often nations are considered to be democratic or non-democratic rather than to possess different amounts of democracy. Voters may be classified as Democrats, Republicans, or Independents. It is difficult to think of these categories as ordinally arranged, let alone deriving from an interval scale. Clearly, what we have is a kind of differentiation of objects into categories that are determined not by their order, but simply by their differences. Blacks are different from whites, men are different from women, democracy is different from totalitarianism, and Democrats are different from Republicans, not in quantity, but in quality. This kind of measurement is called *nominal*. It simply means that we call different phenomena by different names. A *nominal scale*, in a sense a contradiction in terms, simply means a series of categories into which observations of a given property can be classified.

This should not be thought of as an inferior kind of measurement. In politics it is often the only kind possible. And nominal variables are often of the greatest importance in determining political behavior. Race is measured by a two-category nominal scale; yet no one can doubt that this variable is importantly linked to very critical kinds of behavior that should be researched.

All three kinds of measurement—interval, ordinal, and nominal —are applied to political phenomena. Fortunately, all can be employed in achieving the goals of political behaviorism—the discovery of valid general propositions. As we shall see shortly, each has a role in the explanation of the political world.

Explanation

It is clear that measurement contributes to each of the distinguishing features of the political behavioral approach outlined in Chapter 1. To effectively concentrate on facts, one must measure them. To make generalizations, one must make repeated observations of similar phenomena and compare them. The only way to make truly valid comparisons is by evaluating phenomena with respect to a common standard—a measuring standard. It is easy to see why measurement is a basic procedure of political behaviorism.

However, one of the characteristic features of the political behavioral approach is in itself procedural—the emphasis on explanation rather than description. Unlike the other characteristics of the discipline, which reflect orientations, explanation involves procedures whose nature is not self-evident. It therefore deserves special discussion.

The term *explanation* has several meanings, all of which have one element in common—they all involve *accounting* for something in some way, manner, shape, or fashion. To explain sometimes means to *elaborate*. For example, a student may say, "I am really ready for the English exam tomorrow." If pressed to explain, he may say, "Well, I've studied very hard, I know the material, and I've psyched out the prof." Or, he may say, "I got a copy of the exam in advance." To explain can mean to *rationalize or justify*. A motorist, asked to explain why he was driving 50 miles an hour in a 30 mile zone, may say, "I was taking my wife to the hospital." There are other similar, less formal meanings of the word. As we saw in Chapter 1, the political behaviorist seeks to explain phenomena in the sense of learning their *causes*. Of course, attributing causes to observed events is a very common kind of explanation, indulged in by politicians, editors, and, indeed, almost everyone in the course of normal discussion. But even in this sense, accounting for political behavior can fall short of the criteria for explanation we will employ in this section. For example, one could explain political behavior simply by presenting a statement of one's own belief. Asked to explain civil disorders in urban areas, one might reply, "They are due to outside agitators." In one sense, this is an explanation. But it is really just a hypothesis. Although it is a statement of cause and effect, it is not, in and of itself, an explanation in the political behaviorist's sense of the term. It may be completely untested. Only if there are data which establish a connection between the variable "existence of urban riots" and the variable "presence or absence of outside agitators" will the

42

political behaviorist accept this statement as an explanation. The point is that explanation, as we see it, requires data.

TABLES

As students of political behavior, we may be interested in participation in demonstrations by American university students against U.S. military activities. The degree of participation varies from student to student, and to understand it we shall have to measure it. We shall also have to look for its causes. Let us assume that we have reason to believe that the generalization "permissive child-rearing practices are related to (cause) antimilitary activity" may be true. We have introduced a second variable, the permissiveness with which the students were raised, and it too must be measured. We are now embarked on the attempt to explain antimilitary demonstrations as being caused by permissive child raising. Let us assume that we conduct a survey of a sample of 200 students. We might measure the amount of participation in demonstrations (the first variable) by asking the students how many such activities they had participated in. Let us assume that the data allow students to be measured, with respect to this variable, in terms of no demonstrations, one demonstration, or more than one. We might also ask each student a series of questions about his early family life involving, say, participation in family decisions, the frequency of punishment, and the degree of independence permitted in social relations with peers. His answers would indicate a permissive or nonpermissive relationship with his family with respect to certain types of situations. Depending on how many "permissive" answers each subject gave, he would be assigned a permissiveness index score—high, medium, or low.

With these basic steps taken and our data now collected, how do we go about determining whether permissiveness explains (causes) participation in demonstrations? Very simply, we determine whether there is a relationship between the two variables. We can begin by setting up a *table* in which to display our data. Across the top of our table, we indicate our *independent variable*. This term is applied to variables which one employs to do the explaining. In this case, permissiveness is to explain demonstrating, so permissiveness is the independent variable. The term independent is well chosen, because permissiveness is not thought to depend upon any other variable with which we are concerned in this study. The possible scores people may be assigned determine the column headings, which appear across the top of the table. We thus have:

CHILDHOOD PERMISSIVENESS
(INDEPENDENT VARIABLE)

High	Medium	Low

In each of the columns, we will show how people who have the same score on the independent variable behave.

Down the left side of the table, we indicate the *dependent* variable. This is a term one applies to variables that he wishes to explain. In this case it is demonstration behavior. The term *dependent* is used because we are investigating the proposition that this variable depends upon permissiveness, another variable in the study. The possible values of the dependent variable determine the rows of the table. We add them thus:

Number of Demonstrations (dependent variable)	CHILDHOOD PERMISSIVENESS (INDEPENDENT VARIABLE)		
	High	Medium	Low
None			
One			
More than one			

We are now ready to start filling in the blank table with data. Each student must be assigned to one of the nine "cells" of the table. This is easy to do, as each subject has been measured with respect to the two

relevant variables. We take the data on one of our subjects and discover
(1) that he is low in permissiveness and (2) that he has participated in no
demonstrations. He is thus assigned to the upper-right-hand-corner cell
of the table. A second student's data indicate that he was treated very
permissively and that he has participated in more than one antimilitary
demonstration. He is therefore assigned to the lower-left-hand-corner
cell. We continue in this way until all 200 students are accounted for.
Our table can now be reproduced, using numbers to indicate how many
students have been assigned to each cell. Let us assume that we have
obtained the following results:

Number of Demonstrations (dependent variable)	CHILDHOOD PERMISSIVENESS (INDEPENDENT VARIABLE)		
	High	Medium	Low
None	12	17	36
One	15	41	14
More than one	42	13	10
Total	69	71	60

Looking at these raw figures, we begin to get the feeling that our
variables may indeed be very strongly related. However, it is generally
easier to interpret data in percentage form, so we perform a few calculations and arrive at a table in final form, such as might appear in the
professional literature of political science (Table 2-1). Notice that in this
table, as in many one will encounter in the literature, the vertical rules
and some of the horizontal rules have been omitted. Also notice that we
have calculated the percentages so that each column adds to 100%
(discounting the effects of rounding). That is, the 12 in the upper-left-
hand cell of the original table, for example, has become 17.4% because
12 is 17.4% of 69, the total number in the left-hand column. We have
done this because we wish to compare the way the different values of the
independent variable are distributed. After all, what we are asking in
this study, is "Does the independent variable make any difference in the
way people behave?" In order to find out, we must know whether
people with a given score on this variable behave differently with

TABLE 2–1

**Childhood Permissiveness and Student
Demonstration Behavior**

Number of Demonstrations	PERMISSIVENESS		
	High (N = 69)*	Medium (N = 71)*	Low (N = 60)*
None	17.4%	23.9%	60.0%
One	21.7	57.7	23.3
More than one	60.9	18.3	16.7
Total	100.0%	99.9%†	100.0%

* N refers to the number of subjects recorded in each column. It tells us how many people the table is talking about.

† Because of rounding, this column does not add to exactly 100%.

respect to the dependent variable from those with other scores. That is, as far as participation in antimilitary demonstrations is concerned, do people who have a high permissiveness index score behave differently than those who have a medium or low score? This is easy to answer if we compare the columns. By placing the independent variable at the top of the table, we have made sure that the addition will be *down*, rather than across; this is more convenient and easier to read. Calculating the percentages in such a way that they added to 100% to the right (i.e., making the 12 in the upper-left-hand cell 18.5% because 12 is 18.5% of 65, the total number of subjects in the upper row) would be incorrect because we are not asking whether variations in demonstration behavior make a difference in some variable. We are asking what *happens to* demonstration behavior. Treating the data in this way could produce highly misleading results. To avoid this possibility, and to display data in the most readily interpretable form, it is a good rule of thumb always to place the independent variable at the top of the table and to have the percentages add down. Most research reports subscribe to this rule.

Let us return to the substantive results of Table 2-1. Clearly, they bear out our hypothesized relationship. Most students who were treated very permissively, we see from the left-hand column, have participated in more than one demonstration. Inspection of the center column reveals that most students treated with a moderate degree of permis-

46

siveness show some tendency toward demonstrations (most have been involved in one), whereas a look at the right-hand column shows that students with a nonpermissive upbringing generally shun demonstrations. There appears to be a definite connection; permissiveness appears to be one of the causes of participation in demonstrations. Permissiveness explains demonstrating.

In a table of this kind, explanation is indicated when there is a concentration of large values in the cells along one of the diagonals. In this case, the diagonal from the lower left to the upper right contains high values, and from this we infer a connection between the variables in the anticipated direction (a positive connection). If the high values had fallen along the opposite diagonal, that is, in the upper left, center, and lower right cells, the table would have shown the exact opposite of our hypotheses—that nonpermissiveness was associated with (explained) demonstration behavior! Research in the social sciences sometimes produces this kind of result. If the values are approximately the same in all the cells, so that there is no pattern, the variables are assumed to be unrelated and the search for new explanatory factors is continued. The same conclusion would be reached if large values were concentrated in one row of the table—for example, if 65% of the students in all three columns participated in no demonstrations at all. Though such data would indicate a generally low level of participation in demonstrations, they would tell us nothing about the cause of such behavior.

Table 2-1, as we have noted, does support the generalization that permissiveness and participation in demonstrations are associated. Nevertheless, it is clear that some of the students interviewed constitute exceptions to this generalization. For example, 17.4% of those who were raised very permissively, unlike most of their cohorts, engaged in no demonstrations at all. This is not surprising, for as we saw in Chapter 1, scientific generalizations are at best only partially true. That is to say, any one independent variable will not explain all the variance of a dependent variable. In this case, factors other than a strict upbringing cause students to refrain from demonstrations. It is to these other factors that we must look for an explanation of the behavior of 17.4% of the permissively treated students. What these factors are can be learned only through the discovery of other partially true generalizations, perhaps expressed through additional tables identical in format to Table 2-1.

The importance of the independent variable as an explanation of behavior is indicated by the values in the cells on the diagonal. The more observations there are in these cells, and the fewer "exceptions" (observations in other cells), the stronger the relationship between the two variables is and the more it explains. If a generalization were completely true, if it completely explained the behavior of every individual studied, *all* the observations would be in the cells of the diagonal, and the value in each of these cells would be 100%. This would indicate complete knowledge of the subject of interest; it is a condition not likely to occur unless the relationship in question is trivial.

In the course of reading the literature of political behavior, one quickly becomes aware that explanatory inferences are drawn from other kinds of presentations, as well as tables. This is because it is possible to express relationships between variables in different ways, depending upon the circumstances and the level of measurement. Table 2-1, which deals with demonstration behavior and parental permissiveness, clearly reports data on *ordinal* variables. Each variable is divided into categories that are ranked from high to low. A similar table would be appropriate for nominal measurements. For example, we might be concerned with individual personality structure and its possible effects on political loyalties. Some persons' personalities cause them to interpret human relationships in terms of rigidly structured hierarchical patterns. Others are more inclined toward equalitarian postures. Suppose our data—answers to a series of survey questions—allow us to divide subjects into two groups, authoritarians and equalitarians. This classification constitutes a form of nominal measurement. Since we are also interested in the partisan loyalties of our subjects, we ask them to classify themselves as Democrats, Independents, or Republicans. Since these categories are not ordered, they too comprise nominal measurement. We can test the hypothesis that personality structure affects party identification by arranging our data as in Table 2-2.

Since personality structure is the independent variable (cause), it dictates the column headings, while party identification, the dependent variable (effect), determines the rows. Since the categories are not arranged in any order, one need not find a diagonal trend in order to determine a relationship. It is necessary only that the columns have different distributions. In this case, an inspection of the columns reveals that the largest proportion of both authoritarians and equalitarians are

TABLE 2–2

Personality and Party Identification

Party Identification	Equalitarian (N = 117)	Authoritarian (N = 241)
Democratic	48%	47%
Independent	35	23
Republican	17	30
Total	100%	100%

Source: Robert E. Lane, *Political Man* (New York: Free Press, 1972), p. 46. Copyright © 1972 by The Free Press, a Division of Macmillan Publishing Co., Inc.

Democrats. However, this should not be taken to mean that both equalitarianism and authoritarianism lead to being Democratic. In fact, as far as being Democratic goes, authoritarianism or equalitarianism makes no difference at all. Being Democratic does not *depend* upon this personality variable; it is not related to it and it is not caused by it. The large Democratic figures in both columns can be taken to indicate that there were more Democrats than Republicans or Independents in the sample. Some differences, however, do appear in the second and third rows. Personality structure does appear to affect the distribution of Independence as opposed to Republicanism. Republicans are more likely to be authoritarians, and Independents are more likely to be equalitarians. In short, personality has some effect on political affiliations, though it is hardly dramatic.

GRAPHS

When it comes to the expression of relationships between variables measurable on an interval scale, tables are often less efficient than graphic presentations. If one can measure along a continuous dimension, there is no point in dividing a variable into discrete categories. Suppose that we are concerned with the proposition that white resistance to black participation in normal political channels is concentrated in areas where the population has little education. Indeed, there are numerous studies which show that racial discrimination and prejudice are related to low levels of education. This proposition is also consistent

49

with the assertion that racial difficulties can be solved if only people can be educated. Ignorance, it is argued, leads whites to perform unwise, discriminatory acts. White ignorance therefore explains low black participation. If this is so, it is reasonable to argue that in the American South, where there is considerable variance in black participation from area to area, there will be a positive relationship between the amount of education whites possess in a given county and the proportion of the black population of the county registered to vote. As it happens, county-by-county aggregate data on both these variables are available.[10] Since they are continuous variables, they can be used as the axes of a graph, as in Figure 2-1.

FIGURE 2—1

The Median Percentage of Voting-Age Blacks Registered to Vote, by Median School Years Completed by Whites

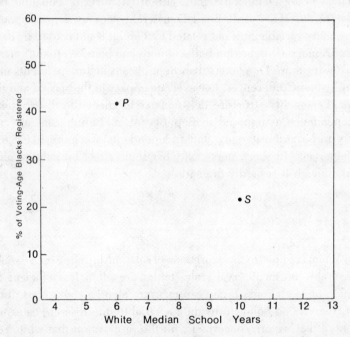

The arrangement of elements in the figure has several similarities to Tables 2-1 and 2-2. Again, the dependent variable (effect) is positioned on the left, and the independent variable is arranged horizontally, albeit this time the label appears at the bottom rather than the

50

top of the array. We are now ready to measure the median number of school years completed by whites and the proportion of eligible blacks registered to vote in each Southern county. Let us say that the whites in Pansy County have a median of six years of education; similarly, let us assume that 42% of the black population is registered. Rather than being assigned to a cell of a table, Pansy County is assigned to a point *P* on the graph. As information on other counties is obtained, they too are assigned points on the graph. This gives us a *scatter diagram*, a pattern of points from which we can infer a relationship. The more closely the points are clustered in a diagonal pattern, the greater the association between the two variables and the greater the explanatory power of the independent variable. Drawing a line that summarizes our findings will make the graph easier to interpret. One way of doing this is to take all the counties with a given median level of white education and calculate the median proportion of blacks registered in these same counties. We can then enter a summary point above that educational level on the graph. For example, suppose that there are five counties with a median educational level for whites of ten years, and that the proportion of blacks registered in these counties is, respectively, 16, 20, 22, 24, and 27%. The median number of blacks registered in these counties is therefore 22%. We can now enter a point S on the graph corresponding to ten years of education for whites and a black registration rate of 22%. A similar point can be calculated for all counties where the educational level is higher or lower. (Remember, just as we compared observations within columns of the independent variables in examining tabular data, we now compare distributions at different *values* of the independent variable.) We then connect the points with a line, the slope or curve of which will enable us to interpret the relationship between the variables. (See Figure 2-2.) Notice that we could have made a table with these data. We could have divided our measurements of the independent variable into, say, low, medium, and high levels of education. For example, we could have defined the level of education as low, where the median number of years of schooling for whites was below six, medium where it was between six and nine, and high where it was above nine. By drawing vertical lines at 6 and 9 on the graph, we could create table columns. By dividing the values of the dependent variable into similar categories and drawing horizontal lines at the dividing points, we could create rows. The resultant cells would be filled in with values equivalent to the number of points on the scatter diagram that fell within them. But since our data are more finely measured (by an interval scale), we need not do this; instead of tables we have graphs, which, though logically equivalent to tables, are more precise.

We can see from Figure 2-2 that our two variables are strongly related, but not in the direction we predicted! As the level of white education goes up in these counties studied, the black registration rate

FIGURE 2–2

The Median Percentage of Voting-Age Blacks Registered to Vote, by Median School Years Completed by Whites

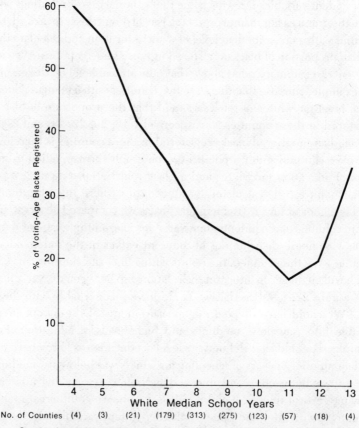

| No. of Counties | (4) | (3) | (21) | (179) | (313) | (275) | (123) | (57) | (18) | (4) |

Source: Adapted from Donald R. Matthews and James W. Prothro, *Negroes and the New Southern Politics* (New York: Harcourt Brace Jovanovich, 1966), p. 128. © 1966 by Harcourt Brace Jovanovich, Inc. Used with the publisher's permission.

goes down. This is a *negative* relationship, negative not because it is the opposite of what we expected, but because as the values of one variable get higher, those of the other get lower. In other words, the diagonal slopes down and to the right rather than up and to the right. This finding, which is a real one, is not as astonishing as it may seem. The premises on which we based our initial prediction were false. (After all, it is to discover whether our premises are true or false that we conduct research.) The authors who discovered this relationship interpret it as follows:

> Short of the highest levels, the more educated the whites the more actively and effectively they seem to enforce the traditional mores of the region against Negro participation in elections. The usual effect of an increase in average schooling for whites in the South as a whole appears to be to give the white people more of the skills that are needed to express effectively their anti-Negro sentiment.[11]

Only where the level of education is very high is the negative relationship reversed. This slight reversal, incidentally, might be worth some interpretive comments. First, because of the very small number of counties with such high white educational levels, the overall social impact of the trend they represent is probably quite small. Second, it hints that higher education may be different in its political effect from lower education, and suggests the desirability of further research on the topic.

CORRELATION COEFFICIENTS

Explanatory relationships between political variables are sometimes reported without presenting arrays of data in tabular or graphic form. There are indicators which can be derived from these forms, and to save space, if for no other reason, one may wish to use them. In the case of interval or ordinal data, *correlation coefficients* can be calculated. These coefficients are computed in such a way that they range from -1.00 for a perfect negative relationship through 0.00 for no relationship at all to 1.00 for a perfect positive relationship. For interval data, the *Pearson product-moment correlation coefficient* is most commonly used. It is based on the best possible straight line (regression line) that can be drawn through a scatter diagram to summarize all the points. If such a straight line were drawn in Figure 2-2, it would slope down and to the right. As it happens, the correlation coefficient for the data reported in Figure 2-2 is $-.26$. This is a moderate correlation indicating a substantial relationship. However, it does not, as usual, in studies of political behavior, bespeak a completely true generalization. There are exceptional counties whose position on the scatter diagram is quite far from the regression line. Hence there are other, unknown causes of black registration rates. The closer the points are to the line, the larger the absolute value of the correlation; if all the points in the diagram fell exactly on the line, the correlation coefficient would be -1.00 and the dependent variable (black registration) would be completely explained. This kind of result is not obtained in political research.

It is easy to see that in presenting data on several relationships at the same time, a great deal of space could be saved by noting correlations rather than presenting large arrays of data. Correlations can convey some impression of the magnitude of the relationship between two variables without requiring the reader to scrutinize a great many graphs; attempting to keep many graphs in mind at once can be confusing, not to mention time consuming and tiring. For this reason, scholars often resort to correlations.

There are, however, some liabilities to this mode of presenting data, and sometimes it is wise to refrain from the use of correlations, or to use both correlations and graphs. The correlation of $-.26$, which describes the data in Figure 2-2, conceals the interesting upturn at the high end of the education distribution and it does not tell us how much registration to expect in a county with a given level of white education.

In measuring variables on ordinal scales, one often presents data in tables such as Table 2-1. But again, one may wish to take advantage of correlation coefficients. In this case, they are calculated directly from the entries in the table. It is not necessary to describe their computation here; their purpose, as in the case of interval data, is to express the degree of relationship between two variables in a concise, easily interpretable form. Coefficients for ordinal data may be thought of as somewhat analogous to Pearson correlation coefficients. Several different

54

correlations may be computed, but those most commonly used are perhaps Kendall's *tau* (sometimes τ) and Goodman and Kruskal's *Gamma* (γ). Which one is used depends on the features of the data one wishes to emphasize; since they are both tools that man has created, they have features that he has put there. They have no cosmic validity, for they are both quite arbitrary conventions. However, both range between -1.00 and 1.00, and either provides a good indication of the strength of relationship between two ordinal variables. These correlations are especially convenient when one has large tables with many cells; such arrays, especially if several must be considered simultaneously, are difficult to keep in mind. Often, research results will be presented in tabular form and the corresponding ordinal coefficient will appear beneath the table as an addendum. The same kinds of reservations mentioned in the discussion of interval correlations, however, attend their use.

Nominal data involve a special problem. One cannot calculate correlation coefficients between nominal variables. Correlation answers the question of what happens to the magnitude of the dependent variable as the independent variable gets larger (or smaller). Since nominal variables are not defined in terms of magnitudes, the idea of correlation is not applicable. One is, therefore, obliged to describe relationships between nominal variables more in terms of the basic data array than may be the case for ordinal or interval relationships.

These examples do not cover all of the ways in which research results may be presented, though they do treat of the most common and most basic ones. Sometimes other measures of association are used (even with nominal variables), and different techniques are often used to examine the relationship between variables measured on different scales. But knowledge of these techniques can be acquired as it is needed and as the sophistication of one's work increases.

SIGNIFICANCE

We seek empirical evidence of relationships in order to explain phenomena. Accordingly, prominent diagonals in tables or graphs of one's data are regarded as demonstrating success in achieving one of the chief goals of the study of political behavior. However, since we are often dealing with *samples* of people (or collectivities), we cannot really be sure—even if the sample is not biased—that expressed relationships are in fact characteristic of the whole population. If we select a random sample of 500 people from a population, there is some possibility that the 500 will not be representative of the whole. It is possible, though not likely, that we selected 500 oddballs. In that event, the relationships we would report would not be the basis for good generalizations; our conclusions would be false. The notion of *significance* addresses this problem. It has to do with calculating the odds that a relationship one finds in a sample is not characteristic of the entire population. In political behavior literature we often see statements like "This relationship is significant at the .05 level" in reference to a particular finding. This simply means that there are five or fewer chances out of a hundred that the sample relationship (evidenced by a table, graph, or correlation coefficient) is not in fact characteristic of the whole population. "Significant at the .01 level" means one or fewer chances in a hundred of this kind of error; "significant at the .001 level" means one or fewer chances in a thousand. Of course, the fewer the chances of error, the greater one's confidence can be in the relationship expressed. Often significance is expressed in this form: $p < .05$. This simply means that the *probability* (p) of error is less than five chances in a hundred. As a rule, a probability of error greater than .05 is regarded as too large for reporting a relationship as valid. In the case of interval or ordinal data, we speak of the significance of correlation coefficients rather than of raw data arrays. Knowledge of the coefficient and a few other characteristics of the data allow such calculations. In the case of nominal data, significance is calculated from a statistic known as *chi-square* (χ^2). This statistic, which can vary from zero to infinity, is calculated from the raw data array. Its interpretation depends on the number of "degrees of freedom" that are associated with the table. A table is said to possess more degrees of freedom (sometimes abbreviated "d.f.") the larger the number of rows and columns. We can determine, from standard published values printed as appendices to statistics books or manuals, whether a chi-square of a given magnitude is significant for tables of the size in question. Chi-square and the accompanying statement of the significance are often presented directly below tables of data in the literature.

The actual procedures for calculating significance are not particularly difficult, but this is not the time to go into them. As long as one understands what significance means, learning how to compute it can wait until one has had some formal training in statistics. As a closing note, it should be pointed out that some authors do not use significance tests in reporting their data. This may be because they feel the implications of their findings are clear enough without it or because their data arrays are too complex to allow a meaningful test of significance. For some relationships involving several variables simultaneously, no tests have yet been devised.

CONTROL VARIABLES

We have mentioned many times that dependent variables—the things we wish to explain—often have several simultaneous causes. Thus one may observe relationships between a number of independent variables and a single dependent variable; all of them may be significant, but the generalization that each represents can be only partially true. How can one sort out the relative importance of several independent variables, particularly when the independent variables may be related to each other in some way? Sometimes what one takes to be an independent variable may be heavily affected by *another* independent variable. The situation then becomes quite complex. For example, we may suspect that both income and education (independent variables) are related to partisan preferences (dependent variables). Thus, there should be a discernible relationship between income and party and also between education and party. But since income and education are related to each other, we do not know to what extent each of these relationships reflects the operation of the other independent variable. Education itself may have no effect; the relationship between education and party that we observe may occur only because education happens to be associated with income, which really does have an effect. For example, let us assume that a sample survey of a voting population has been conducted, measuring three variables: income, education, and partisan preference. Tabulating the data indicates that there is a relationship between income and party (see Table 2-3) and another between education and party (see Table 2-4). However, both relationships are incom-

57

TABLE 2–3

Income and Party Preference

| Party | INCOME | | | |
Preference	Below the Mean		Above the Mean	
Republican	35%	(15)	75%	(15)
Democrat	65	(28)	25	(5)
Total	100%	(43)	100%	(20)

TABLE 2–4

Education and Party Preference

| Party Preference | EDUCATION | | | | | |
	Less than Highschool		Highschool		More than Highschool	
Republican	37%	(6)	44%	(16)	72%	(8)
Democrat	63	(10)	56	(20)	28	(3)
Total	100%	(16)	100%	(36)	100%	(11)

plete. Both tables reveal exceptions to the generalization implied, and both independent variables may be among the multiple causes of party preferences. (As in earlier tables, the independent variable in each case is at the top of the data array and the dependent variable is at the side.)

In order to determine whether education has a real effect on party, and its apparent effect is not just an incidental artifact of education's relationship with income, we must *control* for income. That is, we must determine whether education is related to party *regardless of* income. If it is, the education-party relationship should show up among people with low incomes and people with high incomes. Thus, we need additional tables—one for people with incomes above the mean and one for people with incomes below the mean—in the same form as Table 2-4. The two panels in Table 2-5 provide the necessary information. Notice that the first panel is concerned only with the 43 people with incomes below the mean and the second panel is concerned only with the 20 high-income subjects.

TABLE 2–5

Education and Party Preference with
Income Controlled

PERSONS WITH INCOMES ABOVE THE MEAN

Party Preference	Education		
	Less than Highschool	Highschool	More than Highschool
Republican	31% (4)	37% (10)	33% (1)
Democrat	69 (9)	63 (17)	67 (2)
Total	100% (13)	100% (27)	100% (3)

PERSONS WITH INCOMES BELOW THE MEAN

Party Preference	Education		
	Less than Highschool	Highschool	More than Highschool
Republican	67% (2)	67% (6)	87% (7)
Democrat	33 (1)	33 (3)	13 (1)
Total	100% (3)	100% (9)	100% (8)

The strong relationship indicated in Table 2-4 is clearly *not* repeated in Table 2-5. Among persons with incomes below the mean, there is no relationship at all between education and income, while among people with higher incomes, the relationship is very slight and not significant. Thus, we say that the relationship *disappears* when controlled for income. Education has no effect of its own on party. The apparent relationship in Table 2-4 is due merely to the fact that education happens to be associated with income.

One could, of course, look at Tables 2-3 and 2-4 and suggest with equal logic that income has no effect on party and that the apparent relationship in Table 2-3 is due to the fact that income happens to be related to education, a variable which really has some impact. In order to test this, we would have to test the relationship between income and party while controlling for education. That is, we must determine whether income is related to party regardless of education. To do this we need three tables, one for each level of education measured, or one three-part table such as Table 2-6. It can easily be seen from this table

TABLE 2–6

Income and Party Preference with Education Controlled

PERSONS WITH LESS THAN A HIGHSCHOOL EDUCATION

Party Preference	Income	
	Below the Mean	Above the Mean
Republican	31% (4)	67% (2)
Democrat	69 (9)	33 (1)
Total	100% (13)	100% (3)

HIGHSCHOOL GRADUATES

Party Preference	Income	
	Below the Mean	Above the Mean
Republican	37% (10)	67% (6)
Democrat	63 (17)	33 (3)
Total	100% (27)	100% (9)

PERSONS WITH MORE THAN A HIGHSCHOOL EDUCATION

Party Preference	Income	
	Below the Mean	Above the Mean
Republican	33% (1)	88% (7)
Democrat	67 (2)	12 (1)
Total	100% (3)	100% (8)

that the strong relationship between income and party persists regardless of the level of education. According to the data available to us, then, this is a valid relationship. It is not an artifact of a relationship between education and income. We have more confidence in the relationship because of its ability to persist despite the control.

Since the data above involved a nominal variable, tables and subtables were employed in determining the relationships and in manipulating the controlled variables. In the case of ordinal and interval data, it is possible to control variables through the use of *partial* correlation coefficients. For example, if the correlation between independent variable A and dependent variable B was .47, one might question whether this correlation was an artifact of the fact that B was heavily influenced by the additional variable C, which happened to be related to A as well. Computations that tell how much of the original relationship between A and B remains after C has been taken into account result in partial correlations (or *partials*). The partial correlation between A and B when C was controlled might be .44. This would indicate that the relationship had "withstood" (persisted despite) the control and was largely valid in its own right, since .44 is only slightly lower than .47. Had the partial correlation been substantially lower than the original correlation, .47, and approached .00, we would have concluded that the controlled variable C was a prominent factor in the apparent effect of A upon B.

Controlling variables is clearly one way of learning a great deal about the relationships one discovers. It can prevent us from attributing undue importance to results. But there are obvious problems. When should controls be used, and for what variables? Of course, there is no ready answer. When one has reason to suspect the presence of the effects of another independent variable, one controls for that variable, provided the information needed to do so is at hand or can be obtained. But frequently one does not suspect the action of other variables. Indeed, one may have no idea whatever what other forces may be at work. Social life is clearly very complicated—as the imperfect relationships that are reported show—and in all probability any dependent variable we may be working with is affected by a great number of independent variables that not only have not yet been measured, but haven't even been thought of. Even if one does have reason to control a given variable, it may not be measured in a given study and there may be no way of approaching it. One must then remain in ignorance of its effects. Controlling variables can be very revealing, but controls cannot solve all a researcher's problems or illuminate all the puzzling relationships he encounters. Like all the tools used in the study of political behavior, it works—but to a limited degree.

Conclusion

The basic acts which the student of political behavior performs are measurement and, once measurement is accomplished, explanation. In order to make valid empirical generalizations, we must evaluate political events in terms of some sort of objective standards rather than subjective preferences. Casual observation is not enough. Yet developing standards of measurement is no easy task. We may wish to measure properties of people or of collectivities of people, depending on the problem we have chosen to investigate, and we may need nominal, ordinal, or interval scales. Once adequate measurements are available, we can attempt an explanation of the phenomena that concern us. To the political behaviorist, the term *explanation* means demonstrating a *relationship* between two variables. If we know what factors are related to a phenomenon, we have explained it. Explanatory relationships can be expressed in a variety of ways, such as through tables, graphs, and correlation coefficients.

This, in a nutshell, is the process of the acquisition of knowledge in which the student of political behavior is engaged. It is basically simple, and we should be aware of this simplicity. However, we must also be sensitive to the fact that the findings of political behavior research are subject to many qualifications. Any given relationship one might discover is partial and incomplete; there are always other, uninvestigated independent variables. New research may reveal new explanations of phenomena. Moreover, imposing a control may make a relationship far less exciting than it originally appeared.

Thus the process of measuring human variables and demonstrating the relationships (or the lack of relationships) between them may be subverted by any number of difficulties that can arise at any point. This may seem discouraging at times and lead some to believe that knowledge cannot be discovered in this way. This is an unduly pessimistic stance, but we should be prepared to admit that our knowledge is always partial, tentative, and subject to many qualifications. In any event, we must continue with this incremental, halting process of discovery. The alternative is to become a political theologian, a political historian, or some other kind of political scientist not concerned with systematic knowledge. These scholars too have important roles; but the utility of systematic knowledge, as we have shown, is very great and it ought not to be neglected.

Fortunately, it has not been. Despite the problems involved, behaviorists have persevered. Their research has resulted in a considerable body of findings which assess relationships between a variety of independent variables and a great many kinds of significant political behavior. It is to an assessment of some of these findings that Part II is devoted.

Notes

1. Charles F. Cnudde and Donald J. McCrone, "The Linkage Between Constituency Attitudes and Congressional Voting Behavior: A Causal Model," *American Political Science Review*, Vol. 60 (March 1966), 66-72. See also Warren E. Miller and Donald E. Stokes, "Constituency Influence in Congress," *American Political Science Review*, Vol. 57 (March 1963), 45-56, which is discussed in detail in Chapter 6 of this book.

2. Dean Jaros and Gene L. Mason, "Party Choice and Support for Demagogues: An Experimental Examination," *American Political Science Review*, Vol. 63 (March 1969), 100-110.

3. See John P. Robinson, Jerrold G. Rusk, and Kendra B. Head, *Measures of Political Attitudes* (Ann Arbor, Mich.: Institute for Social Research, 1968), pp. 459-460. This volume discusses a great variety of scales of interest to political scientists.

4. Dean Jaros and Robert I. Mendelsohn, "The Judicial Role and Sentenc-

ing Behavior," *Midwest Journal of Political Science*, Vol. 11 (November 1967), 471-488.

5. For some interesting possibilities in this area, see Eugene J. Webb *et al.*, *Unobtrusive Measures: Non-reactive Research in the Social Sciences* (Chicago: Rand McNally, 1966). A fascinating study involving the direct observation of committees at work is reported in James David Barber, *Power in Committees* (Chicago: Rand McNally, 1966). See especially pp. 20-22.

6. See, for example, John C. Wahlke and Milton G. Lodge, "Psychophysiological Measures of Political Attitudes and Behavior," *Midwest Journal of Political Science*, Vol. 16 (November 1972). A journal called *Experimental Studies of Politics*, devoted to this single procedure, has recently appeared; Volume 1 was published in 1971. Research employing the experimental technique is also cited in Chapter 6.

7. See the section "Comparative Politics: Democratization" in Chapter 3.

8. The section "American State and

Local Politics" in Chapter 3 discusses policy outputs as objects of analysis.

9. W. S. Robinson, "Ecological Correlations and the Behavior of Individuals," *American Sociological Review*, Vol. 15 (June 1950), 351-357.

10. Donald R. Matthews and James W. Prothro, *Negroes and the New Southern Politics* (New York: Harcourt Brace Jovanovich, 1966), Chapter 5.

11. *Ibid.*, p. 128.

PART II

Research in
Political
Behavior:
An Eclectic
Survey

PROLOGUE

Choices of
Substance
and Approach to
Explanation

Suppose a person has decided that the political behavior approach has some potential; suppose he chooses to accept the discipline of political behaviorism. Such a person soon finds that the discipline he has chosen is not very confining, that he must still make a series of choices that reflect his personal interests and needs. The field of political behaviorism is largely unrestricted in terms of both substance and nature of explanation. What one investigates and how one investigates it are not dictated by convention. This may be confusing and disorienting at first, but it is characteristic of all young sciences. Conventions and favored outlooks have not yet developed. The process of making one's own choices may be an onerous task or a great luxury depending on how one looks at it. We feel that it is the latter and that students who like to keep their options open will share this feeling.

There are three types of choices with respect to the substance and approach of investigative research with which we will be concerned in Part II. Of course, in the actual process of research or learning, these choices need not be made in any particular order. Individual interests and situational differences will determine in what sequence decisions are reached. But choices must indeed be made. The order in which we choose to present areas of decision, though rather arbitrary, helps to keep the task in perspective.

As we saw in Chapter 2, the political behaviorist must decide whether he wishes to study collectivities of individuals such as countries, precincts, or courts, or individuals as such—as citizens, revolutionaries, legislators, and so on. The distinction between the behavior of collectivities (behavior at the macro level) and the behavior of individuals (behavior at the micro level) is an important one, and the student must keep constantly in mind the type of activity with which he is dealing. Chapter 3 is devoted to some examples of the behavior of collectivities, while Chapters 4-6 deal with individual behavior.

Second, the behaviorist must, like any other scholar, make some substantive choices about what he wishes to investigate. Which collectivities or individuals should he study, and what kind of behavior on the part of these collectivities or individuals will he investigate? Should he analyze revolutions among the countries of the world or educational policies of American states? Should he study the civil-liberties decisions of judges or the participation of citizens in the elective process? Chapters 3-6 present a great many possible foci of interest: many kinds of behavior of many kinds of collectivities or individuals. The range of investigative topics for the political behaviorist is very wide.

Third, since a behaviorist is very much in the business of asking why particular kinds of political behavior occur, he must choose an approach to the process of explanation. How, in the most general sense, can he account for the political behavior he sees? What kinds of causes may produce it? Behaviorists must constantly choose where and how they will search for the roots of behavior, and in so doing they determine the types of independent variables that will characterize their hypothesis. In the following chapters we suggest several categories of causes, or independent variables. Indeed, Chapters 4-6 are differentiated on the basis of their approach to explaining the political behavior of individuals. Each examines a different type of independent variable.

The chapters that follow contain a great many examples of what researchers in the field of political behaviorism who have made some of the choices just discussed have done. They are examples of current research in the field. Given the emphasis on choice that has character-

ized this book, it should come as no surprise that there is no special logic in including these particular examples, no compelling reason for the order in which they appear, or any reason why they could not be replaced by other examples of equal quality. They were chosen because, as a group, they reflect a great many of the interests and concerns of contemporary political behaviorists. They are a good sample of what people in the field are choosing to do, and they are representative of good, clearly formulated research. Some are topically relevant; others illustrate an important point particularly well. But there is nothing sacred about these examples, and they are certainly not exhaustive of all political behaviorists' interests. In a sense this section is a selective, annotated catalog of current behavioral research. Browsing through a catalog is one of the best ways of finding out what kind of options one has.

Since there is no great unfolding logic to the chapters that follow, and since there are equally valid alternatives to the material included here, it is appropriate that students should have some leeway in choosing what they will read. We feel that the first section of all the chapters in this part should be read by most students, though no great difficulty would be caused by eliminating one of Chapters 4-6 entirely. Substantive sections within each chapter (marked A, B, and so on) are definitely parallel, and a student's own interests, his other assignments, the areas emphasized by instructors, or other criteria can legitimately be used in selecting among them. We feel that most people's interests will be broad enough to dictate reading most of these sections.

Ideally, appropriate research literature from professional journals or books should be read along with these chapters. Hopefully, this literature will be more meaningful in the context of this book. Again, what literature one chooses to read will depend on one's interests. In a more directed classroom setting, an instructor may want to suggest particular reading material. In any event, some sampling of political behavior research should be considered by the reader. It is the existence of such research, after all, that justifies this book; it is to the understanding of such research that it is dedicated.

3

The Political
Behavior of
Collectivities:
Macro-Level
Concerns

In today's troubled world, it is of the greatest importance to understand and explain the behavior of *revolutionaries*, persons actively engaged in the attempt to bring about the collapse of established political orders. What are the conditions under which this kind of behavior occurs? Who are revolutionaries? What motivates them? But, to reiterate a point made in Chapter 2, being able to explain revolutionary behavior in individuals is *not* the same thing as explaining the occurrence of revolutions in nations. Obviously, the presence of persons willing to perform revolutionary behavior is a necessary condition of revolutions. But it is not the only condition. Variables such as the strength and orientation of police and military organizations, logistics, financial resources, communications, and even terrain clearly play great roles as well. Revolutionary behavior and revolutions are similar phenomena, but they are not identical and explaining each is a distinct and separate task.

As we noted in Chapter 2, though much of what is called the behavioral approach is directed at explaining individual behavior, a great many very interesting problems involving collectivities are being studied by political scientists. Revolution is only one of them. In fact, this kind of *macro-level* study is at the core of some of the substantively specific subdisciplines of political science. Comparative politics is, almost by definition, an intellectual enterprise that seeks to make statements about collective political phenomena; it has, in fact, come to mean the study of nations. Often, of course, this implies nothing more than making a series of descriptive statements about specific foreign nations: for example, Great Britain has a parliamentary form of government; France has a judicial system based on Roman law. But there is no reason why one cannot make explanatory general statements about nations as well. In fact, such statements are probably much more useful than a series of discrete descriptive comments. Modern students of comparative politics have of course taken this path. Two of the more prominent kinds of studies today are those that seek to make general statements about *internal violence* (including revolution) in nations and those that seek to explain the *democratization* of nations. The behavior of nations in other spheres—international aggression, for example—could beneficially be approached in the same fashion.

The study of state and local politics is very much like comparative politics. Descriptive statements about institutions, policies, and political competition in various states or cities abound. Again, this is unfortunate, for there are obviously potential bases for general, explanatory statements about these units of government and their politics—for systematic comparative state or local studies. Some scholars have seen this. Attempts have been made to explain states' *policy outcomes* (for example, state expenditures or levels of service in various areas) by analyzing data on all fifty states.

It is easy to see that other features of states could be examined through these kinds of studies and that the behavior of other kinds of collectivities, such as counties or municipalities, could be illuminated by the same kind of treatment.

72

Section A

Comparative Politics: Internal Violence

Gathering data from several nations in order to do comparative research always involves particularly knotty problems. Measurement is difficult to say the least. The problem of an absence of standards mentioned in Chapter 2 is especially acute in this area. Suppose, for example, one wishes to study (compare) judicial systems. Does he include the study of some legislatures that have the power to overrule formal courts? It is hard to secure agreement on whether such legislatures should be included or not. Furthermore, courts in various countries keep different kinds of records. In some instances, they are quite incomplete. Some nations, particularly "primitive" or "undeveloped" ones, collect virtually no political data of any kind. Is it possible to get *comparable* information on the judiciary in many nations when it is not even clear what institutions should be considered part of the judiciary and when parallel records are lacking? Clearly this kind of problem requires a special effort in the area of measurement.

Though problems exist in all comparative studies of this type, they are particularly pronounced in the study of domestic conflicts. Information about the dependent variables must often come from news sources that may be unreliable. Data of this type may also be deliberately withheld by central governments. Assuming that a reasonable amount of information is available, what kinds of events should be taken as manifestations of domestic violence? If an event is adjudged violent, of what kind of violence is it an example? After all, it only makes sense to distinguish between strikes, subversion, and revolution, and between organized and unorganized violence.[1] Different types of violence undoubtedly have different political implications. And even a given violent event may be characterized by many kinds of motivations and activities. Knowing exactly what sort of violent event one is dealing with is no easy task.

In addition to the obvious problem of differing standards for data collection and reporting, there is clearly the question of researcher judgments in classifying the available information. Many evaluations of violent episodes have to be made; and because of the absence of clear standards of measurement, there is no assurance that any two researchers will evaluate the data in the same way. Confidence in a giv-

73

en hypothesis about domestic political violence will develop only as repeated positive results are reported by a variety of investigators.

However, these problems, though knotty, have not deterred imaginative researchers, for the subject of internal violence is both fascinating and of extreme significance for the modern world. Some investigators have begun with the plausible premise that political violence is an aggressive response to some sort of frustration experienced by the population of a nation. Ivo and Rosalind Feierabend[2] posit that the frustration level of a nation is a function of *want formation* and *want satisfaction*. They argue that in nations where few wants have developed among the population (for example, in extremely undeveloped nations) governments should have relatively little trouble in generating satisfactory policies and the level of domestic political violence should be low. Similarly, in nations that have developed very extensive systems for meeting the wants of their citizens (perhaps in the most developed countries), felt deficiencies should be few and the level of political violence should be low. Extending this logic slightly, it follows that countries which are in a transitional state (neither very undeveloped nor highly advanced) should, by virtue of their relatively high level of want formation and their relatively low potential for satisfying those wants, experience the highest levels of domestic violence.

The Feierabends assigned instability scores to eighty-four nations for the period 1955-1961. These scores were based on the occurrence of such violent events as demonstrations, assassinations, *coups d'état*, and civil wars. Nations' satisfaction levels were measured by their gross national product, the mean caloric intake of their citizens, the number of physicians in the population, and similar variables. Their level of want formation was measured by the degree of popular literacy and by urbanization, on the thesis that urbanized, literate people demand more. The findings of this research are varied. In general, the hypotheses are supported. For example, indices of want satisfaction are indeed related to stability. Table 3-1 reports data on the caloric intake and number of physicians in the eighty-four nations. The authors have *dichotomized* both variables in each table (that is, they have divided the possible different values into only two categories). Furthermore, these variables are, in this dichotomized form, regarded as nominal. Clearly, these want satisfaction factors have something to do with domestic violence. An examination of the chi-square statistics shows that these

TABLE 3—1

The Relationship Between Want Satisfaction and Stability in 84 Nations

	DAILY CALORIC INTAKE PER PERSON			NUMBER OF PEOPLE PER PHYSICIAN	
Domestic Violence Condition	Below 2,525 (N = 47)	Above 2,525 (N = 30)	Domestic Violence Condition	Above 1,900 (N = 46)	Below 1,900 (N = 32)
Unstable	83%	33%	Unstable	87%	41%
Stable	17	67	Stable	13	59
Total	100%	100%	Total	100%	100%
Chi-square = 17.42, 1 degree of freedom, $p < .001$			Chi-square = 11.41, 1 degree of freedom, $p < .001$		

Source: Adapted from Ivo K. Feierabend and Rosalind L. Feierabend, "Aggressive Behavior Within Polities, 1948–1962: A Cross-national Study," *The Journal of Conflict Resolution*, Vol. 10 (September 1966), 260. Used by permission of the publisher, Sage Publications, Inc.

results are significant at the .001 level; that is, the probability of such a relationship occurring by chance is less than one in a thousand in both cases.

However, the hypothesis that modern and traditional countries enjoy relative stability while transitional nations experience more domestic violence does not fare so well. The authors trichotomized a variable called *modernity* (composed of indicators of technological advancement) to produce a classification of nations as modern, transitional, or traditional. They then sought to determine whether nations in different categories had different levels of domestic violence—that is, whether they had different instability scores. A *mean instability score* was determined for the nations in each of the three categories. (Notice that instability is treated as an *interval* variable in this case.) As Table 3-2 shows, the transitional nations did in fact have the highest scores, indicating the highest levels of domestic violence. Thus far, the data conformed to the original hypothesis. However, the authors then sought to determine whether the differences in the means were significant. To do this they used a device known as the *t test*, which is appropriate for dealing with differences between means or proportions. The significance or nonsignificance of the *t* value that emerges from the calculations is determined by consulting standard statistical tables.

TABLE 3–2

The Relationship Between Modernity and Instability in 84 Nations

		Mean Instability Score		
Modern countries	(N = 24)	268	Difference between modern and transitional countries	$t = 6.18$ ($p < .001$)
Transitional countries	(N = 37)	472	Difference between modern and traditional countries	$t = 3.71$ ($p < .01$)
Traditional countries	(N = 23)	420	Difference between transitional and traditional countries	$t = 1.53$ ($p > .05$)

Source: Adapted from Ivo K. Feierabend and Rosalind L. Feierabend, "Aggressive Behavior Within Polities, 1948–1962: A Cross-national Study," *The Journal of Conflict Resolution*, Vol. 10 (September 1966), 262. Used by permission of the publisher, Sage Publications, Inc.

Since the *t* for the difference between transitional countries and traditional countries turned out not to be significant at the .05 level, the authors were obliged to reject their hypothesis about the relationship between modernity and domestic violence.

Though not all the Feierabends' expectations were met, it seems very likely that the satisfaction of citizens' wants has something to do with levels of violence. It is undeniably true that violence is not likely to occur in countries where the level of want satisfaction (as defined here) is high.

The potential for extending this kind of analysis should be obvious to everyone. In these kinds of relationships, additional variables almost demand to be controlled. In fact, two kinds of controls suggest themselves. First, if the researcher has a series of independent variables that he knows are related to domestic violence, it is logical to control for *type of country*, to see whether the violence-producing factors are the same everywhere, or whether some are operative, say, in elitist countries but not in more "polyarchic" states (those where there are several identifiable power centers). Similarly, the tremendous cultural differences in the nations of the world may have an effect on how domestic violence comes about. Controlling for *cultural factors* would reveal whether different variables were operative in, for example, Latin as opposed to Anglo-Saxon nations.

Gurr,[3] analyzing 119 nations on the basis of 1961-63 data, imposed exactly these kinds of controls. Reasoning in a fashion similar to the Feierabends, he argued that domestic violence occurs in response to some kind of *relative deprivation*. Of course, if this should turn out to be the case, there is no reason why the nature and cause of the deprivation should not be different from one cultural area to another. Thus Gurr found that, in African nations, levels of civil violence were associated with levels of group discrimination and the potential, within nations, for separatism. In Eastern European nations, however, the picture was totally different. There, increases in school enrollment and expected economic growth, factors associated with what the Feierabends would call want formation, were prominently associated with violence, while discrimination and separatist potential were not related at all. Though deprivation may be involved in both cultural areas, the modes of deprivation appear to be quite different.

Furthermore, it is possible that many of the independent variables suggested to explain domestic violence are *related to each other*. For example, Table 3-1 provides data on two independent variables: caloric intake and the number of people per physician. Countries that have poor diets are, in general, very likely to be the same nations that have relatively few physicians. Accordingly, it would be appropriate to control the caloric-intake table for physicians or, for that matter, other relevant variables in order to determine whether calories have any independent effect. Gurr also faced this problem, since he was attempting to deal with many independent variables at the same time. Among these variables was *institutionalization,* which he hypothesized to be negatively related to civil strife. This variable is composed of measures of party stability, government (as opposed to private) expenditure levels, and union membership. The argument that if there are established institutional and organizational patterns for accomplishing social goals the impetus to use violent means will be less is quite plausible. Gurr treated institutionalization and nine other independent variables as measurable by interval scales. Among these variables were such factors as economic deprivation and "coercive force size" (the size of the police and military forces available to the government). Interval measurement was similarly applied to indicators of three different kinds of domestic political violence: conspiracy, internal war, and "turmoil," as well as a total-magnitude variable that combined the three specific measures of violence. Since interval measurement prevailed, Gurr was able to calculate correlation coefficients for the several relationships that might exist. The correlations between institutionalization and the four violence variables were $-.35$, $-.23$, $-.26$, and $-.33$, respectively. They indicate a moderate degree of relationship and tend to confirm the hypothesis.

However, many of the independent variables in Gurr's study could be related; accordingly, he controlled each relationship for each of the nine other independent variables. This gave him *partial* correlation coefficients, partial, as we noted in Chapter 2, because they tell us what part of a relationship remains when the effect of all other variables is taken into account. If partial correlation coefficients are not notably different than the uncontrolled correlation coefficients (called *zero-order correlations*), we conclude that the variable exerts an effect in its own right. If the partial is much closer to zero, we conclude that the magnitude of the "zero-order," uncontrolled relationship was due largely to the interrelationship of the independent variable with the control variables. Controlling for the nine other variables (all at the same time), Gurr found partials between institutionalization and the four domestic political violence variables of $-.09$, $.11$, $-.05$, and $.07$, respectively. Clearly, most of the apparent impact of this variable disappears under the impact of the control variables. Institutionalization in its own right accounts for very little domestic political violence. We must look elsewhere for an explanation.

Among the vast number of other possible causes of domestic violence is *external violence*. It has frequently been argued that stability and calm within a nation is maintained by uniting all citizens against a foreign enemy. The converse—that the unity of a nation is lost if it does not have an opponent—is also a respectable argument in the study of foreign relations. Tanter[4] sought to determine whether there was any substance to this kind of argument. Using a technique for grouping variables called *factor analysis*, he was able to investigate levels of *turmoil* (defined by the number of domestic demonstrations, riots, strikes, etc.), *revolutionary violence* (defined by the amount of organized violent activity such as guerrilla warfare, purges, etc.), and *subversive violence* (defined by the amount of unorganized, highly violent activity and incorporating the number of people killed within a nation). These three dependent variables were tested for association with indicators of international violence in which countries were engaged. Three such international-conflict variables were a *diplomatic* factor (which incorporated such actions as expelling other countries' ambassadors; making threats, accusations, or formal protests; and moving troops), a *war* factor, and a *belligerency* factor (which incorporated such actions as the severance of diplomatic relations with other countries, limited military activity, and antiforeign demonstrations by citizens).

Do the latter three variables partly explain the former? Since he considered his variables to be interval, Tanter was able to proceed with correlational analysis. Using data on seventy-seven nations for the years 1955-1957, he found only very limited relationships. (See Table 3-3.) The *multiple correlation coefficients* in Table 3-3 are similar to ordinary correlation coefficients, except that they indicate the *combined* effect of several independent variables on a single dependent variable. The correlation between diplomacy, war, and belligerency, taken together,

TABLE 3–3

**The Impact of Given Nations' International Conflict Behavior
on Their Domestic Conflict Levels, 1955–1957**

	Multiple Correlations Between the Three Independent Variables (Diplomacy, War, and Belligerency) and Dependent Variables
Turmoil	.37
Revolutionary violence	.27
Subversive violence	.14

Source: Adapted from Raymond Tanter, "Dimensions of Conflict Behavior Within and Between Nations: 1958–1960," *The Journal of Conflict Resolution,* Vol. 10 (March 1966), 55. Used by permission of the publisher, Sage Publications, Inc.

and turmoil is .37. Taken singly, each of these variables would have a much weaker relationship to turmoil. (It should be noted that multiple correlation coefficients are always reported as positive. One must look at the individual correlation coefficients to determine whether the relationship of any given independent variable to the dependent variable is positive or negative.) Though it is clear that some relationship is present—particularly with turmoil—it is equally clear that internal violence and international violence are to some degree independent of each other.

Still another determinant of domestic political violence may be a very simple one—the force that a government is able to mobilize against those who would engage in political violence. That standing armies "preserve domestic tranquility" is a venerable political principle. Bwy,[5] investigating instability in twenty Latin American nations during the period 1958-1960, constructed a scatter diagram to show the relationship between unorganized, "anomic" domestic violence (different levels of which he assigned interval values) and force, measured by the proportion of the gross national product spent on military defense. (See Figure 3-1.) Though one might reasonably expect a *negative* relationship between force and domestic violence (the more government force available, the more violence can be suppressed), the data reveal that the relationship is in fact *curvilinear*. That is, the line which best fits the points on the scatter diagram is a curve with a single peak in the middle. (The single deviant case of Mexico can be explained by

80

FIGURE 3–1

The Relationship Between Unorganized, Anomic Violence and the Force Available to Government

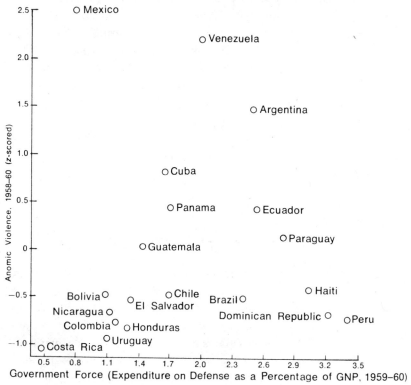

Government Force (Expenditure on Defense as a Percentage of GNP, 1959–60)

Source: Adapted from Douglas P. Bwy, "Political Instability in Latin America: The Cross-cultural Test of a Causal Model," in John V. Gillespie and Betty A. Nesvold (eds.), *Macro-Quantitative Analysis* (Beverly Hills, Calif.: Sage Publications, 1971), p. 128. Used by permission of the publisher, Sage Publications, Inc.

other, very unusual circumstances that prevailed there.) It is clear that the most domestic violence occurs where *moderate* amounts of government force are available. The relationship is more complicated than we may have originally thought. Bwy argues that large amounts of force do in fact prevent people from acting violently, but he further suggests, as do some of the authors cited earlier in this section, that high levels of want satisfaction also have this effect. It is precisely those countries that spend little on the military which may have funds available for pursuing

81

other public policies that satisfy citizens' wants. These countries buy butter rather than guns. "Just as fear of punishment inhibits aggressive actions . . . , so also can relative systemic satisfactions."[6]

What makes for a country beset by political violence? What makes for its opposite, tranquility? It appears that factors like satisfaction, external conflict, and the force available to the government have something to do with the problem. However, it is also clear that though the studies which have been done to date are very intriguing and represent very innovative work on the part of many scholars, nothing in the way of a complete set of answers is available. Not much work has been done. And problems of measurement and data make us treat these studies very tentatively. The opportunities for advancing our knowledge in this area, for really learning something about this important political phenomenon, are many and exciting.

Section B
Comparative Politics: Democratization

The democratization of nations has been a topic of fervent interest among scholars and holders of political power alike. At least since the time of Aristotle, thinkers have wondered what kinds of conditions were responsible for the occurence of different forms of government —among them democracy. Various practical and ethical considerations have kept this concern alive and viable for centuries. For example, in relatively modern times, it was assumed in many quarters that European culture reflected a kind of social and political maturity—an inevitable and desirable end state toward which all other civilizations were destined to progress. This kind of thinking led to the concept of the "white man's burden" as well as to a certainty of the superiority of Western institutions. The same type of thinking was evident in the tremendous confidence of the West during the latter part of the last century and the beginning of the present one. Democratic principles of government, it was believed, were destined to sweep the entire world as soon as people could be educated to the obvious benefits of those principles. War, injustice, and other sources of human misery were destined to disappear as a consequence. Western democracy was regarded as the ultimate in political development. Moreover, increasing government sophistication and productiveness were regarded as inextricably linked with expanding democracy. Indeed, political development and democracy were thought to be the same. Institutions such as the League of Nations reflected this outlook, which also had an important effect on thinking about the less technologically advanced areas of the world. Though vestiges of it linger on, this naivete was harshly dispelled by later events of the twentieth century. Perhaps it was the realization that democracy is not automatic that kindled a new fiercer interest in research on the topic.

Many new nations have emerged from colonialism in the last thirty years, and it is only natural that there should be great curiosity about their political future. Furthermore, recent decades have seen great world conflicts often perceived in ideological terms, as conflicts between democracy and fascism or democracy and communism. What are the independent variables affecting the outcome of such momentous confrontations? Who shall emerge victorious and thus govern the future of the world? Finally, the problems of a supermodern and tremendously complex civilization, such as that which increasingly characterizes the democratic West, have led to a dramatic loss of confidence. Technology may make lighter some of man's burdens, but it makes the world a very complex and interdependent place; the sense of identity is lost. Physiological disease may be on the decline, but mental disease is on the increase. Technology may mean improved communications and therefore greater educational opportunities, but it may also mean increased manipulation of the masses. Man is comfortable, but his life-sustaining environment is being destroyed. Can democratic political institutions survive in the face of such new and awesome problems? Are competing ideologies favored by modern conditions? An abiding interest in democracy and its antecedents is easy to understand, and an *immediate* interest in them is, if anything, easier to understand.

The study of democratization involves great problems of definition and measurement. Which characteristics of a nation should be taken to indicate democracy, and which its absence? Even if there is agreement on the variables that make a nation democratic, how shall they be amalgamated to produce comparable values for each nation? When one is dealing with a topic that has emotional significance for as many people

FIGURE 3–2

Distribution of Index of Democratization over Time, 1800–1950

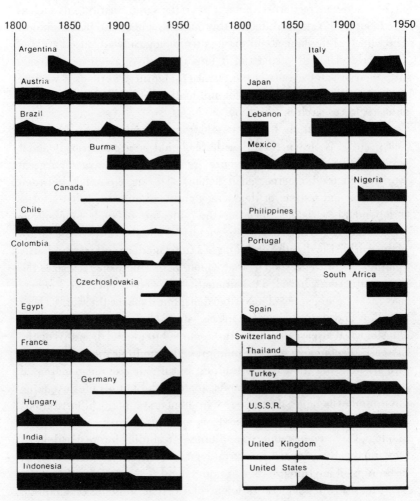

Source: William Flanigan and Edwin Fogelman, "Patterns of Political Development and Democratization: A Quantitative Analysis," in John V. Gillespie and Betty A. Nesvold (eds.), *Macro-Quantitative Analysis* (Beverly Hills, Calif.: Sage Publications, 1971), p. 458. Used by permission of the publisher, Sage Publications, Inc.

as does democracy, there is bound to be controversy over what indicates its presence and what does not. The selection of variables at this stage will necessarily involve some degree of arbitrariness.

Flanigan and Fogelman[7] have done some very interesting research that has helped to determine the scope of the concept of democratization. They collected information on twenty-nine countries for which good data were available not only for the present, but for several decades in the past. This emphasis on the time dimension is rare, especially in cross-national research. In this case, it provides some very valuable insights. The authors collected data on the countries for each decade from 1800 to 1960 for which statistics were available. (Some of the countries did not even exist during the earlier periods.) Historical data on four kinds of practices were assembled. Both formal and actual practices with respect to succession to the highest executive offices were examined; succession by either election or parliamentary investiture was regarded as democratic. The presense of opposition parties in electorate or legislature (also regarded as a component of democracy) was noted, the extent of suffrage was assessed, and the incidence of "suppression directed against individuals, groups, or organizations that participate in the political process" was measured. Scores were assigned for different kinds of practices and combined into an overall *index of democratization.* It was then possible to make *descriptive* statements about democracy by observing the values of the index for each country over time. These data are presented in Figure 3-2. The *narrower* the bar for each country, the higher the democratization index. (The absence of a bar for a given period indicates that the country in question did not exist or that data were not available.)

Some interesting implications emerge from this research. It is clear that countries do not regularly change from relatively nondemocratic states to progressively more democratic states. There is no evidence of a "once democratic, always democratic" dynamic. Democracy does not represent an irrevocable "advance." This alone should lay to rest some widely held, but erroneous, views on the nature of this political form. For one thing, it should clearly demonstrate that democratization and "political development" are not the same thing. Nations rarely become less complex, sophisticated, or productive—that, is, less developed —but they clearly do become, on occasion, less democratic.

Having data that are broken down by time periods also allows some other fascinating discoveries. Though democratization and political development are clearly not identical, they do appear to be related. Flanigan and Fogelman measured development among the twenty-nine nations studied by taking into account certain kinds of government publications; countries that published large amounts of census information, reports on trade and commerce, and government statistics were regarded as politically developed. "The underlying assumption is that the ability of a government to adopt complex policies is indicated by the volume and kinds of information that the government collects and publishes."[8] This publication variable correlated highly with other indicators of political development such as government employment. It also showed, in general, an increase in most nations over time, not the more variable pattern of democratization. The relationship between political development and democratization means that in general the more democratic a nation is the more politically developed it is. (The fact that there are some considerable exceptions—particularly well developed nations that are nondemocratic—suggests that this is not a simple relationship, however.) If two variables are related, it makes sense to ask which of them may be considered independent and which dependent. Which is antecedent to the other? Does political development lead to democracy or vice versa? Time-series data help to answer this question. Flanigan and Fogelman's information clearly indicates that in countries which are both democratic and developed, democracy usually preceded development by several decades! Countries that experienced approximately simultaneous development and democratization did not in general remain democratic. The question of timing is apparently very important. The implications for the presently developing areas of the world are obvious. If the same time relationship is to hold, what are the prospects for democracy in the new nations of the world?

Further food for thought lies in the finding that nations which have been able to sustain democracy developed it during periods of high *economic* development and only after some kind of prior experience with participatory institutions (such as parties or legislatures), perhaps during a colonial period. Indeed, there do appear to be conditions necessary for the occurrence of democracy in nations, and they are not quite the same conditions as those necessary for political development.

The relationship of democracy to variables suggesting national

86

wealth has been prominent in much other research on this aspect of comparative politics. Levels of democracy have repeatedly been found to be related to national wealth, levels of communications (e.g., the number of radios per capita), industrialization, and levels of education. Indeed, this kind of statement might be regarded as part of the conventional wisdom of contemporary comparative politics. However, the way in which these variables are linked is anything but clear.

One of the most interesting attempts to deal with this problem is that of McCrone and Cnudde.[9] Relying on the previous thinking and the less systematic observations of others, they posit that democratization may be the result of a communications process. That is, variables such as those mentioned above have their observed relationships to democracy because they are involved in communications in a particular way. Obviously, the level of communications technology tells us something about communications processes; but, depending on how they are related, the other variables may also tell us something. According to a commonly accepted viewpoint, democracy can occur only if there is a developed communications system. There must be an informed citizenry in democratic polities, it is argued, and this can only occur if the mass media of communication function widely and effectively. Alternatively, democracy may be possible only when there are high levels of social cohesion, which prevent the collapse of the political system in the face of policy disagreements. Only through a developed communications system can society be prevented from lapsing into a segmental parochialism and isolation that would make social cohesion impossible. In any event, the development of communications is seen as an immediate antecedent to democracy. How, in turn, do communications systems come into being? Only educated, literate persons can accomplish this, it is argued. There must exist a stratum of relatively intellectual people who both demand a communications system and operate the necessary communications devices. How, it may be asked, does such an intellectual elite develop? It can occur, according to this paradigm, only in an urbanized context, for it has been true historically that "cities alone have developed the [necessary] complex of skills and resources [including] literacy."[10] Thus, it is implied that democratization is a particular developmental sequence dependent upon the ability of a society to communicate. The expectation is that the key variables are "causally related" in the following way: Urbanization leads to education, which in turn leads to the development of mass communications, which finally leads to democratization. It is a three-step operation.

In order to test the adequacy of this model of the democratization process, McCrone and Cnudde employed a technique known as *causal analysis*. They relied on data similar to those used in the other studies we have discussed here. In order to measure democracy, points were assigned to each country on the basis of whether there were competing sets of leaders for government offices and whether parties and elections were the legitimate devices for political succession. Communication-development indices were assembled from data on newspaper consumption, the number of telephones, and so on. Measures of education reflected literacy rates and university enrollment. The degree of urbanization was determined by the proportion of people living in cities with a population of over 100,000. In all, seventy-six nations were studied. The indices thus assembled were assumed to be interval variables. Thus, correlation coefficients—which are necessary for causal analysis—could be used. The relationships found by McCrone and Cnudde between the four variables are shown in Figure 3-3. The authors' prediction is that there is a causal path from U to E to C and finally to D. Of course, it is not necessary that the actual causal path be this one. Any other sequence is logically possible, and the conclusions and implications about the nature of democracy would be altogether different. The purpose of causal analysis is to reveal which of the possible causal paths might be the correct one.

The analysis hinges on a mathematical property of correlation coefficients. The correlation between any two of three interrelated variables may be assessed in comparison to the magnitude of the product of the other correlations that exist between the variables. That is, if the correlation (r) between variables A and $B = .50$, and that between B and $C = .80$, we may determine how closely the correlation between A and C approximates $.50 \times .80$, or $.40$. If it does equal or is not substantially different from $.40$, we are justified in inferring that the relationship between A and C depends totally or largely on the intervening position of B. Using causal analysis, we would argue that A causes B, which in turn causes C, and that there is no independent causality from A to C. If the correlation between A and C (abbreviated rAC) is considerably different from $rAB \times rBC$, we would argue that there is a connection

FIGURE 3–3

The Relationships Between McCrone and Cnudde's Variables

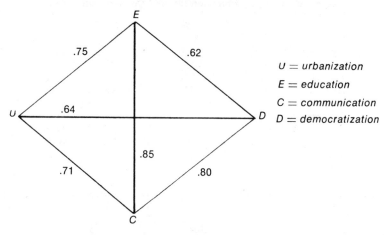

$U = urbanization$

$E = education$

$C = communication$

$D = democratization$

Source: Adapted from Donald J. McCrone and Charles F. Cnudde, "Toward a Communication Theory of Democratic Political Development: A Causal Model," *American Political Science Review,* Vol. 61 (March 1967), 75.

between A and C that does not depend on the intervention of B. That is, the proposition that A causes B, which in turn causes C, is rejected.

Given the data in Figure 3-3, it is possible to test McCrone and Cnudde's paradigm. Let us first consider the left half of the diagram. The authors argue that the causal path is from U to E to C for the reasons given above. This would require, because of the mathematical properties of correlation coefficients, that $(1)\,rUE \times rEC = rUC$, since the only connection between U and C is posited to depend on E. However, it is logically possible that urbanization first produces communications development, which development is a necessary antecedent of the development of literacy and education. That is, the causal path could be from U to C to E. If this were the case, we would expect that $(2)\,rUC \times rCE = rUE$. Finally, it is also logically possible that urbanization spawns both education and communication, but through separate mechanisms. Both may be independent consequences of urbanization. If this is the case, the only relationship between E and C should be that which is necessary because of their joint relationship with U. That is, we expect that $(3)\,rUE \times rUC = rEC$. Table 3-4 presents the values predicted for

89

TABLE 3—4

Possible Relationships Between
Urbanization *(U)*, Education *(E)*, and Communication *(C)*

	Predicted Value	Actual Value	Difference
$rUE \times rEC = rUC$	$(.75)\ (.85) = .64$	.71	.07
$rUC \times rCE = rUE$	$(.71)\ (.85) = .60$	.75	.15
$rUE \times rUC = rEC$	$(.75)\ (.71) = .53$	.85	.32

Source: Adapted from Donald J. McCrone and Charles F. Cnudde, "Toward a Communication Theory of Democratic Political Development: A Causal Model," *American Political Science Review*, Vol. 61 (March 1967), 76.

each possible causal path and compares them to the values actually observed.

On each line, the actual values for the first two relationships are taken from Figure 3-3 and multiplied to obtain a predicted value for the third relationship. This predicted value is compared with the actual value for the third relationship (also taken from Figure 3-3). It is clear that one model (as anticipated, $rUE \times rEC = rUC$), produces a value that is close to the predicted value. Thus the authors can feel confident that urbanization does lead to education and that education in turn is responsible for the development of communication. There is little evidence of any impact of urbanization on communications that does not depend on education as an intervening variable.

If the causal path *U* to *E* to *C* is the correct one, there are only two possible ways to integrate *D* into the causal linkage. Turning our attention to the right side of Figure 3-3, we see that McCrone and Cnudde's original prediction is that $rEC \times rCD = rED$; that is, *E* causes *C*, which in turn causes *D*, and any relationship between *E* and *D* is totally dependent upon the intervention of *C*. The only logical alternate causal path involving these variables and accepting the *E* to *C* causal link is that *E* causes *C* but also independently causes *D* through a different mechanism. In this scheme, communications development is dependent upon education but has nothing to do with democratization; instead, democratization is a direct result of education. Thus, any relationship between *C* and *D* is a consequence of the *E* to *D* and *E* to *C* relationships: We would predict $rEC \times rED = rCD$ for this alternate.

TABLE 3–5

**Possible Relationships Between
Education *(E)*, Communication *(C)*, and Democratization *(D)***

	Predicted Value	Actual Value	Difference
$rEC \times rCD = rED$	(.85) (.80) = .68	.62	.06
$rEC \times rED = rCD$	(.85) (.62) = .53	.80	.27

Source: Adapted from Donald J. McCrone and Charles F. Cnudde, "Toward a Communication Theory of Democratic Political Development: A Causal Model," *American Political Science Review*, Vol. 61 (March 1967), 76.

The data in Table 3-5 demonstrate that McCrone and Cnudde's hypothesis fits the data much better than the alternate hypothesis. It appears that the causal path *E* to *C* to *D* should be preferred on the basis of the empirical evidence. Putting the two halves of the analysis together, it appears that among the seventy-six nations studied the process of democratization is as McCrone and Cnudde expected: Urbanization leads to the spread of literacy and education; education in turn leads to the development of communication networks; finally, communications—no doubt because they create an enlightened and informed citizenry—appear to be directly antecedent to the development of democratic government as defined in the study. (McCrone and Cnudde present other data that confirm this finding.)

The implications of this kind of causal process for the political future of the world are enormous. No student of comparative politics can possibly ignore these kinds of data, for, though they do not present a complete picture by any means, they may well indicate some very basic dynamics in the way collectivities called nations come to have the political features they do. To quote McCrone and Cnudde,

[there are] nations with a relatively low level of communications development which are defined as being relatively highly developed [democratically]. In this case, the democratic political system does not have sufficient communications development to maintain the regime. In terms of our model, this nation is likely to experience severe difficulty in maintaining democratic political competition and may even collapse. The dangers of attempting to

91

impose a democratic regime on socio-economically underdeveloped nations in the post-World War II world are indicated by
this type of analysis.

Stepping further back in the chain of causation, we may also find
nations which are experiencing communications revolutions, but
without prior developments in urbanization and education. In this
case, disruption of the regime may occur because the citizenry has
not been prepared for the sudden exposure and communications
development may bring social disintegration, rather than social
cohesion.[11]

Though these findings are very exciting, like all empirical findings
in political science they are subject to qualification and discussion. Work
that has to do with the *development* of a collectivity has a certain
temporal implication to it. In the case of the work just cited, we tend to
think of urbanization as preceding educational development in time;
communications development takes place in a given nation *before*
democratization. Yet the data examined did not allow us to compare
conditions in nations over time. All the data collected were for the same
period, and the analysis proceeded on the basis of what was related to
what in the various nations. Any conclusions about temporal sequences
are inferences, and not directly demonstrable. This, of course, should
not be taken as an indictment of the research. It is only meant to remind
the reader that one kind of approach cannot attack all aspects of a
research problem at the same time.

Other researchers have chosen to investigate the time-related
problems implicit in this work more directly. Winham[12] collected similar data to that used by McCrone and Cnudde, but on a decade-to-
decade basis for the period from 1790 to 1960. However, his data
concerned only one country—the United States. This restriction was
necessary because sufficient information for so long a period is just not
available for most nations. One could argue that such a study is no longer
an explanatory one, seeking to make generalizations about collectivities
called nations; that it is no longer a study in comparative politics. It
is, however, a comparative study nonetheless. What are compared are
blocks of time rather than nations. What is explained is not what happens to nations, but what happens over time. Of course, the results of

92

such work constitute in one sense a case study. The extent to which they apply to other nations is problematic. However, one could consider these decades of American history to be a sample of all decades of history experienced by all nations. Perhaps to assert that the findings of such research can be generalized to apply to all nations' experiences or lack of experiences with democracy is not so bizarre after all.

Winham finds that comparing decades in the history of the United States leads to results similar to those produced by comparing nations at a given point in time. That is, there are strong interrelationships between communications, urbanization, education, and democratization. Those decades that had higher levels of democratization also had, in general, higher levels of the other three variables. (Though Winham does not report it, a causal analysis would suggest the same causal paths among these four variables as McCrone and Cnudde's report.) Winham attempts to determine the chain of causality among these variables by a procedure known as *time-lagging*. His reasoning is as follows. The correlation between democratization and communications development in his data is .723. This correlation corresponds to a scatter diagram in which the vertical axis represents the democratization variable and the horizontal axis represents the communications variable. Each point on the graph is determined by the values of the two variables for a given decade. Such a graph tells us nothing about time sequences however. Winham argues that if communications cause democratization, high communications development should stimulate *later* (not simultaneous) democratization. Accordingly, he argues that democratization at any given time should be correlated with communications development at that time (as it is), but correlated more highly with communications development levels that prevailed at *previous* times. Similarly, one would reason that democratization at any point in time should be correlated less highly with communications development levels in subsequent periods. Since data for each decade exist, it is possible to test these assumptions simply by correlating values for democratization with values for communications ten and twenty years before and ten and twenty years later.

When the values for democratization are correlated with the values for communications ten years before, the relationship between the two variables increases from .723 to .765; when the differential is twenty

93

years, it increases to .780. When values for democratization are correlated with values for communications ten years later, the relationship decreases to .670; a twenty-year differential of this kind produces a decrease to .554. It seems that communications development at a given time has consequences for democratization at a future time, and not vice versa. The thesis that communications is an important determinant of democratization is clearly reinforced by these time-series data.

However, Winham's time-series data do not correspond entirely to the previously suggested causal patterns. The initial "first in line" position of urbanization, in particular, fails to emerge in the time-series data for the United States. Time-lagging suggests that urbanization may be partly dependent upon prior education levels and prior communications development—a conclusion at variance with that suggested by Cnudde and McCrone's work. Writing about the relationship between education and urbanization, Winham remarks: "it is probable in U.S. development—and perhaps in development elsewhere—that *rural* education developed skills and expectations in the population that led people to migrate to urban areas."[13] Similarly, he notes that "communications could have been an agent in the urbanization of society through the process of providing information to rural populations about new opportunities and a new way of life."[14]

In addition to providing some interesting insights into the process of democratization in a particular nation, this study provided some evidence about the interrelations among key variables in the general process of democratization and also suggested some specific new patterns that may have more general applications and that may help to account for the imperfect relationships encountered in studies of many nations.

Thus, the question of how democracy comes about in nations has provoked some reasonable, if partial, answers. Democracy is capable of ebbing and flowing; its acquisition is not necessarily a continuous process. Democracy appears to depend upon variables that indicate economic or technological modernity—high levels of education and literacy, of communications development, and of urbanization—though the way in which these variables interact is not necessarily the same everywhere. Political development is not a precondition of democracy. In fact, nations that develop before they democratize do not maintain democratic forms of government. In a very real sense, this is an impressive body of knowledge. Though there are clearly many questions left unanswered, it is very possible to speculate on the political future of the many developing nations of the world today.

Comparative politics, in the best sense of the term, means more than making discrete statements about a variety of nations. It means the making of general, explanatory statements about nations; that is to say, accounting for features of nations by explaining variance in them. Another way of putting it is to say that the behavioral approach to the study of politics has a contribution to make in studying the behavior of collectivities called nations. The foregoing two sections were designed to suggest that many critical and interesting questions—ones which great minds have contemplated for centuries—can be illuminated by a systematic, empirical approach. Of course, the two behaviors of nations examined here by no means exhaust the possibilities for research. Any other behavior that nations perform, from the provision of domestic services through participation in alliances to warfare, can be explained if the data needed to investigate the phenomenon can be found. Such explanation is the goal of scholars with a behavioral orientation to both comparative politics and international relations.

Section C
American State and Local Politics

Perhaps no other area of political science has been as much the province of the political anecdotalist and the political engineer as state and local politics. State and local government has historically been regarded as the most corrupt and debased kind. Reformers have railed against political bosses, patronage, and "machines" for well over a century. Political scientists, along with journalists, businessmen, and many others, have participated in the reformist tradition fully and enthusiastically.

Because of the large number of offices, personalities, and policies involved, state and local politics is bound to generate a great number of personality clashes, bizarre situations, and apparently novel behavior. The swirling mass of people and events involved on the politics of the many states and localities generates lots of interesting stories. Many have chosen to become experts on a particular city or state by learning a number of these stories. Every political science department has at least one member who can relate interesting tales about prominent figures and particular elections. This man is always a specialist in state and local politics.

The work of these people has often resulted in notable scholarship. However, despite the tradition of engineering and anecdotalism, there is no reason why the study of state and local politics should be restricted to the specific and particular. In fact, just the opposite is the case. All kinds of questions about why some states act in certain ways while others do not practically cry out to be answered. General, explanatory analysis is clearly called for. Moreover, data are relatively easy to acquire. The American states keep relatively good records on political and governmental matters. There are no language barriers to comparative analysis. The structures of the various states and of the various localities are sufficiently similar so that congruity of data is more the rule than the exception. Indeed, compared to cross-national investigations, studies of the states or municipalities present strikingly few problems.

Several imaginative scholars have taken opportunities offered for research in this area. Considerable attention has been focused on explaining state policy outputs in various areas. Why are some states frugal, say, in the area of public education, while other states are relatively generous? What leads a governmental unit to pursue one policy rather than another? If we have some notion of how democracy functions in this country, it is not difficult to come up with some hypotheses on this kind of problem. In general, we would expect that various *political features* of the states would provide an explanation of their behavior. For example, one might well postulate that competition among political parties, institutions that supposedly channel public demands to the officers of government, would make a difference in the policies enacted. People clearly become very exercised about who wins partisan elections; it is not unreasonable to link this concern with elections to expectations of differential policy performance by government. Similarly, there is a great deal of concern in most democracies about the level of citizen participation in elections. People are urged to exercise the franchise, to view voting as a public obligation. Citizen participation supposedly means a healthy polity. It is supposed to make a difference.

96

Surely, extrapolating from this conventional wisdom of politics, it is not unreasonable to expect that government policies will, in part, be dependent upon the level of citizen participation. Similarly, it is not unreasonable, in view of recent political events in America, to expect that legislative malapportionment will result in policies favorable to particular groups and that "equitable" apportionment will have altogether different implications for public policy.

Another reasonable hypothesis is that the policies of governmental units are dependent upon *economic conditions*. We have already seen how economic variables dramatically affect behavior of nations. It requires no great insight to guess that particular kinds of policies of states or municipalities may result from the same kind of impetus. Economic development—urbanization, industrialization, and increases in the level of wealth and education—is likely to create different kinds of demands upon government than a condition of underdevelopment. Demands for urban services, facilitative fiscal policies, and various particularistic amenities by a population highly specialized economically are likely to present an irresistible configuration.

Political features and economic conditions, particularly as they affect state tax and expenditure policies, have generated a great deal of interest among political behaviorists. Undoubtedly the most comprehensive treatment of these kinds of variables has been rendered by Dye.[15] Dye investigated four political factors: party control, party competition, the level of electoral participation, and the degree of legislative malapportionment. Party control was measured simply by the percentage of Democratic seats in the legislature (separate measures were used for the upper and lower houses) over a ten-year period and the percentage of Democratic successes in gubernatorial elections during the same period. Competition was measured on the basis of the proportion of legislative seats held by the majority party and by margins of victory in gubernatorial races. Participation was measured by the proportion of eligibles casting votes in gubernatorial and congressional elections. Legislative apportionment was gauged by calculating the minimum proportion of people in a state that could elect majorities to the houses of the state legislatures (that is, by adding the populations of the smallest districts necessary to make a majority of the total number of districts), by an urban-representation index that compared the population of urban legislative districts with the state average, and by a technical measure that examined the distributions of district sizes for statistical properties which caused them to deviate from normal distributions.

Since economic and social census data by states are readily available, Dye had no difficulty in acquiring information on the chief economic variables in the study: industrialization, urbanization, wealth, and education. Statistics on the proportions of the population engaged in industrial occupations and living in urban areas were available, as was information on mean family incomes and mean school years completed.

Dye examined a staggering total of fifty-four dependent policy variables for each of the fifty states. As Table 3-6 shows, these variables are largely expenditure or revenue measures (per capita) obtained from state budget documents. They tell how much money is spent on different kinds of services to "the public." There are some other ratios and rates (such as the number of policemen per capita) that reveal policy outputs. These too are easily available from official state records. A few variables, such as school dropout rates, reflect the consequences of policy. Though this assemblage of statistics by no means provides a comprehensive description of state policy output, it is an impressive collection of information on what states are doing in many important areas of public service.

The data Dye collected constituted interval scales in the true sense of the term. Unlike some of the measures used in cross-national research, variables such as the proportion of seats Democratic or the average salary of public employees are unambiguously interval. Accordingly, the use of Pearson correlation coefficients is completely appropriate.

Dye's analysis is extremely comprehensive, but the most interesting aspect of it for our purposes is his attempt to assess the relative importance of political and economic factors in explaining various kinds of state policy. Of course, many of the simple relationships are not too hard to visualize. In general, states that are economically developed can afford higher levels of public service; it is not surprising, then, to find that many of the economic factors correlate positively with many of the policy variables. Similarly, governments that must face a highly participatory citizenry (rather than an apathetic one) or that operate in a partisan competitive milieu are presumably in a much more precarious situation. Since the threat of losing office always exists, they are presumably more likely to be responsive to public needs. It is thus perhaps to be expected that participatory and competitive states should have, for example, higher per-pupil expenditures for education. But Dye's most fascinating findings result from considering many of the variables simultaneously. Since so many variables are involved in this type of analysis, multiple correlations are necessary; since we wish to isolate the impact of certain variables, other variables must be controlled, and partial correlation coefficients will play a role.

A summary of Dye's findings is presented in Table 3-6. The first column contains multiple correlations that demonstrate the combined impact of the four economic variables studied plus the four political variables. In many cases, the correlations are quite large. Column two contains multiple correlation coefficients that indicate the impact of the four economic variables alone, while column three contains the multiple correlation coefficients that indicate the impact of the four political factors alone. A comparison of these columns is very revealing. First, the coefficients in the economic-development column are almost always larger than those in the political-factor column for any given variable. The impression that economic variables are more important than political ones is reinforced by comparing columns one and two. Often, the multiple correlation coefficient for all the variables is not much greater than the correlation coefficient for the economic variables alone. That is, the contribution of the political variables to explaining the variance in policy outputs seems in most cases rather marginal. Adding the political variables doesn't make much difference.

Since the economic variables and the political factors are related, it is wise to impose controls on these relationships. The effect of the economic variables without the contaminating influence of the political factors is demonstrated in column four, while the fifth column reveals the impact of the political factors when the effect of the economic variables is controlled. Though controlling political factors reduces the economic variable-policy relationship (column four entries are smaller than column two entries), much of the relationship remains in most cases. That is, controlling the political variables does not eliminate the economic variables' effect. On the other hand, controlling the economic variables does in some cases cause the relationship between political factors and policy variables to virtually disappear. In most cases, the size of the relationship in column three is drastically reduced. This implies

99

TABLE 3–6

A Comparison of the Effects of Economic Development Variables and Political System Variables on Policy Outcomes in the American States

	Total Effect of Economic Development and Political System Variables	Total Effect of Economic Development Variables	Total Effect of Political System Variables	Effect of Economic Development Variables, Controlling for Political System Variables	Effect of Political System Variables, Controlling for Economic Development Variables
Education					
Per pupil expenditures	.86	.85	.58	.61	.04
Average teachers' salaries	.91	.90	.43	.78	.05
Teachers with B.A.	.85	.70	.64	.54	.47
Teachers with M.A.	.64	.60	.33	.34	.08
Male teachers	.73	.70	.56	.32	.10
Pupil-teacher ratios	.80	.70	.74	.24	.30
Dropout rate	.91	.82	.79	.54	.48
Mental failures	.88	.79	.81	.32	.39
Size of school districts	.69	.52	.67	.05	.28
State participation	.74	.49	.70	.13	.41
Federal participation	.74	.50	.37	.48	.40
Welfare					
Per capita welfare expenditures	.52	.41	.41	.12	.12
Per capita health expenditures	.57	.42	.40	.18	.16
State participation in welfare	.52	.41	.40	.17	.16
State participation in health	.57	.42	.40	.18	.16
Federal participation in welfare	.85	.85	.54	.62	.04
Unemployment benefits	.85	.84	.57	.60	.07

(continued on next page)

TABLE 3–6 (continued)

	Total Effect of Economic Development and Political System Variables	Total Effect of Economic Development Variables	Total Effect of Political System Variables	Effect of Economic Development Variables, Controlling for Political System Variables	Effect of Political System Variables, Controlling for Economic Development Variables
OAA benefits	.82	.74	.69	.37	.27
ADC benefits	.87	.80	.75	.44	.35
Blind benefits	.82	.78	.63	.43	.13
General assistance benefits	.86	.81	.66	.54	.24
OAA recipients	.62	.59	.41	.25	.05
ADC recipients	.66	.55	.50	.25	.20
Unemployment recipients	.78	.76	.43	.52	.09
General assistance cases	.55	.43	.44	.14	.14
Highways					
Per capita highway expenditures	.81	.75	.64	.40	.10
State participation	.56	.48	.34	.22	.10
Federal participation	.65	.65	.39	.35	.00
Funds from highway users	.50	.42	.18	.23	.09
Highway fund diversion	.59	.51	.31	.29	.12
Rural-urban distributor	.55	.52	.41	.16	.04
Public Regulation					
Government per population	.87	.83	.53	.66	.27
Number of bills introduced	.59	.57	.28	.29	.04
Number of laws enacted	.53	.48	.23	.25	.06
Public employees	.75	.73	.46	.46	.07
State employees	.65	.54	.25	.39	.19

(continued on next page)

TABLE 3–6 (continued)

	Total Effect of Economic Development and Political System Variables	Total Effect of Economic Development Variables	Total Effect of Political System Variables	Effect of Economic Development Variables, Controlling for Political System Variables	Effect of Political System Variables, Controlling for Economic Development Variables
Public employees' salaries	.88	.86	.44	.72	.12
Correctional expenditures	.78	.72	.34	.56	.19
Policemen	.80	.79	.26	.62	.38
Prisoners	.67	.27	.60	.14	.41
Crime rate	.77	.63	.28	.57	.33
Gambling revenue	.45	.40	.22	.17	.04
Divorce rate	.64	.37	.26	.24	.17
Parolees	.45	.49	.42	.28	.22
Taxation					
Total revenue per capita	.84	.81	.51	.61	.12
Total taxes per capita	.89	.87	.61	.66	.16
Debt	.71	.67	.40	.40	.07
State percentage of total revenue	.68	.40	.60	.17	.36
Federal percentage of total revenue	.71	.64	.39	.42	.17
Income taxes	.42	.32	.16	.15	.09
Sales taxes	.45	.33	.25	.15	.10
Alcohol and tobacco taxes	.40	.35	.25	.11	.05
Motor fuel taxes	.53	.38	.28	.23	.17
Property taxes	.80	.58	.73	.23	.46

Source: Thomas R. Dye, Politics, Economics, and the Public: Policy Outcomes in the American States (Chicago: Rand McNally, 1966), pp. 286–287.

that the economic variables exert an influence in their own right, but that the apparent impact of political variables is largely an artifact of their relationship to the economic variables:

> Again the evidence seems conclusive: economic development variables are more influential than political system characteristics in shaping public policy in the states. . . . Forty-seven of the fifty-four key policy variables listed are more closely related to economic variables than to political variables. These are the policy outcomes for which the coefficients in the fourth column are larger than the coefficients in the fifth column. For these forty-seven policy outcomes the effects of all economic variables under controlled conditions are greater than the effects of all political variables under controlled conditions.[16]

This rather jolting conclusion that political variables have relatively little effect on public policy outcomes has been confirmed by several researchers. It is very difficult to escape the conclusion that the relationship of such variables as party competition and voter participation to policy is due to the fact that the former are related to economic conditions. However, there is some contour to the picture. Walker[17] was interested not so much in policy outcomes and expenditures as indicators of service, but in other aspects of policy. Particularly, he was interested in the decision to initiate policies in the first place. He was concerned with diffusion of innovation, with the rapidity with which states adopt new policies. Over the years, especially since 1870, many new and "progressive" kinds of legislation have been developed at the state level. After an idea has been introduced, most states, sooner or later, get around to enacting legislation on the topic. Some states are leaders in adopting the new and others are laggards. Why? This is an important question. How long people will have to wait for a particular policy, if it is adopted at all, depends on the answer. Walker collected information on the adoption of eighty-eight kinds of state legislation —from licensing pharmacists and other health-related professionals, through the establishment of legislative reference bureaus, through home rule for cities, to the establishment of provisions for criminal probation. Each state was scored on each of the eighty-eight policy variables on the basis of how quickly they enacted legislation after the idea was introduced. All eighty-eight scores were summed to provide an *innovation index* for each state. Because of the previous work done on state policy and because it makes good sense independently, Walker tested the proposition that economic variables and political factors affected state innovation scores. Rich states, he hypothesized, should be innovative, as should competitive, well-apportioned ones. In general, high correlations were obtained between economic variables and innovation and also between political variables and innovation. But when the economic variables were controlled, the values of the coefficients for the relationship between the political variables and policy generally declined, as in Dye's research. The relationship between the index of party competition and innovation was originally .54; when all four economic variables were controlled, it declined to .12. However, one variable, apportionment of the legislature, continued to be strongly related to innovativeness in policy regardless of the impact of the economic variables. Originally .65, the correlation between equality of apportionment and innovation declined only to .58 when the four indicators of economic development were controlled. Apparently this political variable, at least, does have an effect, if not on expenditures and services, then on the degree of innovation in state policies.

Fry and Winters,[18] while not challenging the findings of previous scholars, offer an interesting new insight to this problem. Like Walker, they focused on a different dependent variable. They argued that the important thing about policy outputs and public services may be not how much is spent on a given policy area or the magnitude of services rendered, but rather who pays for and who benefits from the enactment of policies. Instead of explaining budgetary levels, one should, they argued, account for how politics *redistributes* values, how it allocates benefits and costs. This is a reasonable approach if we think of politics as a device for settling conflicts within society, as a process that produces winners and losers. Surely, in addition to producing policies that are "mutually" beneficial, politics causes some people to get more and others to get less.

Fry and Winters relied on data collected by the Tax Foundation. The Foundation looked at all the taxes imposed by each state and then determined what proportion of each tax was paid by persons with various incomes. It further considered all the expenditures made by each state for all types of public services and then sought to determine

104

what proportion of the benefits produced by each policy was enjoyed by persons with various incomes. This is not as difficult as it sounds. As Fry and Winters point out, "elementary and secondary education expenditure benefits [for instance] were assumed to be distributed according to the number of children under eighteen in families in each income class, so that if 20% of children under eighteen were in families with an income of $4000 to $4999, 20% of expenditures on elementary and secondary education were assigned as benefits to that income class."[19] A simple ratio of benefits to expenditures could thus be calculated for each income class for each state. Fry and Winters then assigned each state a *redistributive ratio* based on the benefits-received to taxes-paid quotient of people with annual incomes of less than $4000. For reasons much the same as those offered by Dye, they sought to determine the impact of various economic variables, as well as political factors, on this redistributive measure. Very similar indicators of income, industrialization, urbanization, and education were assembled, as well as one of income inequality. Of course, data for all such indicators are easily available, largely from the U.S. Census. Many of the political variables used (participation, Democratic vote, party competition, and apportionment) were similar to those used by Dye, but several others having to do with the legislature and interest groups were added. The same basic kind of analysis was performed on these data as Dye performed on his. Fry and Winters' conclusions, however, are quite different:

> The most interesting and significant finding in this study . . . concerns the relative importance of political and socioeconomic variables in determining redistributive fiscal policies in the state. . . . previous studies of policy outcomes in the states have been hard pressed to find an independent impact for the political variables considered, and where the relative impact of political and socioeconomic variables has been examined, the socioeconomic variables have predominated. In the present analysis, these findings are reversed. Not only do the political variables have an independent impact on redistributive policies in the states; they also account for considerably more of the variance in redistribution than do socioeconomic variables.[20]

Table 3-7 contains a summary of the results of this study.

TABLE 3–7

**The Effects of Economic Variables and Political Factors on
Redistributive Policies in the American States**

Total Effect of Economic and Political Variables	Total Effect of Economic Variables	Total Effect of Political Variables	Effect of Economic Variables, Controlling Political Variables	Effect of Political Variables, Controlling Economic Variables
.75	.42	.62	.52	.68

Source: Adapted from Brian R. Fry and Richard F. Winters, "The Politics of Redistribution," *American Political Science Review,* Vol. 64 (June 1970), 520. Entries are multiple correlation coefficients or multiple partial correlation coefficients, as appropriate.

The research we have reviewed here makes it very clear that while economic considerations are extremely important in determining the policies of state government—so much so that the reformist view that merely changing the form of political institutions will produce dramatically different results appears rather naive—there are ways in which political variables exert systematic effects on policy. One cannot argue for a simple kind of economic determinism. The policy picture in the American states is one of considerable contour—all of which is by no means known to political scientists.

Local politics is an area of study that also contains many collectivities that can be systematically examined. Of course, units of local government themselves are the most obvious subjects for investigation. Lineberry and Fowler[21] analyzed 200 American cities in an attempt to deal with an age-old political question—the effects of institutional reform. During a later part of the nineteenth century and early in the twentieth century, city politics in particular were regarded as corrupt and dishonest. And in many cases, they were. This phenomenon was due partly to the kinds of political demands that were made upon urban governments, not the least of which emanated from newly arrived ethnic populations whose votes were assiduously sought by politicians. Urban government responded to the particularistic needs created by ethnic and socioeconomic divisions. Particular ethnic populations were able to capture given wards, control given aldermen, and exert influence in party organizations. Benefits and payoffs were thus assured. The irrationality of such a scheme, the lack of consideration for "the interests of the city as a whole," spurred institutional reform. In many areas, city managers or city commissions were substituted for the mayor-council form of government. Nonpartisan elections were introduced, as was "at-large" rather than ward-based election of city representatives. All these reforms were supposed to eliminate the responsiveness of government to particularistic and ethnic interests so that enlightened rationality, or the interest of the whole, could prevail.

The reform movement, however, did not touch all cities. Though the efforts of the reformists were vigorous, many cities retain "unreformed" governments to this day. This situation offers a superb opportunity for comparative research. Are reformed and unreformed cities different in their politics? Are they differentially responsive to particularistic, ethnic interests? In short, did reformers achieve the effect they desired by changing the institutional structure of American municipalities?

Lineberry and Fowler reasoned that if city politics are responsive to ethnic interests taxation and expenditure policy should be associated with the extent to which the population is composed of ethnic minority groups. Thus, if reformers have achieved their goal, this kind of relationship should be most pronounced in unreformed cities. They collected data (from the U.S. Census) on the proportion of population that was foreign born or of mixed parentage and the proportion of children in private schools (which are mostly parochial) as indicators of ethnicity. They then correlated these variables with total city taxes and total city expenditures (from official budgets) for each kind of city. The results are indicated in Table 3-8. It appears that there is at least a modest relationship between these indicators of ethnicity and taxes and expenditures. Moreover, in general, the strength of these relationships is greater in cities that have unreformed governmental institutions. Reformism has produced an effect, and it is the effect, for better or worse, that its advocates intended. The institutional structure of government can, it would seem, affect political happenings very significantly—in this case apparently modifying the power of minority groups.

Though the study of state and local politics has generally been the province of political anecdotalists and political engineers, there is no reason why it should not be studied from other points of view as well.

107

TABLE 3–8

Correlations Between Ethnicity and Religious Heterogeneity and Outputs in Reformed and Unreformed Cities

Correlations	TYPE OF GOVERNMENT			TYPE OF ELECTION		TYPE OF CONSTITUENCY	
	Mayor-Council (N = 85)	Manager (N = 90)	Commission (N = 25)	Partisan (N = 57)	Non-partisan (N = 143)	Ward (N = 73)	At-Large (N = 127)
TAXES WITH							
Ethnicity	.49	.26	.57	.61	.43	.56	.40
Private-school attendance	.38	.15	.37	.33	.37	.41	.25
EXPENDITURES WITH							
Ethnicity	.36	.02	.21	.48	.21	.44	.13
Private-school attendance	.34	−.01	.07	.25	.24	.40	.05

Source: Robert L. Lineberry and Edmund P. Fowler, "Reformism and Public Policy in American Cities," *American Political Science Review*, Vol. 61 (September 1967), 713.

Considering units of government (states or municipalities) as collectivities offers a great many opportunities for behavioral research. Indeed, most of the assertions made by anecdotalists or engineers about state or local politics are capable of translation into explanatory propositions, many of which can be tested through studies of collectivities. Suppose an anecdotalist tells us that the only reason Governor Jones carried so many counties was because of his road- building program. We can generalize from this and ask whether there is, among the collectivities called counties, an observable relationship between votes for an incumbent and miles of new roads completed. A political engineer may argue that a new law providing for an expanded public defender's office will result in fewer convictions of poor people accused in local courts. Data comparing conviction records for localities (collectivities) that have an extensive public defender system with those that do not would reveal whether this proposition is generally true. One need only use one's imagination to see the many possibilities for research of this type. It is time for the study of local politics to be supplemented by the systematic study of collectivities.

Studying Collectivities: A Recapitulation

Tremendous numbers of important political concerns involve the behavior of collectivities. Comparative politics and state and local government represent only the most developed areas of research. Many additional areas are amenable to the behavioral approach. What kinds of colleges and universities experience political protest? What kinds of courts make libertarian decisions? The list of questions about collectivities is virtually unlimited. It is not surprising, then, that a full understanding of the behavioral approach to the study of politics requires some knowledge of this class of objects. Given the great potential in this area—which results from the momentous nature of the subject—there can be no doubt that a lot of effort will be invested in macro-level political studies in the future.

Notes

1. John V. Gillespie and Betty A. Nesvold (eds.), *Macro-Quantitative Analysis* (Beverly Hills, Calif.: Sage Publications, 1971), p. 32.
2. Ivo K. Feierabend and Rosalind L. Feierabend, "Aggressive Behavior Within Polities, 1948-1962: A Cross-national Study," *The Journal of Conflict Resolution*, Vol. 10 (September 1966), 250.
3. Ted Gurr, "A Causal Model of Civil Strife: A Comparative Analysis Using New Indices," *American Political Science Review*, Vol. 62 (December 1968), 1104.
4. Raymond Tanter, "Dimensions of Conflict Behavior Within and Between Nations: 1958-1960," *The Journal of Conflict Resolution*, Vol. 10 (March 1966), 42.
5. Douglas P. Bwy, "Political Instability in Latin America: The Cross-cultural Test of a Causal Model," in Gillespie and Nesvold (eds.), *op. cit.*, p. 128.
6. *Ibid.*, p. 123.
7. William Flanigan and Edwin Fogelman, "Patterns of Political Development and Democratization: A Quantitative Analysis," in Gillespie and Nesvold (eds.), *op. cit.*, p. 441.
8. *Ibid.*, p. 444.
9. Donald J. McCrone and Charles F. Cnudde, "Toward a Communication Theory of Democratic Political Development: A Causal Model," *American Political Science Review*, Vol. 61 (March 1967), 73.
10. *Ibid.*, p. 78.
11. *Loc. cit.*
12. Gilbert R. Winham, "Political Development and Lerner's Theory: Future Tests of a Causal Model," *American Political Science Review*, Vol. 64 (September 1970), 813.
13. *Ibid.*, p. 818.
14. *Ibid.*
15. Thomas R. Dye, *Politics, Economics, and the Public: Policy Outcomes in the American States* (Chicago: Rand McNally, 1966).
16. *Ibid.*, p. 296.
17. Jack L. Walker, "The Diffusion of Innovations Among the American States," *American Political Science Review*, Vol. 63 (September 1969), 881.
18. Brian R. Fry and Richard F. Winters, "The Politics of Redistribution," *American Political Science Review*, Vol. 64 (June 1970), 508.
19. *Ibid.*, p. 511.
20. *Ibid.*, p. 521.
21. Robert L. Lineberry and Edmund P. Fowler, "Reformism and Public Policy in American Cities," *American Political Science Review*, Vol. 61 (September 1967), 701.

4

Explaining
the Political
Behavior of
Individuals:
Group or
Social Factors

Social groups, associations, and organizations are important to politics. The idea that large numbers of people, because of common membership in some sort of group, can be induced to perform the same political acts or believe in the same political norms has fascinated thinkers for centuries. Aristotle, for example, believed that social classes exhibited characteristic behavior. He argued that it was necessary for a state to have a relatively large middle class and few very rich or very poor citizens in order to enjoy political stability. Otherwise, the characteristic acrimony between the rich and poor would be too destructive. In a way, contemporary scholars, like Aristotle, also think of politics as a clash of groups. Ecology groups, student groups, consumer protection associations, and ethnic minorities are viewed as the dynamic new forces in today's public life. And they are opposed, allegedly, by groups

representative of the older establishment: labor unions, business associations, and the military.

The continuing relevance of groups is reflected in a prominent
focus of empirical political science that might be called the "group basis
of politics" approach. The fundamental principle of this approach is that
all significant groups have political interests and therefore all significant
political activity reflects intergroup conflicts. That is, the prime moving
force in the operation of any political system is controversy not between
isolated individuals, but between groups of individuals who are bound
together by some common interest, economic, religious, or otherwise.
A significant proposition of this approach is that public policy is the
result of governmental institutions' responses to interest-group efforts.
Somehow, policy reflects a synthesis of all the "pressures" such groups
apply to public officials or offices. The validity of such an approach
obviously can be determined only from macro-level research. In order
to test Aristotle's hypothesis, for example, we would have to gather
information on a number of nations and determine whether there was a
positive relationship between the size of the middle class (calculated
from census or other demographic data) and political stability (measured
in terms of the amount of revolutionary behavior or domestic violence)
among them. The policy hypotheses could be approached by studying
the decisions of public agencies. We would expect that legislation
passed by representatives, for example, would be beneficial to groups
that had articulated specific interests in public policy. Moreover, such
groups should, in some sense, have more "strength" than competing
groups. Legislation that is favored by no group or only by weak groups
should not be passed.

Although, as we saw in Chapter 2, there are some systematic
macro-level studies of the impact of lobbying, there are few comprehensive assessments of the impact of groups on politics that rely upon
the systematic analysis of data from a behavioral viewpoint. This, of
course, is not to imply that there are no good studies in this area; in fact,
there are a great many and they have made a clear contribution. Much of
this research focuses on the enactment of—or the failure to enact—some
important piece of legislation, say, for example, that approving Britain's
entry into the Common Market.[1] It then goes on to examine the activities of interest groups that were involved in the debate over the
policy, and tries to establish likely connections (or account for the lack of

112

apparent connections) between the two.[2] Many interesting case studies emerge from such efforts, but the ability of group activity to explain policy outputs remains, from a scientific point of view, relatively unexplored.

Much of the group basis of politics approach is based on the principle that we stated at the outset of this chapter: that members of groups exhibit similar political behavior. It is at least implicit in many hypotheses that group power is in part dependent upon the likemindedness of members. If group members do not do something substantially in unison—vote, support a revolutionary leader, demand policy changes—it is difficult to see how their actions can be translated into political power. Unity of behavior gives them something to sell to political policy-makers or would-be policy-makers in return for policy payoffs or the promise thereof.

Though it is not logically necessary that such unity exist for a group to have power—the leaders could fool policy-makers or provide them with other things they valued such as money from a private fortune or personal services—it seems likely that it is critical in a large number of cases. Thus, the group basis of politics approach implies an interest in the questions of how, when, where, and under what circumstances group memberships influence human political behavior. This, of course, is totally different from the question of whether groups influence policy. For one thing, it is a micro-level question. We are concerned here with explaining individual human behavior in terms of independent variables having to do with membership in groups or associations. Furthermore, even if it should turn out that the group basis of politics is largely unsupported by macro-level research, interest in the group determinants of political behavior at the individual level would still be fully justified. We still need to understand and explain behavior, regardless of whether its effect on governmental policy is achieved through groups.

In this sense, the group explanation of individual behavior is a broader concern than the group basis of politics. The latter is really concerned with the behavior of mass publics who may be organized into groups. It is really a question of citizen behavior. But there is no logical reason why group or social factors should be thought of as potential determinants of citizen behavior only. Indeed, *all* political actors, including officeholding elites, live in a social context and are surrounded by members of groups, formal or informal, to which they belong. If

113

masses are influenced by their group membership, it is likely that persons in very rarified political strata—say, Justices of the Supreme Court—are also.[3]

Thus, the political importance of groups is reflected in two conceptually related but quite distinct approaches to political study. We should keep clearly in mind that these approaches are *not* the same, though they are sometimes lumped together under the heading "group" approaches without any explanation of their differences. The group basis of politics could be investigated in a systematic study of the behavior of political collectivities, as was discussed in Chapter 3. However, this chapter is devoted to the general hypothesis that individual political behavior—regardless of type—may be partly explained by membership in groups. We shall investigate the questions of how, why, when, and under what circumstances this occurs.

Primary and Other Groups

People possess at least three kinds of group memberships in the course of a relatively normal lifetime. First and most obviously, people are members of *primary* groups. These are groups that involve very regular, face-to-face contacts. Immediate associates like one's family, friends, or co-workers constitute primary groups. Only hermits and recluses avoid primary-group contacts—and even these had a primary group life at one time. Someone cared for them as infants, or they would not have survived. Primary-group life, it goes without saying, is tremendously important to all persons in all societies. Most people are acutely conscious of their primary groups. In addition, there are *secondary* groups, made up of people who share one or more traits. Professional, religious, or labor organizations are good examples of such groups. Membership in a mass political party (such as the British Labour Party or the French Communist Party) would amount to membership in a secondary group. So would membership in any kind of pressure group. Usually, we may think of secondary groups as having some sort of formal organization. Close personal contact on a regular basis is less likely to occur in such groups, but relatively asymmetrical relationships (such as that between an editor of a club bulletin and its readers or that of participation in mass meetings) are more likely. Like primary-group membership, secondary-group membership is something of which one is likely to be quite conscious. Most people in modern societies consider their secondary-group memberships to be quite important. Finally, there are what may be called *categoric* groups. Categoric-group members merely share some characteristic that assigns them to an identifiable category. High-school graduates constitute a categoric group, as do all persons under the age of thirty, all persons residing in communities with a population under 15,000, women, and people with blond hair. As the term "categoric" implies, these are just ways of classifying people. Typically, there is no formal organization involved in categoric-group status, and in many cases people are not particularly conscious of the fact that they are members of given categoric groups. Of course, there are exceptions to this: There are conditions under which social classes become acutely conscious of their status, and organizations such as women's liberation groups are based on categoric status. In the case of the exceptions, we can easily see how they might be very politically relevant. But even when no organization or consciousness is present, categoric-group membership may be of great importance in explaining individual political behavior.

Sources of Group Influence

Although the ways in which groups influence people are many and complex, we can isolate several general dynamics that make the impact of these associations on political behavior more understandable.

SECTION A
GROUP MEMBERSHIP AND
EXPOSURE TO COMMON STIMULI

Perhaps the most widely accepted generalization in social science—and one shared by casual observers—is that people from different social backgrounds behave in characteristic ways. We expect people from the working classes to read rather different kinds of material than the middle classes. Relatively few members of the middle classes have the magazine *Modern Romances* in their homes, while even fewer

115

working-class people receive the *Atlantic Monthly*. People from cities are typically more knowledgeable and "sophisticated" than those who have a rural background. Boys from homes in which the father is absent adjust much more poorly to their peers than boys from normal, two-parent homes. Part of the reason for these clear differences in behavior on the part of people with different backgrounds may be that the backgrounds imply different patterns of influences. For example, middle-class people typically receive more education than members of the working classes, and this undoubtedly has something to do with the kinds of material they choose to read. Persons raised in an urban environment receive more communications and experience contacts with many more people than their rural counterparts. The greater level of stimulation imparts both information and motivation to action. Boys from fatherless homes typically do not receive the extensive training in interpersonal relations with other males that most boys do.

In other words, the circumstances of one's life determine to a large degree the kinds of influences that impinge upon one. Thus, members of a given group—be it primary, secondary, or categoric—may exhibit characteristic behavior because they have shared certain experiences; they have experienced a common set of stimuli, while members of other groups have experienced other sets of stimuli.

One of the earliest and most popular areas of investigation among political behaviorists has been the extent to which "background factors" function as determinants of various kinds of mass actions. Among the researchers' favorite subjects has been one that has fascinated Western scholars and philosophers for centuries—participation in democratic politics. No doubt because of the old proposition that democratic societies must have high rates of citizen participation to be healthy, the search for the antecedents of political activity has been vigorous. For example, we noted above that residence in a rural area tends to diminish social participation whereas residence in an urban area increases it; survey research has demonstrated that this is generally true in politics as well as in other fields. An interesting exception to this rule was examined by Tarrow.[4] Tarrow found that peasants in rural France were somewhat *more* inclined to be politically active than French workers resident in the large industrial cities. Among the many data he reported were some from a survey of a national sample of the French electorate. Respondents were queried as to whether they had (1) voted, (2) attended campaign meetings, (3) read election posters, and (4) tried to persuade others how to vote. These items were used as an index of political participation, and respondents were given a score based on the number of positive answers they gave. (Voting plus at least two of the other activities gave one a "high" score, voting plus one other activity gave one a "moderate" score, while voting alone or no activity at all gave one a "low" score.) The results are displayed in Table 4-1. The respondents were also asked about their occupations. As the table shows, farmers were not dramatically more participatory than workers; however, the amazing fact is that they were not *less* participatory than most other occupational groups.

Tarrow believes that this curious pattern is partly due to the fact that French peasants have been subjected to influences not common to most other rural populations. Rural education has always been considered important in France, especially during the Third Republic. The result has been a higher rural literacy rate than in surrounding countries. Education, as we know, is a stimulus to participation. In addition, French rural communes tend to be small in population and organized around a central village. These villages have large numbers of elected officers, relative to size of their populations. Indeed, the number of offices is so large that, in one study, fully one-fifth of the rural residents were found to have held public office. In other words, the rural French are impelled by the smallness of their communes and their institutional arrangement to take a more active role in public affairs. Being a member

TABLE 4–1

The Relationship Between Political Participation and Occupation in France

Participation Index Scores	Farmers (N = 91)	Professionals, Executives (N = 59)	Artisans, Tradesmen (N = 127)	Clerical Workers (N = 162)	Factory Workers (N = 257)
High	24.0%	27.0%	20.5%	19.0%	15.0%
Moderate	35.0	35.5	36.0	41.0	37.0
Low	41.0	37.5	43.5	40.0	48.0
Total	100.0%	100.0%	100.0%	100.0%	100.0%

Source: Adapted from Sidney Tarrow, "The Urban-Rural Cleavage in Political Involvement: The Case of France," *American Political Science Review*, Vol. 65 (June 1971), 346.

of the categoric group "rural resident" has dramatic implications for political behavior.

Many scholars have shown the relationship of education to political involvement and participation more directly. Time and again survey research in the United States has indicated that more educated people are more likely to vote, to seek information about political issues, and to become involved in the political process in other ways.[5] This is not at all surprising, for the stimulus of education probably heightens interest in many aspects of life (not only politics); allows people to understand politics better, so that participation does not have an aura of futility; and is responsible for people attaining positions in life upon which politics impinge more directly, thus giving them a greater "objective" interest in politics.

What has been said about the categoric groups defined by education is also generally true of those defined by other elements of socioeconomic status (SES) such as occupation and income. Persons with a high income or a high-status occupation are likely to be more immediately affected by politics; few people are as directly involved as the business executive whose firm has government contracts. Nor have such people suffered the feelings of futility that often accompany the efforts of the relatively poor to assert themselves in what is essentially a middle-class society. It is not at all surprising that persons in families of low status should be relatively nonparticipatory. They receive few stimuli that encourage participation and many that discourage it.

It has often been suggested that lower-class persons, because of their inability to achieve much in the way of desirable goals, become despairing and withdrawn, or alienated. (We shall return to this notion in a later chapter.) In a sense, they are seen as constituting a frustrated but silent and withdrawn reservoir of discontent. Periodically, it seems, this supposed reservoir of discontent is rediscovered. Thinkers with revolutionary or reformist goals look to it for mass support for dramatic changes in society. Since the people in this reservoir are not participating in the normal political affairs of society, they can perhaps be stimulated to action of another sort—protest or revolution. Great power and great changes may stem from activating the alienated and nonparticipatory lower-class masses.

This theme, common at least since Marx, seems especially relevant to contemporary social protest, to concern with the urban poor, and to the articulation of black demands. Indeed, there seems to be a good deal of validity to the hypothesis of lower-class withdrawal and discontent. But on the other hand, there is often a tendency on the part of reformers to misperceive the sources of their support; what may seem to be the voice of the deprived masses, liberated at last after years of silence, may in fact be the sound of a small but articulate segment of the middle class that is no newcomer to political action at all. At least in the beginning stages of political change, support is often concentrated in the elite, not the masses.

Jackson has studied the political protest activity of black college students.[6] Selecting subjects from three universities in the South, he inquired into individual participation in seven types of political protest activities: leading or organizing black protest activities; participating in wade-ins, kneel-ins, or sit-ins; participation in riots; picketing; joining or attending meetings of an Afro-American group; donating money to a black cause; and taking part in mass demonstrations, marches, and the like. Responses to this inquiry were used as the basis of a scale of protest activities, and all subjects were assigned a score according to their degree of participation. Information was also gathered on the black students' family backgrounds.

Is it true that the most deprived blacks, those upon whom the burden of discrimination falls most heavily, those who have been the most nonparticipatory, jump into protest activity most readily? Or, are the most frequent protestors those who have received the most stimuli to social participation, that is, the more privileged? Part of the answer to this question is given in Table 4-2, which shows the relationship between protest activity and the educational level of the subjects' parents. It is at once evident that parental education is positively related to protest activity. The children of the most educated black families are most likely to protest. Additional evidence confirms this finding for the other dimensions of status. Jackson reports that the Gamma coefficient for the relationship between a family's occupational status and protest is .39; that between reported family income and protest is .44. (Notice that these coefficients are comparable in magnitude to the coefficient, .47, reported in Table 4-2. As we mentioned in Chapter 2, Gamma or other coefficients may be reported rather than displaying an entire table of ordinal data. To save space, Jackson used only one table, but reported all three coefficients.) Black protest can hardly be regarded, then, as a great

TABLE 4–2

**The Relationship Between Black Students' Protest Activity and
the Education of Their Parents**

LEVEL OF EDUCATION

Level of Protest Activity	Highschool or Less (N = 286)	Some College or College Graduate (N = 103)	Professional or Graduate Education (N = 59)
Low	61.5%	35.9%	16.9%
Medium	11.9	18.4	25.4
High	26.6	45.6	57.6
Total	100.0%	99.9%*	99.9%*
	Gamma = .47, p < .0001		

* Does not add to 100% because of rounding.

Source: Adapted from John S. Jackson, "The Political Behavior and Socio-Economic Backgrounds of Black Students: The Antecedents of Protest," *Midwest Journal of Political Science*, Vol. 15 (November 1971), 679.

demonstration of discontent on the part of the most deprived, the inarticulate, and the normally withdrawn. Indeed, participation in protests can be explained by the same variables that explain participation in "normal" political activity such as voting and working for candidates. Indeed, Jackson shows that though protest activity has been increasing among black students over the last few years, so have less dramatic, conventional forms of political involvement. Rather than rejecting conventional participation in favor of, first, apathy and withdrawal and then protest, blacks are more vigorously pursuing *both* kinds of political activity. And particular categoric groups (those high in SES) are taking the lead in both areas. Perhaps, then, the "reservoir of discontent" hypothesis does not do too good a job of accounting for this kind of political behavior. Indeed, just the opposite kind of group-participation relationship appears from the one which this notion suggests.

Two rather different kinds of stimuli to which status groups may be exposed are suggested in an interesting study by Weissberg.[7] Weissberg was interested in a behavior called "diffuse support." It is likely that for any government to function adequately in the modern world there must be a rather generalized feeling of goodwill toward the government on the part of substantial numbers of its citizens. Clearly, no ruling group today can disregard how its citizens feel toward it and maintain itself by force alone. It must get citizen support. In part it does this by enacting satisfying policies—or at least so we are told by many normative theorists. However, it is clearly not true that most citizens support the political systems under which they live only so long as the stream of satisfying policies is continuous. Significant portions of the citizenry may be receiving no tangible benefits from the operation of government at any given time. At some particularly difficult junctures, periods of war or depression, for example, virtually no one may be satisfied by policy outcomes. However, there usually exists a generalized feeling that the government is good, honest, and strong, which enables rulers to weather crises and periods of adversity. Such generalized support may be thought of as a kind of primitive patriotism or loyalty.

A particularly intriguing variant of political behavior research has demonstrated that young children exhibit extremely high levels of diffuse support for government figures and institutions. This may signal something that political philosophers and practitioners have argued for a long time: that patriotism may take root at a very young age. However, there is some question about exactly what these youthful orientations presage for adult behavior. Do they persist to the age of functioning citizenship or do they wane, to be replaced by attitudes acquired later? There have been several studies of such diffuse support among different age groups designed to chart its growth or decline. Not surprisingly, the rather exaggerated positive image of political authority held by children erodes somewhat with age. It is clear that, at least in the United States, increased knowledge and sophistication—which comes with age—leads to a more critical assessment of public authority.

Weissberg examined the opinion of adolescents in this regard. He looked at three separate groups: university students who were "predominantly middle and upper-middle class," technical school enrollees of the "lower-middle and upper-lower" class, and a group of "very low status" delinquents confined to state institutions. To the extent that these groups reflect SES differences (and they do), we would expect, on the basis of the argument spelled out above, that there would be some specific differences between them. Lower-status youngsters are not subjected to stimuli that make for sophistication; they remain relatively underdeveloped in a cognitive sense. Logically, then, they should continue to demonstrate more of the idealization of political authority characteristic of children than others in their age group. And, indeed, just such SES differentials in idealization have been noted among older preadolescent children. These data are consistent with the common knowledge that working-class people today express the greatest opposition to most forms of racial or youth protest.

The delinquents in Weissberg's study, on the other hand, had been the direct object of restraint imposed by government. They had been convicted and imprisoned by public authorities. If these stimuli have any impact, we would expect the delinquents' attitudes toward public agencies to be relatively unfavorable. This supposition, of course, is not tremendously different from the alienation-protest hypothesis discussed earlier in the chapter.

The subjects in each of Weissberg's three samples were asked to evaluate various agencies of public authority according to *semantic differential scales*. These devices simply ask respondents to place the object to be evaluated somewhere on a seven-point continuum, the ends of which are defined by polar adjectives such as "good-bad" or "smart-stupid." A subject may place an object at the extreme positive point (e.g., smart) and receive a score of seven, at the extreme negative point (e.g., stupid) and receive a score of one, or at some intermediate point for which he receives an intermediate score. Table 4-3 shows the data Weissberg obtained by asking his subjects to rate the honesty or dishon-

TABLE 4-3

Adolescents' Ratings of Political Authorities' Honesty (Mean Scores)

	University Students	Technical Students	Delinquents	p*
Federal government	3.83	4.89	4.65	<.05
State government (Wis.)	4.00	4.88	5.02	<.05
City council	4.36	5.01	4.79	<.05
Courts	5.09	5.19	4.43	<.05
Police	4.39	5.52	3.45	<.05

* Significance is determined by using a technique called *one-way analysis of variance*. Chi-square or correlation coefficients would be inappropriate with these kinds of data. [Note added.]

Source: Robert Weissberg, "Adolescents' Perceptions of Political Authorities: Another Look at Political Virtue and Power," *Midwest Journal of Political Science*, Vol. 16 (February 1972), 159.

esty of various branches and levels of government, using a semantic differential scale. The entries in the table are simply the average score for each group. Even though the middle-class university students had, in a sense, received more from the system, they invariably regarded the public agencies or institutions as less honest than their lower-class counterparts in the technical training institution did. It would seem, then, that the latter, because of their lack of exposure to sophisticating stimuli, may have continued to idealize the agencies of the establishment despite their own relatively unfavorable social positions.

The delinquents, on the other hand, had somewhat mixed reactions. To be sure, as a result of their unfortunate experience with the law, they appeared to be less favorably inclined toward courts and the police. However, they did not appear less supportive of other, more general agents of government. Indeed, the delinquents' evaluations of the more general agents were as positive as those of the technical students and notably higher than those of the university students.

Obviously, the kinds of stimuli groups receive can have a dramatic impact on their behavior. But the patterns evident among Weissberg's subjects, though explicable, give one cause to contemplate. One could argue that sophistication is a greater solvent of diffuse support than even punishment by incarceration. If one were very cynical, one might think about the implications for social control. From this standpoint it would be possible to argue that it is better to have an unsophisticated citizenry than a sophisticated one. Unsophisticated ones, it appears, can even be severely punished without destroying diffuse support, whereas sophisticated populations are dubious of political authority even when in possession of all the fruits their superior status has brought them.

Occasionally, we can observe groups whose political behavior seems very obviously to be the consequence of a peculiar set of stimuli. For example, few people would deny that black protest activity is at least partly due to the discriminatory treatment blacks have experienced over the years. Indeed, it seems likely that discriminatory stimuli are the reason race today is no longer merely a categoric group but the basis for many secondary groups that possess a very great degree of self-consciousness. Aberbach and Walker[8] analyzed data from an extensive survey of blacks and whites in Detroit, a city with a considerable history of racial disturbance. They were concerned about political trust, a form of diffuse support such as we have already discussed. Not

123

surprisingly, they found that blacks were less trusting of government when trust was measured by a five-item index that dealt with both national and local government. Furthermore, political trust among blacks was negatively related to willingness to participate in riots or other forms of political protest. But the most relevant finding of this study, for our purposes, concerns the impact of discriminatory experiences. To determine this impact, blacks in the sample were simply asked (by black interviewers) about such events. The number of incidents reported were then summed to create a discrimination index.

Such stimuli, we would expect, would cause an increase in willingness to participate in riots. Aberbach and Walker's data on this point are reported in Table 4-4. There we see the relationship between discriminatory experiences and willingness to riot when the variable political trust is controlled. This control is used not to determine whether the relationship between discrimination and trust is spurious (as it would be if only people with little trust in government experienced discrimination), but rather to glean additional information on when and how discrimination produces its effect. Experiences with discrimination clearly affect blacks who are relatively trusting as well as those who are

TABLE 4–4

The Relationship Between Discrimination and Blacks' Willingness to Take Part in Civil Disturbance

Willingness to Partici-pate in Riots	LOW TRUST REPORTED EXPERIENCES			HIGH TRUST REPORTED EXPERIENCES		
	Few (N = 122)	Medium (N = 31)	Many (N = 61)	Few (N = 139)	Medium (N = 37)	Many (N = 44)
Yes or Maybe	30%	60%	71%	22%	30%	36%
No	70	40	29	78	70	64
Total	100%	100%	100%	100%	100%	100%
	Gamma = – .65			Gamma = – .26		

Source: Adapted from Joel D. Aberbach and Jack L. Walker, "Political Trust and Racial Ideology," *American Political Science Review*, Vol. 64 (December 1970), 1214.

not. However, the effect of discrimination is clearly much more pronounced among those with little trust in government:

> When trust is low, experiences of discrimination have a very powerful effect . . . but trust seems to serve as a dike which blunts somewhat the political effects of these experiences. Persons who are low in trust seem to interpret each experience of discrimination as further proof that the political system is evil . . . while those who are trusting have a less severe reaction to these experiences. High levels of trust are resources which governments can use to gain time. . . . When trust is low, injustices have a stronger and more immediate impact since the reservoir of good will has been destroyed.[9]

These findings demonstrate the importance both of diffuse support and of the stimuli blacks as a group experience.

Our review of the proposition that group members may exhibit similar political behavior because of exposure to common stimuli has covered a variety of examples. And we have by no means exhausted the possibilities by this sampling of the research. There is evidence, for example, that Congressmen who are members of foreign-relations committees vote differently on foreign-relations roll calls than their colleagues with different committee assignments. Is this because these men receive different information or encounter different demands as a consequence of their position? It is reasonable to think so. Many other situations in which groups may have experienced characteristic stimuli come readily to mind.

Social background characteristics—education or, more generally, SES—may be a kind of summary indicator of important experiences or real interests. Associations between such characteristics and diverse kinds of political behavior are thus quite understandable. However, it should be evident that this kind of interpretation is not adequate to account for all the group-related political phenomena we can observe in the world. For one thing, we have not spoken of primary groups as a basis for the receipt of common stimuli. There is no logical reason why they should not be. However, it is usually true that the stimuli of the type we have been discussing have a much wider incidence than primary groups. They are likely to be experienced by a whole social class or race, not just a small group. On the other hand, we have noted in passing such phenomena as parents communicating political norms to their children. Primary-group influences, though they operate in different ways, can have visible political effects. There are other kinds of group dynamics, and it behooves us to examine them.

SECTION B
THE REFERENCE GROUP:
INTERNAL STIMULI

Many groups, particularly primary and categoric ones, are capable of generating influences of their own that affect their members. Though such influences are not totally independent of the external common stimuli discussed in Section A, they are more than just relayed incarnations of them. In fact, group influences *as such* have a tremendous effect on all aspects of a human being's existence. Let us examine some common examples of group-specific behavior. Italians eat more pasta than residents of other countries, while Swedes prefer limpa bread. To be sure, these preferences may have been determined originally by external stimuli such as the availability of particular foodstuffs, but over the years they have become more than that; they have become part of the national culture. American Jews generally choose to live in urban settings rather than rural ones. Divorce is less common among Catholics than among Protestants. Some families—for generation after generation—are very rigid in rearing their children, while others, with equal consistency, are very permissive. The examples of such behavior could be multiplied indefinitely. The point is obvious: Groups are able to get their members to conform to definite standards of behavior even when the reasons for such behavior are subjective or no longer exist.

The source of much of this conformity is interpersonal interaction within groups. Somehow, associating with other Italians or other Swedes in secondary or, as is more likely, primary groups leads one to prefer certain foods. A preference for urban settings is somehow communicated among Jews. Such processes are pervasive in human experi-

126

ence from infancy forward. In fact, much of the process by which an infant acquires the characteristics of a human person is eminently social. A totally helpless and inarticulate organism becomes a child and then an adult not only through physiological maturational processes, but also through the mental process of learning. This learning—sometimes called *socialization*—takes place in response to the actions of *significant others*. These significant others are, for most infants, their parents. From a child's earliest days significant others dispense rewards and impose punishments. Many of the earliest movements and actions of an infant are probably random. The capability of moving limbs or crying is present, so the infant engages in these behaviors without any purpose. However, certain of these movements and actions result in rewards from the parents, while others result in punishment. Crying at certain times or in certain ways is rewarded with food or a changed diaper. Laughing or making gurgling sounds is encouraged; it is rewarded with affection. On the other hand, hurling food about, continuing to creep (rather than beginning to walk), and calling out at night are discouraged by punishments ranging from admonitions in a disapproving tone of voice through minor physical violence. The child, of course, learns to repeat actions that elicit rewards and to avoid those that result in punishment. In this way, the originally purposeless movements and actions of the infant acquire meaning. They acquire meaning because significant others impart meaning to them. Crying now means something. Throwing food means something. It is no longer random behavior.

It is in this way that a child learns to talk, interact with others, and perform a host of other behaviors. Most of what an individual becomes is thus socially induced. Surprisingly little of what we might call "humanness" is biologically inherited. Indeed, there are reports of a boy found in India who was supposedly lost in the wilds at birth and reared by wolves. He reportedly exhibited much wolflike behavior, including snarling, walking on all fours, and eating as a quadruped. Needless to say, his initially random actions not having been reinforced or discouraged by human significant others, he exhibited very little of the behavior we associate with human beings. This story suggests that social learning is also an important process in the lives of other species than the human. Evidence confirms this. For example, ducklings hatched under a chicken behave as much like chicks as they are physiologically able to do.

127

Individuals appear to learn to do what is most efficient in their social environments. In so doing, of course, they learn a great many useful and necessary behaviors, such as speech or other forms of communication, without which survival would be difficult. A great many noncritical behaviors and preferences are learned in the same way. Traditions, culture, and political norms are all transmitted by such a process.

It seems especially plausible that the family group should exercise great influence over children. Its ability to control virtually all rewards—food, clothing, shelter, affection, etc.—and to impose a great variety of punishments—deprivation of material comforts, spanking, withdrawal of love, etc.—should logically encourage a child to conform to prescribed norms. Basically the same dynamics are involved in relationships with other groups and at times other than childhood. Though other groups, especially during adulthood, do not control so many rewards and punishments as the child's family, they nonetheless possess a considerable arsenal. Approval, affection, and desirable social interactions—not to mention occasional opportunities for economic, professional, or political advancement—are dispensed by groups. Most people continue to desire these things throughout their lives. To the extent that they do, groups have a continuing potential for influence. The point, of course, is that the process of learning to conform to the norms of the groups to which one belongs, that is, to the dictates and preferences of significant others, is a very basic process which attends virtually all that men—and other species as well—do.

This idea of group conformity as a natural and inevitable process is at variance, to some extent, with the rather disparaging attitude of most people to conformist behavior. Conformity, in common parlance, implies weakness, lack of initiative, and lack of intelligence. It is thought to be a bad thing; no one wants to be labeled a conformist. And, of course, there are differing degrees of conformity and initiative; people vary on such dimensions. Whether we as a society suffer from an excess of "other-directedness," whether we are too conformist, is a frequent topic for debate. It is sometimes argued that groups are engaged in some sort of coercive process, forcing people to conform against their will. Uncomplimentary remarks may be made, say, about labor unions, which are often thought to unjustly demand of their members a conformist stance. Parents seen as preventing their adolescent children from "doing their own thing" may earn similar disapproval. The image of malevolent group leaders crushing free spirits into a conformist mold is a common one. Moreover, there are in fact situations in which groups can exert inexorable pressures on people and cause them great emotional discomfort. This phenomenon too is well worth our attention.

Despite all this, no one avoids conformity to group standards altogether. Moreover, conformity need be neither a sign of weakness nor an indication of group coercion. Individuals do, after all, receive benefits from a group to whose standards they conform. This point is perhaps best illustrated in an "artificial" situation. Imagine an experiment in which a subject is placed in a totally dark room. If a tiny, stationary point of light is exposed to his view, he experiences an illusion that the light is moving. Yet if he is told to describe the movement of the light, he finds it very difficult. This is because there are no standards for judging shifts in position of a single point of light in a world of otherwise total darkness. If a group of subjects is placed in such a situation and told to describe the movement of the light audibly and publicly, an interesting phenomenon occurs. The subjects tend to describe the movement of the light in the same way. The reason for this is clear. In this dark, standardless world, a group norm quickly develops. The subjects need a standard for judging the movement of the light if they are to carry out the task assigned to them. None is available except that provided by others in the same situation. These others thus become significant; they provide a standard. Accepting it provides a reward, a device to use in the completion of a difficult task. In this case, conformity gets one out of a difficult situation; it provides aid in understanding an ambiguous phenomenon. In effect, it gives a person a handle on his world (in this case an artificial one). This hardly smacks of coercion; indeed, subjects in this experiment do not know that they are accepting a group position. They think that the light actually moves in the way they have said it does.

In other words, accepting group standards is very helpful to the individual. It gives him something to go on in a situation that is ambiguous and uncertain. The world is full of such situations—for adults as well as children. Most of the social, political, or religious questions we must make judgments about have no clear and obvious answers. Without group standards to conform to, it is difficult to see how most people could deal with them. Even people who pride themselves on being nonconformists, in the sense that they reject widely held values, are usually found in groups which supply standards on how to go about rejecting the establishment. A person rarely seeks out a new lifestyle by himself. Even those who feel that it would be desirable to resist group influences in order to do their own thing should remember that perhaps the only reason they have an "own thing" to do is that they acquired it from a group.

Although acceptance of group standards is normal and universal, we would be remiss not to point out that there are many conditions which govern the extent to which individuals conform to these norms. At least beyond early family relations, it is not at all reasonable to regard conformity to any given group as necessary or automatic. Some groups may influence a given individual heavily, while others have no effect on him. The influence of a particular group is likely to depend upon how badly the individual needs what the group provides. This in turn is probably a function of how basic the need is and of the probability of its fulfillment through alternate agencies. Obviously, the family provides for very basic needs. A child learns to view much of the world in the same terms as his parents and probably many others in the culture. He needs the standards of this early group in order to think, communicate, and get what he wants from his environment. To reject them totally is out of the question. It is from the family, for example, that he learns a language. Most of us conform to the extent of using the language our parents taught us. It fills a very basic need. However, in many areas, the family's influence begins to wane as the child grows older. Particularly in the provision of less basic things, such as desirable social contacts, the family faces increasing competition from a child's peers. Children receive from their peers what the family once provided, and its influence declines.

Since individuals typically belong to many groups simultaneously, the failure of one group to influence their behavior may signal the success of other groups. The complex social lives of human beings often subject them to certain inconsistencies and stresses. Indeed, the different groups that are important to an individual may impel him to totally incompatible behaviors. The behavior that results from this complex pattern of "cross-pressures," though perhaps a net result of a series of group influences, can hardly be thought of as simple reproduction of the demands of a single group.

This discussion should make the use of the term *reference group* more meaningful. People find it useful to *refer* to groups for guidance in a great variety of ambiguous situations—many of them, as we shall see, political. The reference process, of course, is essentially one of learning. We internalize the norms emanating from a group because doing so is associated with the gratification of various needs.

Since this is the case, we would expect groups to be very much involved in the explanation of political norms and political behavior. People should, at least occasionally, refer to groups for political cues and learn appropriate political responses from them. Not surprisingly, families—a very important group—do indeed have considerable political impact. Surveys of general populations reveal, according to what adults can recall about their childhoods, great correspondences between parent and offspring. This finding, which extends to levels of participation, interest in politics, and party identification, is a classic one in behavioral research and has been part of the conventional wisdom of the discipline for many years.[10] There is, of course, a certain difficulty with this sort of research. The independent variable is not the parents' actual political orientation, but what adults *remember* about their parents' political orientation. For many reasons, a person's memory may be inaccurate—especially about things like politics which are not often highly salient or much discussed in the home. Furthermore, adults, having acquired certain political orientations elsewhere, may assume that their parents must have had similar ones; they may erroneously project their own outlooks onto their parents. Given these problems with recall data, it increases our confidence to note that substantially the same relationship—at least as far as party identification is concerned—is reported by very young children. Even second-grade children are likely to report a partisan attachment, and it is generally the same attachment that they perceive their parents to hold. Indeed, it is difficult to imagine where else these partisan sentiments, at such a tender age, may have originated. Recent surveys of both young people *and* their parents have shown similar results. Of course, when both child and parent are interviewed, there is no danger that one is misperceiving the political views of the other. The uncertainties of recall data are eliminated. Some results of the most interesting of these studies, involving American highschool seniors,[11] are reported in Table 4-5. Both parents and students were asked to indicate partisan attachment using a seven-point scale. Subjects could categorize themselves as strong Republicans,

131

TABLE 4–5

**Correlations Between the Party Identification
of Highschool Seniors and That
of Their Parents ***

ALL FAMILIES	.47
FAMILIES IN WHICH HUSBAND-WIFE POLITICAL CONVERSATIONS OCCUR	
Very often	.54
Pretty often	.49
Not very often	.45
Never	.32

* Correlations are tau-b.

Source: Data from M. Kent Jennings and Richard G. Niemi, "The Transmission of Political Values from Parent to Child," *American Political Science Review,* Vol. 62 (March 1968), 173, 182.

weak Republicans, independent Republicans, independents, independent Democrats, weak Democrats, or strong Democrats. Each parent-child pair was then assigned a position in a seven-by-seven table with parents' party identification as the independent variable and students' party identification as the dependent variable. The resulting tau (ordinal-data) correlation was .47.

Of course, one can argue that such correspondences do not indicate parent-child transfers at all but only that both parents and child are subject to roughly the same set of external stimuli. That is, the parents' orientation is not independent while the child's is dependent; both are dependent. It is external variables that are independent. As we saw in Chapter 2, this sort of situation does sometimes confound. apparent explanatory relationships. But in this case it does not appear to do so. We can see from the last four entries in Table 4-5 that the extent of the parent-child correspondence depends upon an internal family variable, namely the extent to which politics is discussed in the home. If parents talk about politics, transmission occurs; if they do not, the transmission of values is somewhat reduced. Internal rather than external stimuli appear to be at work here. It looks very much as if political party is one of the many norms that constitute the heritage families pass on to their children.

However, some other data from the highschool-senior study are equally interesting. Table 4-6 shows that there are many areas of political orientation, measured by various scales, in which parent-child correspondences are very weak indeed. Party identification clearly represents the area of greatest agreement. How can we account for such divergences in these areas? The best answer appears to lie in the variables' salience. For most people, party is a salient variable. Though there is some reason to believe the overall impact of parties, at least as they are presently configured in America, is declining, party is nonetheless the criterion most often appealed to in making political decisions. It is usually people's most consciously held political characteristic. This is understandable, for many political events in America are organized by party. Most parents probably emit party-related cues quite readily. On the other hand, most other political questions are probably less salient than party to parents or children, or both. At the very least, they are not likely to be as salient over long periods of time. Accordingly, parental influence in such matters is likely to be considerably less.

In general, people's ideas on issues are ill-formed and poorly thought out. As one moves to areas that are more removed from im-

TABLE 4–6

Correlations Between Attitudes of Highschool Students and Those of Their Parents on Several Political Orientations *

Federal government's role in integrating the schools	.34
Whether schools should be allowed to use prayers	.29
Legally elected communist should be allowed to take office	.13
Speakers against churches and religion should be allowed	.05
Political cynicism	.12
Political cosmopolitanism	.17

* Correlations are tau-b.

Source: Data from M. Kent Jennings and Richard G. Niemi, "The Transmission of Political Values from Parent to Child," *American Political Science Review*, Vol. 62 (March 1968), 175, 178, 179.

mediate daily concerns, little communication is likely. Two of the issues in Table 4-6 deal with the public schools. These are likely to be relatively salient attitude areas both for students and their parents who are paying taxes and who have children in the schools. Both generations are immediately affected by these concerns, and they are likely to talk about them. Accordingly, some parental influence is to be expected. And, in fact, rather moderate correlations of .34 and .29 were found. On less concrete issues, involving communists and antireligious speakers, there was little correspondence between the attitudes of parents and children. As the authors of the study point out, "it is improbable that the students are reflecting much in the way of cues emitted from their parents, simply because these topics or related ones are hardly prime candidates for dinner table conversation or inadvertent cue-giving."[12]

For different reasons, expressions of cynicism are not common in the home either. Even if adults believe government to be pernicious, they are likely to sugar-coat their descriptions of it to youngsters. Children are shielded from the seamy side of many dimensions of life. Too, schools probably have great weight in this area, urging trust and confidence in government through civic education programs. Parental influence is probably overwhelmed by school influence. As a group, the highschool seniors were much less cynical than the older generation. Cosmopolitanism, the extent to which one is oriented toward national or international political affairs rather than those at the local level, is also likely to be influenced by nonfamily situations. The fact that students are much more cosmopolitan than their parents may be instructive. It may indicate that there is a maturational effect operating. That is, as people mature, they are exposed to different conditions that regularly influence their behavior. Older people become more attached to their local communities as property-owners and taxpayers. They get more intimately involved with the level of local services as their potential mobility declines. A forty-five-year-old engineer is likely to be vitally concerned about local tax levels and about the snow-removal capability of the city. It is equally probable that his adolescent son could not possibly care less about such matters. Levels of cosmopolitanism may thus be dependent upon experiences and interests. Indeed, we could perhaps use the idea that *age groups* are exposed to common stimuli (in the manner discussed in the first part of this chapter) as an aid in explaining the findings of this study. Or, there may be a generational effect. The world is shrinking dramatically. The interdependence of all parts of the nation and of the countries of the world is evident today as never before. New communication and transportation technology has made dramatic onslaughts on parochialism. Young people experience modern events in ways that their parents do not. The implications of such stimuli are much more momentous for the young. Their entire future is likely to be influenced by them. This generation is thus bound to be different from those before it. Again, age may define a categoric group that is exposed to common stimuli which have dramatic effects on political behavior.

Of course, we have not considered all the possible kinds of political behavior that the family group may influence. Patriotism, all forms of elite behavior, and many other issues have not been discussed. Some are extremely interesting and timely. For example, there is some evidence that youthful political protest behavior on campuses and elsewhere may have roots in the family. Radical students today may be acting congruently with their parents' principles. Their parents may have transmitted politically liberal views to their children, though they may never have tried to actually implement them.[13] However, the data we have seen should clearly demonstrate that the family primary group is only sometimes used as a reference group. Like all reference groups, it is successful in transmitting political values in some instances and it fails in others. The point is that while learning from this group is important, it is hardly determinative. Children may resemble their parents in some respects, but they are obviously not made into political carbon copies of them. Once all the effects of the family, or any group for that matter, have been considered, there is still a great deal of slack left. Some matters may not be salient in the family context. Alternate reference groups or exposure to other stimuli may then be more likely to govern behavior. As we have said before, the failure of one kind of group influence may be explained by the success of another.

Greatly similar political views are observed among the members of groups other than the parental family as well. Husband-wife pairs, groups of friends, work associates, classmates, and members of legislative houses and committees have all been observed to develop group norms that govern important aspects of their political behavior. An interesting example is provided by labor unions. In the United States Democratic voting has been a clear political norm of organized labor. Of course, there is a strong tendency among all working-class citizens to support the Democrats. However—and this supports the idea of influences internal to the group—union members exhibit this propensity much more than nonmembers, even those of exactly the same socioeconomic status. Furthermore, the longer a person has been a union member (and thus the longer he has been exposed to the prevalent norms), and the more he identifies with the organization, the greater is his support of this political norm.[14] Thus, although people may have a tendency to join groups with whose principles they agree, the social support that the group provides for political beliefs seems to exert an independent effect.

Having begun with the family as the original political reference group but come to the conclusion that its effects are mutable, let us examine other groups that may constitute a direct challenge to its primacy. Undoubtedly, as we become a more complex and urban society, the overall influence of the family is declining. If for no other reason, there are an increasing number of sources of competing norms. Chief among these competitors is the peer group. Peer relationships are far more numerous and far more pervasive today than ever before. Langton demonstrated the power of peer groups over traditional values in a study of Jamaican students.[15] He discovered that there were social-class norms relating to a variety of political objects. Working-class students were typically less committed to the idea of political majoritarianism, less supportive of minority rights, less politically involved, less interested in voting, and less supportive of the extant regime than their middle-class counterparts. Though these norms are no doubt partly a result of the exposure of members of this class to common political stimuli, they are probably communicated as group norms from working-class parents to working-class children as well. Some working-class students, Langton discovered, associated almost exclusively with friends of the same social status, while others included a considerable number of upper-class youths in their circle of friends. By inquiring about the type of houses and the amount of money that friends possessed, he classified his subjects as either *peer-homogeneous* (having all working-class friends) or *peer-heterogeneous* (having some middle-class friends). If norms communicated by peers are efficacious, we would expect that peer-heterogeneous students would hold political views at variance with those typical of their class, while peer-homogeneous students would not. If the objective interests of a class (or the norms probably communicated by parents) determine behavior,

136

there should be no difference between the two groups. And, indeed, on all the dimensions studied, the peer-heterogeneous students were notably different from their peer-homogeneous counterparts. In every case, moreover, they were more "middle-class" in their views. The data for the variable "system legitimacy" are displayed in Table 4-7.

Similar data are not difficult to find. A classic study by Newcomb investigated the political attitudes of students at Bennington College in the 1930s.[16] Girls who, as freshmen, held relatively conservative political views typical of their middle-class backgrounds underwent a considerable transformation, gradually coming to favor very liberal, "New Deal" type policy alternatives by the time they were seniors. Though it is difficult to isolate the specific causative agents in something so pervasive as a four-year college experience, it is likely that the changes were peer-mediated phenomena. To be sure, the typically liberal faculty may have been involved in the process, but not necessarily through their teaching. The faculty interacted socially with the students to a high degree and thus may have been able to determine group norms. Indeed, the great liberalizing of outlooks was confined to those girls who depended upon the college for their social lives. Girls who went home most weekends, who participated in much social interaction off campus, were far less likely to undergo this transformation of political ideals.

TABLE 4–7

Peer Environment and the Attribution of Legitimacy to the Political System by Working-Class Youths

System Legitimacy *	Peer-Homogeneous Students (N = 206)	Peer-Heterogeneous Students (N = 193)
Support	45%	33%
Ambivalent	42	51
Oppose	13	16
Total	100%	100%

* This variable was measured by a single question about the honesty of politics and government.

Source: Adapted from Kenneth P. Langton, *Political Socialization* (New York: Oxford University Press, 1969), p. 130. Copyright © 1969 by Oxford University Press, Inc. Used by permission.

These findings about the power of group influences seem all the more striking when we observe that these changes largely persisted for twenty-five years. Newcomb was able to interview the same subjects in the early 1960s and found that the girls' liberal views—particularly if there had been social support for them in other group contexts—had largely been maintained.[17]

The widespread importance of group norms as determinants of political behavior comes up time and again. Many important political phenomena appear to depend upon the operation of group norms. For example, ethnic political behavior—very prominent and extremely momentous in its consequences—has been a topic of great practical and scholarly concern for many years. Although the United States is supposed to be something of an ethnic "melting pot" where national origins lapse into insignificance in a very short time (and the children of immigrants supposedly retain little identification with their ethnic background), it is clear that this is not entirely the case. Given the fact that the children of immigrants and subsequent generations are known to reject many aspects of their native culture, often imitating American slang, customs, and behavior with an almost humorous fidelity, the persistence of ethnic political behavior has mystified observers for some time. If the ethnic identity has been lost, how can we account for the curious persistence of voting patterns over generations?

Apparently, the bafflement over this state of affairs has been due to a failure to distinguish between *acculturation* on the one hand and *assimilation* on the other. With respect to ethnic populations, *acculturation* has occurred. That is, separate ethnic communities have *not* been able to maintain distinct cultures. The presence of ethnic neighborhoods, restaurants, fairs, and the like notwithstanding, ethnic populations have not generally been able to maintain their own art, artifacts, language, law, or learning in unmodified form. The battle to maintain indigenous ways has largely been lost as newer generations adopted the American language, American dress, American forms of recreation, and acquired American attitudes with respect to work and material wealth. Indeed, it is perhaps because ethnic interest in the Old World culture has been so minimal, so truly quaint, that we find fairs, festivals, and the like so charming.

Though acculturation—the disappearance of subentities distinct from the dominant American culture—has definitely occurred, assimila-

138

tion has not progressed to anywhere near the same degree. By *assimilation* we mean the absorption of an ethnic group by the host culture in terms of *social relations*. There would be no social distinction between an assimilated minority and the native host population; minority citizens would not be more likely to associate with their own kind and members of the host population would not prefer other natives. In terms of a social system, an assimilated minority would have disappeared.[18]

Although a general relationship between these two processes would seem likely, and although one would certainly assume that an assimilated minority would also be acculturated, there is no necessary reason why the reverse should be true. Indeed, for the American ethnic, it has not been true. Though acculturated, he has remained unassimilated. He tends to maintain many of his personal contacts with other ethnics. Social relations continue to exist within the confines of the ethnic population for many generations after cultural identity has largely vanished. This is not obvious, but it has been shown to be true by any number of studies of ethnic life. It is undeniable that ethnics persistently identify themselves as ethnics and thus respond favorably to other ethnics. Though the reasons for this phenomenon are complex and manifold, two are particularly appealing. First, there is no guarantee that a host population will accept even an acculturated minority as social equals. Even though an ethnic population mimics American ways of life, native Americans may still exclude them from social relations and force them into interpersonal contacts among themselves. Distinctions on the part of the host population force ethnic self-identification. Second, many ethnics may not want to be totally assimilated. In a modern, industrial society, assimilation into the dominant culture, which is rather homogeneous and featureless, may threaten one with loss of identity. Being able to think, for example, "I am Italian" may provide some protection against being psychically swallowed up by an impersonal and complex modern lifestyle.

If this interpretation of the impact of the ethnic group on political behavior has any validity, we would expect ethnic behavior to be more prominent in areas where the opportunities for intraethnic social contacts are greater and less prominent where they are fewer. Though ethnic political behavior can take many forms, certainly one of the most discussed is the tendency of ethnics to vote for candidates who bear a characteristic ethnic surname. In some areas, it is said, a winning ticket must include both an O'Connor and a Goldberg on the ballot. Lorinskas and others have presented some interesting data on the incidence of such voting in different kinds of areas. [19] They began by locating samples of Polish-American voters in Chicago and in a rural Illinois county. These people were then subjected to an interesting research technique. They were asked to "vote" in a "straw," or hypothetical, election. Several of the choices they were asked to make were those they would have to make in a real election to be held a few weeks later. Thus, the research attempted, as do many polls, to learn voting preferences before the fact. However, the "ballot" also contained some mythical candidates running for mythical offices (e.g., Sanitary Canal District Committeeman). In these contests, a "candidate" with a Polish surname (Stanley J. Lipinski) was always run against a nonethnic opponent (Michael E. Harper). The party affiliation of these mythical candidates was manipulated to suit the researchers' purposes. This quasi-experimental research design has some advantages. There is considerable control over the possible independent variables that may affect behavior. We know that the subjects are not choosing a candidate because they like his personality because the candidates, being mythical, are unknown to the subjects and have no personality. We know that they are not responding to the relevant issues surrounding the office because the office does not exist and no issues could therefore be relevant to it. The only bases for choice were ethnicity of surname and party because these were the only variables the subjects were allowed to know about.

Half of the Chicago subjects were given ballots that identified Lipinski as a Democrat, and half were given ballots that identified him as a Republican. The same arrangements obtained in the ballots presented to the rural Polish-Americans. The resulting "votes" are displayed in Table 4-8. The rural ethnics are probably less acculturated than their urban counterparts, for they are not so heavily bombarded with communications about and observations of the dominant American culture. The cities are "where it's at," and few old folkways could be expected to stand up to such an onslaught. More isolated rural residents might be expected to hold on to their traditional culture a while longer. On the other hand, the urban Polish-Americans are perhaps less assimilated. The urban Pole finds contacts with fellow ethnics far easier. Population concentration and the ease of communication and transportation over

140

The Behavior of Individuals: Group or Social Factors

TABLE 4–8

Support for a Hypothetical Ethnic Candidate Among Urban and Rural Polish-Americans

	Lipinski as Democrat	Lipinski as Republican
URBAN SUBJECTS		
Voted Democratic	61.7%	23.5%
Voted Republican	38.3	76.5
Total	100.0%	100.0%
RURAL SUBJECTS		
Voted Democratic	65.5%	56.3%
Voted Republican	34.5	43.7
Total	100.0%	100.0%

Source: Robert A. Lorinskas et al., "The Persistence of Ethnic Voting in Urban and Rural Areas: Results for the Controlled Election Method," *Social Science Quarterly*, Vol. 49 (March 1969), 895.

short distances give him opportunities not available in rural areas. Institutionalization of ethnicity through clubs or churches is more feasible. The nature of rural life, on the other hand, may require proportionately more contact with nonethnics. The cooperative nature of work on a small farm may insure this. Accordingly, we would expect a greater sensitivity to ethnicity on the part of our more acculturated but less assimilated Poles. This is exactly what Table 4-8 appears to indicate. Regardless of party, urban Poles preferred Lipinski; the same cannot be said for the rural residents.

Of course, as sensitive behaviorists, we should recognize that we could have more confidence in this finding if the party affiliation of the subjects in Table 4-8 was controlled. If more rural residents turn out to be Democrats, we might have some reservations about generalizing the results of this study. Too, it would be most desirable to have some information on the extent and kinds of social contacts the different classes of respondents really have. We have suggested some very great differences, but have presented no data to confirm these suggestions. But, as is often the case, a single piece of research cannot provide

141

definitive results. It is to the researchers' credit that they have given us evidence which allows us to gain some insight into an important kind of group influence on American political behavior.

There is no doubt that many groups influence their members in a way that produces conformity in political behavior. However, no one expects perfect conformity all the time from all members of a group. As many of the examples we have just cited indicate, a variety of conditions govern when a group will effectively determine the behavior of an individual. These conditions are many and complex, and whole books could be devoted to them alone. However, a particularly common set of conditions deserves at least a brief examination here.

As we noted before, few persons can be said to belong to only one relevant group. Interpersonal relations necessarily go on with several sets of associates simultaneously, as with parents and peers. It is likely that, at least some of the time, a person will choose his friends and associates partly on the basis of congruent beliefs and attitudes. One chooses to be with people with whom one agrees. Often a person's total group environment is congruent with a particular set of beliefs. However, as we saw in the discussion of peer relationships, there are increasing possibilities for incongruity of beliefs among one's circle of associates. In the modern world, only the most parochial persons can escape at least occasional contact with a wide variety of views. Thus, inconsistent group norms must be an increasingly common experience. How does an individual handle these kinds of cross-pressures? The classic answer is that the cross-pressured individual withdraws and becomes uninterested in the topic at hand. In this way, he avoids the psychological tension caused by having to balance, rationalize, and live with inconsistent claims on his loyalty. However, this is not always the reaction. A cross-pressured individual may choose one of the horns of the dilemma. The gratifications or rewards received from one group may far outweigh those the other group can provide, and this may govern his choice. If this occurs, however, the individual may feel the need to fully rationalize his choice and thus may become well versed in the matters at issue. Indeed, he may become just the opposite of withdrawn, once he has prepared himself "ideologically" to reject salient group norms.

Merelman studied cross-pressures from parents and peers.[20] He examined several hundred college students, classifying each of them according to whether their group political environment was *congruent*, *role conflicted,* or *limited congruent.* Those who reported that most of their friends *and* their parents were of the same political party were assigned to the first category; those who reported that most of their friends were of a different party than their parents were assigned to the second category; and those who reported that only one group, either their parents or their friends, had an identifiable party affiliation were assigned to the third category. Merelman reasoned that congruents, who experience no cross-pressure and receive consistent social support for a single position, are the least likely to withdraw from involvement in political affairs. Role conflicteds, on the other hand, experience a very direct cross-pressure, and some of them, those who do not rationalize choosing the alternative supported by one group, should withdraw from political involvement. The limited congruents, who are also cross-pressured in a sense, since they do not encounter congruent social support of a particular party, should have some tendency to withdraw. Moreover, since they are not motivated to rationalize a choice of one party, the limited congruents should be more inclined to withdraw from politics than the conflicteds. An interesting test of these notions is reported in Table 4-9. Political involvement or withdrawal is measured by whether the respondent identifies with a political party. Those who have no identification are considered to have withdrawn. Clearly, Merelman's expectations are realized in the table. Withdrawal is appar-

TABLE 4–9

The Relationship Between Group Environments and Withdrawal from Party Identification

	GROUP ENVIRONMENT		
Withdrawal Status	*Congruent*	*Role Conflicted*	*Limited Congruent*
Have party identification (Republican or Democrat)	72%	63%	54%
Have no party identification (Independent, None)	28	37	46
Total	100%	100%	100%
		$\chi^2 = 11.5, p < .01$	

Source: Adapted from Richard Merelman, "Intimate Environments and Political Behavior," *Midwest Journal of Political Science,* Vol. 12 (August 1968), 395.

ently a response to group cross-pressures, but the lesser withdrawal of the conflicteds compared with the limited congruents suggests that there are other ways of dealing with this problem.

We have seen that conformity to group standards is a very common kind of behavior. It is something all of us experience to some degree from the cradle to the grave. Humans must learn many behavior patterns if they are to survive as organisms. They must respond to significant others. They must have guidance, even in order to think. The world is an ambiguous place, and the ability to refer to a group standard in dealing with it may be the only thing that makes it comprehensible at all. It is inevitable that most groups, including parental families, will in the normal course of communicating norms to their members emit some political cues. Political learning takes place even in the absence of a conscious indoctrination program. In a world where citizens are called upon to make manifold judgments about political candidates and issues, it is inevitable that many should be searching for guidance in making these judgments. It is the primary group—and occasionally even secondary or categoric groups—which very often provides that necessary guidance. It is difficult indeed to imagine a world in which much political behavior is not explained by the relations of people to and within groups.

Group Influence on Political
Behavior: A Recapitulation

The mechanisms we have described in this chapter are not the only ones that may produce relationships between group membership and political behavior. Obviously, some groups may impart a very general norm or some sort of psychological orientation to their members. Political behavior may then be a direct consequence of that general norm or psychological orientation, even though the group may not have any political norms at all. For example, religious groups often have characteristic political behavior patterns. Though this phenomenon could be related to an association of the interests of the group with specific political alternatives, there is some possibility that it springs from the deeply held theological principles of the group. It is often argued that the tendency of Jews to support "liberal" or libertarian political policies and minority political protests (despite the fact that they possess a much higher SES than the average American) is due to the fact that social consciousness is a basic and fundamental part of Jewish religious beliefs. Similarly, it is sometimes said that the pronounced Protestant support for Republican candidates and fiscally conservative policies is an outgrowth of a fundamental philosophical compatibility between the Protestant ethic and capitalism. Though it is difficult to validate such assertions in any forthright way, they represent an intriguing possibility that should not be overlooked.

In a somewhat similar way, the basic features of some types of intragroup relations are thought to be projected onto the political world. This argument is most frequently encountered in discussing the political socialization of children. If a child has harmonious relations with authority figures in his primary environment (the family), he will supposedly react to new, more remote authorities (government leaders) in the same way. A projection of the father image supposedly takes place. Impaired family relations, by the same token, supposedly presage later difficulties with political authorities. Though there is little evidence to directly support this notion, it is not impossible for primary-group relations to leave a psychological residue that has some relevance for political behavior. We will consider such dynamics in more detail in the next chapter. As students of political behavior, we should not lose sight of this possible avenue of group influence.

These possibilities, coupled with those we have discussed in more detail—exposure to common external stimuli and the dynamics of relations within groups—indicate that it is probably impossible to adequately understand the behavior of individuals in politics without invoking some group variables. To be sure, the picture one gets from studying groups is not always a clear one, as the research we have cited amply indicates. But the amount of evidence about the importance of group memberships is impressive indeed. We should not be distressed that our look at group influences has provided only a partial picture. An essentially piecemeal approach to understanding is very characteristic of the social sciences. If we find that many questions are still unanswered, that we do not completely understand individual political behavior, then we need to consider some other kinds of independent variables in

145

addition to (not in place of) groups. The following chapters, hopefully, will help us to fill in a bit more our necessarily incomplete view of the roots of political behavior.

Notes

1. Robert J. Lieber, "Interest Groups and Political Integration: British Entry into Europe," *American Political Science Review*, Vol. 66 (March 1972), 53-67.
2. For an excellent collection of examples of various kinds of research on pressure groups, see Betty H. Zisk (ed.), *American Political Interest Groups* (Belmont, Calif.: Wadsworth, 1969).
3. David J. Danelski, "Task Group and Social Group on the Supreme Court," in John H. Kessel *et al.* (eds.), *Micropolitics* (New York: Holt, Rinehart & Winston, 1970), pp. 266-274.
4. Sidney Tarrow, "The Urban-Rural Cleavage in Political Involvement: The Case of France," *American Political Science Review*, Vol. 65 (June 1971), 341-357.
5. Lester W. Milbrath, *Political Participation* (Chicago: Rand McNally, 1965), pp. 122-123.
6. John S. Jackson, "The Political Behavior and Socio-Economic Backgrounds of Black Students: The Antecedents of Protest," *Midwest Journal of Political Science*, Vol. 15 (November 1971), 667.
7. Robert Weissberg, "Adolescents' Perceptions of Political Authorities: Another Look at Political Virtue and Power," *Midwest Journal of Political Science*, Vol. 16 (February 1972), 152.
8. Joel D. Aberbach and Jack L. Walker, "Political Trust and Racial Ideology," *American Political Science Review*, Vol. 64 (December 1970), 1204.
9. *Ibid.*, 1213-1214.
10. Dean Jaros, *Socialization to Politics* (New York: Praeger, 1973), Chapter 4.
11. M. Kent Jennings and Richard G. Niemi, "The Transmission of Political Values from Parent to Child," *American Political Science Review*, Vol. 62 (March 1968), 169-184.
12. *Ibid.*, 175.
13. Jeanne Block, Norma Haan, and M. Brewster Smith, "Activism and Apathy in Contemporary Adolescents," in James F. Adams (ed.), *Understanding Adolescence* (Boston: Allyn & Bacon, 1968), pp. 214-215.
14. Angus Campbell *et al.*, *The American Voter* (New York: Wiley, 1960), p. 325.
15. Kenneth P. Langton, *Political Socialization* (New York: Oxford University Press, 1969), Chapter 5.
16. Theodore M. Newcomb, "Attitude Development as a Function of Reference Groups: The Bennington Study," in Eleanor E. Maccoby *et al.* (eds.), *Readings in Social Psychology*, 3rd ed. (New York: Holt, Rinehart & Winston, 1958), pp. 266-267.
17. Theodore M. Newcomb *et al.*, *Persistence and Change: Bennington College and Its Students after Twenty-Five Years* (New York: Wiley, 1967), p. 39.
18. Many of these points are spelled out in more detail in Michael Parenti, "Ethnic Politics and the Persistence of Ethnic Identification," *American Political Science Review*, Vol. 61 (September 1967), 717-726.
19. Robert A. Lorinskas *et al.*, "The Persistence of Ethnic Voting in Urban and Rural Areas: Results for the Controlled Election Method," *Social Science Quarterly*, Vol. 49 (March 1969), 891-899.
20. Richard Merelman, "Intimate Environments and Political Behavior," *Midwest Journal of Political Science*, Vol. 12 (August 1968), 382-400.

5

Individual
Behavior:
Personal
Factors

In the crudest sense, the behavior of anything, from microorganisms to planets, may be thought of as a function of two sets of factors. Obviously, what something does is heavily conditioned by the forces that act upon it from the outside; its *environment* is important. On the other hand, what a thing does is also heavily dependent upon what it is, upon its own *internal characteristics*. If we place an amoeba in weak acid solution, it contracts, perishes, and ultimately disintegrates. Had we placed the amoeba in distilled water, this behavior would not have occurred. The acid environment was important in the demise of our unfortunate protozoan. However, if we had placed, not an amoeba, but one of several kinds of rotifers in the acid solution, the organism would have survived quite handily. The rotifer has characteristics that render it resistant to acids. It makes no difference to it whether it is in water or a weak acid. It can survive either type of environment because of its own characteristics. Even the behavior of inanimate objects can be thought of as stemming from its environment and internal characteristics. A rock hurled into the air follows a certain path because of the pull of gravitational forces, air resistance, and other environmental factors. However, we have only to try to induce a wad of paper of the same approximate shape to follow the same path to realize that the behavior of thrown objects is also dependent upon inherent characteristics such as their mass and volume.

These observations may seem so obvious as to be trivial, but they illustrate one of the basic conclusions of scientific inquiry. Moreover, thinking along these lines helps us to appreciate the problems attending the systematic study of human behavior. Human behavior too may be thought of as resulting from the two general categories of factors we have just described. Those who have read Chapter 4 will realize quite clearly that there we were discussing the effect of *environmental* factors on the political behavior of human beings. Indeed, at one point, we were quite explicit in arguing that groups are responsible for certain kinds of "environmental" stimuli. In effect, we started with an undifferentiated human organism and argued that some of its behavior was a consequence of the group-mediated experiences its environment imposed on it. However, it was obvious from our sampling of research in this area that all individuals placed in a particular group environment did not behave in exactly the same way. None of the explanatory relationships examined were represented by tables with all the observations in the cells on the diagonal or by correlation coefficients approaching 1.00. In part, of course, this is because people experience a variety of group environments. But it may also be due, in part, to the fact that individuals have different internal characteristics. That is, two individuals placed in exactly the same configuration of group influences may behave quite differently because they are different kinds of people.

Physiological Factors

What kinds of internal characteristics may affect people's political behavior? The relevant internal characteristics of microorganisms or inanimate objects seem to be physical or structural variables like weight or resistance to chemicals. Is the social behavior of humans also affected by physical or physiological considerations? With a little thought, we can quickly see that the answer in many areas is clearly yes. Though a person may learn to appreciate certain kinds of music and even to desire to play a particular instrument, some aspects of the ability to understand and play music are physiologically determined. A person may fail to be a musician simply because there is no music in his environment; significant others may not have encouraged him to understand or enjoy it. However, even if a person's environment is musically rich and he is musically encouraged by significant others, he will not become a musician if he has thick and insensitive eardrums or if he lacks, for example, the dexterity to play notes in time or handle the fingering of a stringed instrument. Thus, a person's career options or his cultural preferences may in some instances be heavily dependent upon his physiological characteristics.

Even political behavior may be governed by physiological variables. It is a truism that in this day of television and other mass media, political candidates must have an attractive physical appearance in order to be competitive. "Image," it is alleged, counts. For this reason, those who are physically attractive may be more likely to be recruited into political life. Of course, in this case the physiological variable is not producing the behavioral effect in question. It governs the receipt of other stimuli that constitute causative variables. However, physiological factors may also affect certain kinds of political behavior directly. Any kind of deep political involvement, whether it be running for office, organizing a protest demonstration, presiding over a patriotic society, or running a group with lobbying interests, takes tremendous physical energy and endurance. Undoubtedly, it is beyond the physical capacities of many persons to undertake this kind of political behavior. A person's energy level—which is determined by his metabolic rate and general health—is probably a significant variable in explaining very intensive political participation.

Personality

Human beings, of course, have other internal characteristics besides physical or physiological ones. In fact, though the effects of physiological variables are terribly interesting and probably represent a significant area of potential study, very few scholars have devoted any

149

attention to them. Most researchers who have examined the role of personal factors in political behavior have focused, instead, on internal characteristics of the mind. It is these internal characteristics of the mind that determine what we call *personality*. Our use of this term is similar but not identical to the way in which it is used in everyday conversation. In casual parlance we may identify a person who has a tendency to be truculent, abrasive, and domineering as having an unpleasant personality. We may argue that he has a relatively permanent disposition to react in a particular way in particular situations. Similarly, we may identify a person who is unusually amiable as having a "good" personality and as likely to react in other, equally characteristic ways. There is something about the mental states of these people that causes them to behave in different ways.

Although the scholar uses the term *personality* to refer to more than the way a person handles interpersonal relations, he too is concerned with the enduring dispositions to act in particular ways. He too argues that there are mental characteristics which govern behavior. At any given time people carry about with them a series of mental states that heavily influence what they do. People do not experience their environment as a *tabula rasa*. Stimuli impinge on the mind, but they interact with what is already there. People do not just stand around waiting to be influenced by independent variables from outside. At the least they possess opinions, attitudes, and beliefs that influence their behavior. It is a crude misconception (sometimes indulged in by students and practitioners of mass media and propaganda) to consider human beings as an undifferentiated, manipulatable mass. The point of this discussion should be obvious: In seeking to understand environmental influences on people, it is erroneous to consider only the properties of those influences. We must also consider what is already in the minds of the people who are subjected to them.

Of course, mental characteristics or dispositions don't just happen. They are not mystically implanted, immutable features of the human organism. They too are capable of being explained and understood. Where does personality come from? No doubt it is partly inherited through the genes, but it is certainly largely if not overwhelmingly a function of environment itself. Environment shapes personality, which in turn shapes behavior. In a very general sense, personality *intervenes* between environment and behavior. This should come as no surprise. All personality theorists attribute an important role to the formative years of early childhood. The environmental influences of the first years leave a great imprint on individuals because the input to enduring mental dispositions is so great. How a person characteristically thinks, responds, and acts is determined, to a considerable extent, by the environment he encounters as an infant or a young child. Thus the introduction of the subject of personality should not be taken as an indication of the limitations of the impact of groups, for groups themselves—especially the significant others that constitute the family—are instrumental in the development of personality. The situation can be represented by the diagram below.

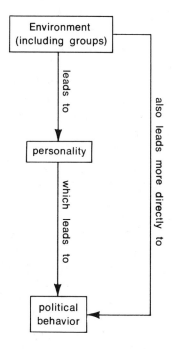

Since environment seems to be involved, ultimately, in all human behavior, why not simply forget about personality and devote all our attention to this apparently more basic factor? Aren't all factors ultimately environmental? Though this may be true in a sense, there are several good reasons for retaining a keen interest in personality. In the first place, suppose that we are able to examine a relationship in which some group variable is independent, some feature of personality is an intervening variable, and a particular behavior is the dependent variable. Logically, we could dispense with the intervening variable and discuss the association between environment and behavior directly. We would still have a legitimate explanatory relationship. However, knowledge about possible intervening variables broadens our understanding of a phenomenon. How is it that the family authority structure (environment) affects the propensity to accord "diffuse support" to the political regime (political behavior)? Perhaps it is because the family variable more or less permanently conditions individual personality in matters of authority relations, and according diffuse support is a function of the possession of these personality features. Being able to identify variables in the middle allows us to know more about the relationship between the variables on the ends.

In addition, there are many situations in which we cannot identify all three elements in the causal chain. The personality an individual possesses at a given time is a function of environment he has experienced *in the past*. Personality, we have noted, has its roots in childhood. We may not be able to investigate the childhood of adult subjects whose here-and-now behavior we are investigating. But we may be able to explain this behavior in terms of here-and-now personality. In this case, we examine only personality as an independent variable and behavior as a dependent variable. Admittedly, we are looking at only part of the picture. But this is usually the case in scientific investigation anyway. We never completely explain anything. It is better to have some understanding of a phenomenon than none at all. If we know that a certain feature of personality is related to a given type of political behavior, we can appreciate that without necessarily being able to locate the antecedents of the personality.

Thus, the study of personality can add a great deal to our understanding of individual behavior. But like any other category of independent variables, it cannot offer a complete explanation. There are no great, universal answers in science. We look for gains in understanding by bits and pieces. Personality is undoubtedly capable of making a substantial, though of course partial, contribution to this understanding.

152

Although there has been considerable disagreement on arriving at a useful definition of personality, we shall not spend much time on definitional problems. We shall simply regard any relatively enduring mental characteristic of a human being as a personality characteristic. However, even this definition is tremendously broad . We shall rather arbitrarily divide the range of such characteristics into two segments. On the one hand, we will discuss those characteristics which emphasize a "deep" inner life and personal needs that must be fulfilled in order to maintain psychic integrity. Such characteristics frequently center on the idea of *ego defense*.[1] People have very private needs; and overt behavior, including political behavior, though it ostensibly has nothing to do with the self, is performed in a way that meets these needs. For example, a particular political act may be undertaken by people who have grave doubts about their own adequacy. The act may be an exercise in self-assurance rather than political rationality. Of course, inquiry into this kind of motivation for behavior is common among researchers interested in psychotherapy and psychoanalysis. One could argue, albeit rather crudely and inaccurately, that many people perform the political behavior they do because they are mentally sick; therapists are often concerned with the same inner needs that may be called upon to explain political behavior.

On the other hand, there is much to be said for studying psychological dispositions that are closer to the surface of the personality. As we noted earlier, people do acquire attitudes and orientations about a variety of objects with which they come into contact. Such everyday, garden-variety orientations need not be thought of as rooted in deep psychological needs. They may simply be learned orientations that anyone exposed to a given set of stimuli could be expected to acquire —such nonexotic phenomena as opinions and beliefs.

SECTION A
DEEP PERSONAL NEEDS

An early and famous report on personality and political behavior was written in 1930.[2] Its author, Lasswell, was interested in the possible personality antecedents of active involvement in political leadership. An investigation of a group of politicians who had been confined to mental hospitals convinced him that many different kinds of public or political action are connected to private motives, frustrations, and intrapsychic conflict. To him, private motives are displaced onto public objects, and the resultant behaviors rationalized in terms of the public interest. In other words, public officials' acts may be performed because they satisfy some inner need—say, for aggression against a weak victim. Lasswell's subjects were, literally, mentally ill—they were undergoing therapy. Their personal needs were perhaps "sick" needs. However, we should not think of the study of underlying needs as always involved with the investigation of the perverse. It is perhaps unfortunate that Lasswell's study and others in this area have had something of this aura imputed to them. Another famous investigation of personality and politics, by McCloskey, also tends to get involved in moralistic arguments that obscure the real point. McCloskey wondered whether different kinds of personal needs contributed to the adoption of conservative or liberal political beliefs. His principal findings were that personality did indeed make a difference: Conservatives were disproportionately characterized by "feelings of worthlessness, submissiveness, inferiority, [and] timidity"; they were, moreover, "hostile and suspicious, rigid and compulsive, . . . inflexible and unyielding."[3] Given these results (which have been challenged on the basis of inadequate definitional procedures), it was quite possible for ardent liberals to impute moral inferiority or other undesirable characteristics to conservatives. This kind of attitude is unfortunate, for it obscures the real contributions of personality research with a screen of moral righteousness. Whether the implications of such research are good or bad according to prevailing standards is not the immediate point at issue. The real issue is, "Can investigating deep psychological needs contribute to our understanding of important political behavior?" It is this question that governs our discussion.

Several kinds of behavior, both mass and elite, have been examined for their dependence on personality antecedents. DiPalma and McCloskey were interested in conformity to and deviance from community political norms.[4] They suggest, as we did in Chapter 4, that conformity is a consequence of *learning* the norms prevalent around one. They argue, however, that certain personality characteristics can impede this learning process, and thus lead to nonconformity. This may occur in two ways: actual cognitive ability may be impaired by personality, or personality may affect the amount of interaction with others from

154

whom the norms may be learned. A person who was greatly introverted, for example, would probably have few contacts with others, and his opportunities for learning commonly held norms would be greatly restricted.

Relying on data from an extensive national survey and another survey conducted in Minnesota, DiPalma and McCloskey constructed conformity indices. These consisted of statements relating to political, social, or economic affairs with which at least 70% of the respondents from all educational backgrounds—college, highschool, and grade school—agreed or disagreed. The items on which there was a high degree of consensus included such statements as "By belonging to the U.N. we are running the danger of losing our constitutional right to control our own affairs," and "I think it is more important to vote for the man than for the party." (Most subjects disagreed with the first statement and agreed with the second.) Individuals were scored on each item according to whether their answer agreed with that of the majority, and the scores were summed into an overall index of conformity. On the basis of these scores, the respondents were divided into five classes: extreme deviants, moderate deviants, middles, moderate conformers, and extreme conformers. A large number of personality characteristics were also measured, using scales whose validity and reliability have been established in the literature. We will concern ourselves here with only two of these characteristics: *acquiescence* and *manifest anxiety*. Acquiescence is an important component of the cognitive features of the personality. An individual who is acquiescent does not think clearly, discriminatingly, or consistently. He tends to capitulate to any suggestion. According to DiPalma and McCloskey, acquiescent individuals should be less able to learn prevailing norms and thus should be more deviant. The data on this point are presented in the first panel of Table 5-1. There we see the mean acquiescence scores for people of differing degrees of conformity. To provide additional information, a control is imposed for educational level. It is clear that deviants are more acquiescent than conformists and that the relationship is most pronounced among those with the least education.

The negative relationship between acquiescence and conformity may seem startling. If we persist in the belief that conformity always means a weak and uncritical acceptance of what others want us to believe, while deviance implies a critical, self-initiated independence,

155

TABLE 5–1

Mean Scores on Personality Measures Among Minnesota Respondents Who Exhibited Differing Degrees of Conformity

Level of Conformity *	General Population	Non-College Educated	College Educated
Acquiescence			
Extreme deviants	7.52	7.68	—
Moderate deviants	5.31	5.74	3.23
Moderate conformers	4.11	4.46	3.32
Extreme conformers	3.53	3.97	2.85
Manifest Anxiety			
Extreme deviants	4.50	4.47	—
Moderate deviants	3.96	4.05	3.48
Moderate conformers	3.20	3.28	3.01
Extreme conformers	3.10	3.18	2.94

* "Middles" were excluded from the analysis to promote clarity.

Source: Giuseppe DiPalma and Herbert McCloskey, "Personality and Conformity: The Learning of Political Attitudes," *American Political Science Review*, Vol. 64 (December 1970), 1065, 1067.

such an association is almost a contradiction in terms. But as the authors point out,

> . . . cultural norms are, in effect, "obscure, subtle, persuasive messages" which seep in over time. . . . The intellectually adept will pay closer attention to public affairs and will usually have a better sense of what is valued and likely to be rewarded. They will read the signals more accurately and have a more acute grasp of the intention and meaning of a given public communication . . . conformity (as herein defined) is by no means the same as yea-saying, suggestibility, or gullibility. . . . An individual who affirms belief after belief regardless of content—indeed, regardless of whether one belief contradicts another—is less likely than someone of greater discrimination to recognize which of the innumerable beliefs he encounters have been approved or rejected by the society. Being suggestible does not necessarily make him conformist; on the

contrary, it makes him vulnerable to many aberrant opinions that a more perspicacious mind would shun.[5]

Perhaps, on the basis of these data, we should reassess what is meant by conformity and what its implications are. Obviously not all kinds of political conformity are explainable in this way. But these findings do suggest that political conformity and the characteristics associated with it are very complex phenomena indeed.

Probably one of the most discussed features of personality is *ego strength,* or *self-esteem.* Supposedly, the valuation a person places on himself governs many aspects of his relationship to the outside world and thus a great deal of his behavior. In particular, DiPalma and McCloskey believe that it affects the confidence with which one approaches others. Accordingly, those low in ego strength should have characteristic patterns of interpersonal relations. "Lacking self-assurance, such people tend to withdraw from social interactions and avoid 'involvement' in group activities."[6] If they are less involved, they will have less opportunity to learn approved community norms and they should therefore show greater rates of deviancy. The second panel of Table 5-1 displays DiPalma and McCloskey's data on manifest anxiety, a facet of ego strength that implies exaggerated worry and uncertainty. Like other aspects of self-esteem, manifest anxiety is indeed related to conformity, and, as we would expect, the relationship is a negative one. Personality can affect this important kind of political behavior apparently by virtue of its impact on social relationships.

Deep personal needs may be manifested in political behavior in other ways as well. *Externalization* is a particularly interesting ego defense. A person with ego problems may not only need to escape contact with others, as we have just seen, but also to project his inner feelings onto some visible, tangible object. Thus, a person with deep-seated feelings of hostility may become intensely involved in politics, attacking political opponents and disfavored policy alternatives with gratifying vehemence. Unable to cope with the hostility within himself, he may externalize it in this way.

Certain kinds of low self-esteem may thus lead to political extremism. Indeed, there is some evidence that both extremism of the right *and* extremism of the left have roots in this kind of personality need.[7] In this sense, then, the old adage that there is not much differ-

157

ence between the far left and the far right appears to be true. This proposition, though fascinating, raises a great many questions. Available data on personality give us no hints as to why some people with low ego strength choose left-wing political beliefs while others choose right-wing ones. To find out, we would have to examine additional variables, some of them environmental rather than personal. Some of these variables may be very broadly situational. People with little ego strength who happened to live in Germany in the 1930s may well have made very good Nazis; on the other hand, those with a similar personality structure who happened to live in Czechoslovakia during 1968 may have found the relatively forcible restoration of hard-line communism altogether acceptable and even desirable.

Some research on the personality antecedents of more vigorous right-wing activity makes this suggestion seem particularly likely. Rohter constructed a sample of 169 rightists by locating persons prominently identified as such in newspapers, authors of right-wing letters to the editor, and members of organizations such as the John Birch Society.[8] These persons, who were very active in supporting right-wing policies, were compared to a group of nonrightists who were equally active politically but who had different leanings. The nonrightists were selected in basically the same way as the rightists. Both groups were then shown a series of items used as an index of "radical rightism." The items dealt with concern over communist subversion and socialism and with actions taken in response to the perceived threat. The index was apparently a particularly good indicator of commitment to radical-right political causes, since those persons originally selected as rightists scored much higher on it than those chosen as nonrightists.

Rohter argued that persons who have certain *cognitive* needs and feelings of *hostility* find radical rightism congenial and included measures of these internal factors in his questionnaire.

Some people, he asserted, "have a general psychological need for uncomplicated, firm, stereotyped views of people and events."[9] Many people, especially in times of great social and cultural change, find the world puzzling and unintelligible. In some, this bafflement and uncertainty creates a great disturbance, an intolerable confusion. Such people are moved to seek an easily grasped explanation for nearly every distressing thing they see. Right-wing doctrine—which tends to attribute all the ills of the world to a communist conspiracy—is remarkably simple.

158

Busing to achieve racial integration, the ecology movement, and fluoridation of water, in addition to more obvious "evils," have all been attributed to communist machinations. The single overriding cause is exactly the kind of massive oversimplification that fills certain psychological needs. Rohter indicates how contemporary right-wing doctrine vividly portrays world events in black and white, evil and moral, communist and Christian, terms. Because it stresses absolutes, a completely anticommunist posture is the only acceptable one. There is no question as to what to believe and feel; the communist conspiracy is everywhere and any compromise with the enemy is equivalent to betrayal.

Similarly, some people have a strong need to express aggression. This is a basic feature of their personality. When such people experience frustration, they tend to blame external objects and to attack those objects in some manner. This personality trait, called *extrapunitiveness*, is also consistent with participation in rightist activities, according to Rohter. The rightist theory of a communist conspiracy provides a concrete target for extrapunitiveness. A desire to justify aggression is also typical of extrapunitive individuals, according to Rohter, and right-wingism provides a convenient rationale. Aggression in the name of pro-Americanism provides an "intellectual, political, and moral" justification for otherwise antisocial and unacceptable behavior.

If these hypotheses are correct, we would expect personality traits that indicate a need for simplicity and clarity or extrapunitiveness to be associated with rightism. Rohter reports that "intolerance for ambiguity," measured by a four-item scale, is related to the rightism index to the extent that Gamma = .46 ($p < .001$), while a lesser relationship (Gamma = .22, $p < .05$) prevails between "closed mindedness" and the same index; a Gamma of .31 ($p < .001$) is observed between the four-item "hostility toward deviants" scale and rightism as measured. There seems, then, to be some empirical substance to the claim that internalized personality characteristics partially explain the contemporary attraction to rightist political beliefs and activity.

Though this is an interesting finding which lends some insight to an apparently significant contemporary political phenomenon, it should be evident that right-wingism is not the *only* kind of political ideology that can fulfill the psychological needs described above. There are other simplistic explanations of the world's troubles besides the bogey of a communist conspiracy. One might, for example, invoke the persistence of capitalism as an economic form. Similarly, extrapunitiveness might be directed against other objects than conspiring communists; American imperialist aggressors may provide a perfect target for rationalized aggression in some quarters. That these personality features happen to be associated with rightism in this country is clearly a consequence of particular place and particular historical time. As usual, one would have to grapple with a great many additional variables to have a complete understanding of these personality needs.

Two extremely interesting personality traits are *power motivation* and *achievement motivation*. The idea that some persons have a strong personal need to exercise power over others has been prominent in political science since the early work of Lasswell, to which we referred earlier. Supposedly, persons who are characterized by this need are attracted to active involvement in politics. Government or party offices carry with them a certain amount of authority. The occupants of such positions can legitimately tell other people what to do. Politics, after all, is the exercise of power, and those who have a strong need to compel others to take certain actions should find political positions particularly gratifying. Accordingly, becoming a politician should be partly explainable by personality characteristics.

Achievement motivation—the desire to advance or improve one's situation in some way—has also been of great interest to social scientists in recent decades. Achievement motivation is very much akin to *ambition*. Although everyone will surely admit that some people seem to be well satisfied with the status quo and others seem not to be regardless of how much they achieve, it is also true that in our culture we think of high achievement motivation as a quite normal and universal thing. Indeed, it is clearly an important part of our lives. Somehow, we induce most members of our society to acquire this personality trait in some degree. However, high achievement motivation is by no means characteristic of all societies. In fact, it is generally characteristic only of modern, developed cultures. It is typically *not* prevalent in the more traditional cultures found in the "developing" nations of the world. In other words, high achievement motivation seems to be a characteristic of modern industrialism.

However, the leaders of the developing nations of the world, since the achievement of their political independence, have attempted to direct their countries along the most rapid path to development and industrialization. The reason is obvious. National wealth, power, and economic independence come with industrialization. "Modernization," as we saw in Chapter 3, involves many problems, but they are not all of a material nature. Many of them involve the motivation of the citizens of the developing nation. Unless the citizens are interested in achieving a higher standard of living, stature in the economic community, and the like, their willingness to work toward the goal of modernization may be quite limited. The lack of achievement motivation in many traditional, tribal cultures is a cause for some concern. Many scholars have wrestled with the problem of how to increase it among people who have no aspirations beyond conforming to traditional mores that have prevailed for centuries.

Though we cannot investigate this truly intriguing problem at this time, we should be able to guess that differences in achievement motivation within a given culture can importantly condition social and political behavior.

Browning and Jacob[10] became interested in a very significant political behavior—the quest for political office. Their examination of the personality antecedents of this activity included the classic question of power motivation. However, they were not altogether comfortable with the classic hypothesis that politicians are more interested in power than persons involved in nonpolitical pursuits. On the contrary, they thought it altogether possible that success in democratic politics is incompatible with the naked exercise of power. Democratic politics, after all, entails deals, compromises, and accommodations. Even the President of the United States is obliged to persuade, cajole, or reward the Congress, governors, local officials, or the military in order to get what he wants. This is of course true of most lesser officials as well. In a democracy, then a power-motivated person might not become a politician at all; instead, he might become an army sergeant, a policeman, or a dean of students. The role of power motivation in politics, Browning and Jacob felt, was very much an open question.

The role that ambition is supposed to play in democratic politics (people are assumed to have some desire to achieve something if they go to the trouble of serving in public office) leads fairly straightforwardly to the proposition that achievement motivation characterizes politicians more than their counterparts in other fields. There seems little empirical reason to question the stereotype of the ambitious politician. With-out some sort of ambition, it is difficult to imagine American politics going forward as we know it.

To test this hypothesis, Browning and Jacob located a sample of elected local officers in two Louisiana parishes (counties) and a sample of businessmen who had been or were officers on at least the ward level or who had sought political office in a middle-sized eastern city. They also had access to a group of politically inactive businessmen in the same city, which they used for comparative purposes. The power motivation and achievement motivation of these subjects was assessed by a device similar to the Thematic Apperception Test widely used in psychological research. Six pictures of people engaged in various kinds of activity were presented to the respondents, and they were asked to make up a story to indicate what was happening in each one. The stories were assumed to reveal deeply rooted aspects of the respondents' personality. They were scored on the basis of whether a power relationship was attributed to the people in the picture or whether someone was seen as striving to accomplish a goal. The results showed the politicians to be only slightly more oriented toward power and achievement than the nonpoliticians. In fact, the differences were not significant, and one could not argue that there were any real differences at all. Though this would seem to disprove the hypothesis that the personality traits studied affected the desire for public office, the authors felt that some additional variables were involved. Not all political offices are equally valuable as bases for the acquisition of power or for achievement. Some local offices do not provide many opportunities for their occupants to enact policies, en-force laws, or distinguish themselves in any particular area. In most places, the office of justice of the peace would be such an office. On the assumption that the potential of most public offices is readily perceived, Browning and Jacob argued that power-motivated persons would seek out the offices with the most potential for its acquisition, while leaving offices with little potential to those not motivated by a desire for power. Similarly, achievement-motivated persons could be expected to pursue only certain political offices. To test this thesis, the authors classified the power and achievement potential of all the local offices in the Louisiana parishes and the eastern city. The achievement- and power-motivation scores of persons associated with each kind of office were them com-pared; the results are reported in Table 5-2.

TABLE 5–2

Mean Motivation Scores of Politicians in Positions with High and Low Potential for Power and Achievement

| | POSITION'S POTENTIAL | | Significance of |
	High	Low	the Difference (p)
EASTERN CITY			
Power motivation	7.9	4.7	.02
Achievement motivation	8.3	6.5	.13
LOUISIANA PARISHES			
Power motivation	5.9	4.9	.26
Achievement motivation	5.9	3.5	.06

Source: Rufus P. Browning and Herbert Jacob, "Power Motivation and the Political Personality," *Public Opinion Quarterly*, Vol. 28 (Spring 1964), 85.

In the eastern city, persons of high power motivation were attracted to the high- as opposed to the low-power-potential positions. The difference was quite significant. (Significance was determined by the Mann-Whitney *U*-test, a device for assessing the difference between such scores.) Although the other differences between groups of politicians are all in the anticipated direction, their levels of significance are not so impressive; the only one we might have confidence in is the difference between high- and low-achievement-potential positions in the Louisiana parishes. Though the evidence does not confirm the authors' expectations in all respects, even partial success is sufficient to bolster the contention that personality is critical in governing behavior. It is the job of science, after all, to determine when and in what circumstances given explanatory relationships will hold. Browning and Jacob showed that the relationship between personality and the pursuit of political office held only for certain kinds of offices. The differences in configurations of scores between the eastern city and the Louisiana parishes suggest that the nature of the political system or the prevailing political culture also has something to do with the conditions under which personality affects behavior. This may well be true. In any event we can only observe that this research, like all good research, has revealed a little more about the complex and never fully knowable phenomenon of political behavior.

Rutherford conducted an especially intriguing investigation that bears on some of the problems we have raised in this chapter.[11] He was able to interview a sample of patients at a mental hospital, all of whom had severe and identifiable personality impairments. This research strategy had several great advantages. For example, it was possible to compare these individuals to samples of the general population with respect to several types of political behavior with a view to identifying differences between the patients and the general population that might be attributed to the former's peculiar personalities. A prominent hypothesis regarding nonparticipation in politics involves the presence or absence of personality difficulties. Supposedly, if a person has a great many intrapsychic difficulties, most of his energies will be consumed in regulating internal tensions. Accordingly, he will have little inclination to participate in social relations of any kind, much less political activity. He will have neither the mental energy nor the social support associated with involvement in public affairs. This is a very general hypothesis that does not depend on the presence of any particular kind of personality difficulty; any kind can supposedly inhibit participation. However, it is of some significance, for there are those who believe that the pressures of modern life, which grow with each passing year, may be responsible for increasing the frequency of emotional disorders. Perhaps, as we evolve more and more into a complex industrial state, we are eroding the necessary conditions of a democratic government by creating personalities that are essentially nonparticipatory. It is interesting, therefore, to note that Rutherford did *not* find the disturbed patients at the hospital to be any less participatory than the general population. He asked them the same questions about political activities (in the days prior to their admission to the hospital) that he asked the national samples, and he discovered no significant differences.

But the knowledge that people with disordered personalities do participate in politics raises the possibility that certain kinds of disorders lead to certain kinds of activity. This brings back the question of the personality antecedents of seeking political office. As we have seen, this is hardly a settled issue. Rutherford, extrapolating from some case studies which suggested that twentieth-century dictators were severely paranoid, wondered whether some degree of paranoia might not underlie democratic political leadership behavior as well. Of course, he was not able to test this hypothesis directly with his sample of mental

164

patients. To be sure, he had some people who were, on the basis of available clinical records, unambiguously paranoid. But none of these individuals had held positions of political leadership. No actual leaders were available to be studied. But there was a surrogate situation of which a clever researcher could take advantage. In the hospital, there had been an effort to organize the wards into "political" units, with the patients themselves running a decision-making body. These "ward councils" had been set up for therapeutic reasons, to provide the patients with opportunities for self-direction that would help them function when they were dismissed from the hospital. Accordingly, they were given real power to allocate funds and could also exercise discretion in other ways.

These synthetic political units supplied a basis for Rutherford's study. He addressed himself to an examination of the individuals who sought and acquired leadership positions on these councils. It was an easy matter to determine whether such leaders were different, personality-wise, from their nonleader counterparts by a simple comparison of the emotional disorders attributed to them. The results of this comparison are reported in Table 5-3. Judging by their "diagnostic type," the council leaders were indeed different from the sample of patients as a whole. Manic-depressives and especially paranoids were present in disproportionate numbers among the "political leaders." Apparently, there was something about this personality need structure that dictated seeking a position of leadership, at least in this "artificial" hospital context. This is not as strange as it may seem. Paranoia does not imply the symptoms one usually associates with mental illness, such as loss of control, anxiety, withdrawal, and inability to function normally. In fact, much of the paranoid's personality remains unimpaired. His anxieties, guilts, and the like are projected onto others, and he remains unaffected by them as a functioning human being. In fact, the paranoid gives the appearance of extreme ego strength, competence, and effectiveness—even to the point of rigidity. His delusions and suspicions are a result of this rigidity, but it may also give him a resilience that is particularly suited to the rigors of political office.

Of course, Rutherford did not mean to suggest by this research that political leaders are in fact psychotic paranoids who are prime candidates for hospitalization. However, he does suggest "that substantial elements of paranoid behavior and belief may be prevalent among" such

165

TABLE 5–3

Diagnostic Typologies of a Population of Mental Patients Compared with Those of Ward Council Leaders

Diagnostic Type	Total Population (N = 93)	Leaders (N = 24)
Sociopathic	1.1%	4.2%
Personality trait disturbance	4.3	0
Manic-depressive	3.2	20.8
Involutional psychotic reaction	7.5	0
Schizophrenic schizo-affective	6.4	4.2
Catatonic schizophrenic	5.4	0
Paranoid schizophrenic	11.8	45.8
Undifferentiated schizophrenic	33.3	20.8
Simple schizophrenic	6.4	0
Hebephrenic schizophrenic	2.2	0
Mental deficiency	4.3	0
Chronic brain syndrome	14.0	4.2
Total	99.9%*	100.0%

$\chi^2 = 30.28$, with 4 degrees of freedom, $p < .001$

* Does not equal 100.0% due to rounding.

Source: Brent M. Rutherford, "Psychopathology, Decision Making, and Political Involvement," *Journal of Conflict Resolution*, Vol. 10 (December 1966), 401. Used by permission of the publisher, Sage Publications, Inc.

persons. This thesis may help us to understand the behavior of political leaders, which is one of the chief goals of political research. In fact, it has some very interesting implications. Paranoid persons are especially sensitive to detrimental remarks about themselves. Accordingly, paranoid tendencies may lead to attempts to control communications and to the imposition of secrecy in order to prevent the transmission of information. Paranoic suspicion may make it difficult to adopt creative and innovative postures, and it would surely inhibit trustful relations with other persons or other nations.[12] The possibility that paranoid personality characteristics are associated with political leadership is certainly worth the attention of serious students of political affairs.

We have seen that internalized features of the human mind represented by deep-seated personality characteristics are important in explaining a wide range of political behavior, both elite and mass. Human minds develop more or less permanent personal needs. These needs—which when they become exaggerated or uncontrolled are defined as mental illness—often require gratification through some kind of tangible, visible behavior. This behavior, even in perfectly normal people, who are not emotionally disturbed, may well take political forms. The deep, inner personality affects the behavior of everyone. It is not mental illness which motivates behavior, but the enduring character of the mind.

SECTION B
THE SURFACE PERSONALITY:
BELIEFS, ORIENTATIONS, AND ATTITUDES

People are often psychically different from one another in ways that do not involve deep, inner features of the personality. They simply learn a variety of different attitudes or to identify with different objects. The fact that people have great or little trust in government officials, that they are Democrats or Republicans, is not necessarily connected to particular patterns of inner needs.

Rather, it appears that human beings have *universal* needs that are strongly conducive to the formation of opinions, attitudes, and orientations and to identifications. Because of the limitations of the human mind, it is probably impossible to confront the world without a set of internalized dispositions of these kinds. Human beings are simply not capable of considering every new event in their lives as a totally unique situation, of evaluating every discrete occurrence on its merits and divorcing it from all previous experience. The sheer weight of decision-making involved would be beyond human endurance. Accordingly, people employ psychic methods for dealing with the events of their lives with some degree of economy and efficiency. These methods involve the holding of relatively permanent mental dispositions toward whole classes of phenomena. If one possesses an attitude (a type of relatively permanent mental disposition), say, a strongly favorable one, about the values of the natural environment, one has some preexisting equipment for evaluating and otherwise dealing with a proposed an-

167

tipollution regulation. Instead of having to start from scratch, one can respond to key signals which evoke stored information and feelings that help to interpret an event.

To be sure, such "surface" orientations are much less enduring than emotional needs. Attitudes and opinions may be learned and unlearned; circumstances may engender or extinguish them. But they are not ephemeral, and they do profoundly influence behavior.

The scope of possible orientations is clearly immense. The variety of opinions and attitudes which people hold toward politically and socially relevant objects seems virtually unlimited. Accordingly, while we will deal with a few types here, we should keep in mind that they represent only a small part of the total possibilities.

Philosophers and social scientists have historically been concerned with a mental state called *alienation*, or *anomie*. The thinking about this phenomenon involves complex and varied theories, but some central themes prevail. Supposedly, human life in a modern, bureaucratized, industrialized society contains the seeds of severe disorientation. Unlike their forefathers, men today must participate in a great number of impersonal relationships. Intimate contacts with workmates, shopkeepers, and even family members have been replaced by institutionalized routines. Man deals not with men, but with corporations, with massive merchandizing chains, and with a remote and impersonal government. Traditional norms have broken down and been replaced by uncertainties. Social and political decisions seem to involve titanic, complex, and remote issues beyond the comprehension of the individual. How can an ordinary citizen relate to the problems of international monetary exchange rates or comprehend the technology that produces environmental pollution? Man sees himself dwarfed, powerless, subject to forces beyond his control. There are no guidelines for behavior in an industrial culture that seems bent only on achieving wealth, regardless of the means employed.

The idea that there is nothing to believe in, nothing to attach oneself to, in modern society has been prominent almost since the beginning of the Industrial Revolution; and many possible behavioral responses to it, including suicide and revolution, have been suggested. Although alienation may be thought of as characteristic of a whole society, it is also possible to distinguish people who experience this feeling in differing degrees. That is, one may think of alienation as a "surface" personality characteristic. As such, it may well affect individual behavior. We would expect a person suffering from feelings of powerlessness and normlessness to be baffled, inarticulate, and nonparticipatory. Indeed, there is no shortage of research which shows that anomie, measured by scales containing such items as "These days a person doesn't really know whom he can depend on" or "You sometimes can't help wondering whether life is worthwhile anymore," is negatively related to political participation of various kinds. This general state of mind, perhaps experienced most acutely by those exposed to the disorienting forces of industrialism, inhibits involvement. In addition, there is some evidence that anomic individuals may attempt deviant political behavior as a response to their condition. Such behavior has been described as rebellion or innovation, terms which are also used to describe important kinds of political nonconformity. A large number of anomic nonparticipants may thus be thought of as forming a reservoir of discontent that may be tapped by proponents of some radical programs.

It is also possible to examine the extent to which people have feelings of confusion and estrangement directed specifically at the *political* world. Recent research has measured the extent to which people feel politically powerless, politically distrustful, and otherwise estranged from the political institutions around them. Not surprisingly, all these dimensions of *political alienation*, like more general feelings of anomie, have been shown to lead to low levels of political participation, low levels of political knowledge and interest, and vacillation. These findings, though significant in themselves, make one wonder whether some of the other findings about anomie might not find a parallel here in the political sphere. Is political alienation related to any kinds of positive political deviancy? Again, the answer appears to be affirmative for certain kinds of rejective behavior. Voting down referenda, protest voting, and support for demagogic candidates all appear to be at least modestly related to political alienation.

Aberbach felt that the 1964 Presidential election represented a unique opportunity to investigate the role of political alienation in voting.[13] The Republican nominee in that year, Senator Goldwater, if not a self-proclaimed extremist, was considered one by many of the mass media. Did citizen alienation lead to a protest vote for this candidate? Goldwater did attempt to appeal to the "forgotten man" in America, seeking perhaps the votes of a previously inarticulate segment of the population, and rejection of a confusing, alienating political system might well be expressed through a vote for this man who promised simple solutions to many ills. Aberbach investigated these questions using a national sample of voters. In addition to voting behavior, he assessed the respondents' general trust in people and general personal efficacy (perhaps dimensions of a wider kind of social alienation) as well as their feelings of political trust and political efficacy. The measure of political trust contained items that reflected confidence in government officials, such as "Do you feel that almost all of the people running the government are smart people who usually know what they are doing, or do you think that quite a few of them don't seem to know what they are doing?" The political-efficacy scale dealt with respondents' feelings about whether citizens like themselves could effect government decisions.

Responses to all four of these measures of alienation were examined for a relationship to the 1964 Presidential vote. Neither of the general alienation indicators produced a relationship, but the political trust measure did. The tau-c correlation (appropriate for ordinal data such as scale scores) between political trust and voting for the Democratic candidate was .39. That is, the more trusting respondents tended to vote for Johnson and the less trusting ones tended to vote for Goldwater. Of course, this relationship alone should not be too convincing to the alert student of political behavior. Political distrust could be associated with other variables. Aberbach took care to guard against this possibility, however. He showed that there is little relationship between trust and party identification, so that the relationship between trust and a Democratic vote could not be taken as a reflection of party preference. Moreover, by examining survey data for other election years, he showed that there was no particular link, in general, between political distrust and Republican voting. In fact, he argued that there was a slight tendency for political distrust to lead to voting for the party *out of power*. That is, politically distrustful people might engage in a kind of protest voting by opting against the incumbents. This is an altogether reasonable expectation, but the 1964 relationship between trust and vote was much larger than that observed for other years, indicating that both extremism and nonincumbency (the Democrats, of course, being in power) were factors in the vote of the politically distrustful.

However, the tendency of political distrust to stimulate voting against incumbents appears to be facilitated by yet another attitudinal variable. As Table 5-4 indicates, the relation between political distrust and voting against the incumbent party is much stronger among persons who are opposed to the government's taking an active role in promoting educational and social opportunities than among those who favor such action. The entries in this table are tau-c correlation coefficients expressing the relationship between political trust and vote for the Democratic candidate. Comparing the 1958 columns with the 1964 columns reveals that there was a much stronger association between distrust and anti-incumbent voting in the latter year, a fact we have already remarked upon and attributed to Goldwater's extremism and consequent appeal to the distrustful. However, a comparison of those strongly favorable to government action in each of three areas cited with those strongly unfavorable shows stronger relationships among those unfavorable. (The relationships for those with intermediate positions on the issues, which are not shown in the table, are between these extremes.) Indeed, in 1958 there is no appreciable relationship at all between trust level and vote among those strongly favoring government action; only among those opposed to government action is there anti-incumbent (i.e., anti-Republican) protest voting by the distrustful. (Keep in mind that a positive coefficient means that the trusting are tending to vote Democratic and a negative coefficient means that the trusting are tending to vote Republican. Also, the Republicans were the incumbents in 1958, and the Democrats were the incumbents in 1964.)

TABLE 5–4

Correlations Between Political Trust and Democratic Vote, by Issue Position and Year

POSITION ON GOVERNMENT ACTION

Issue	Strongly Favorable 1958	1964	Strongly Unfavorable 1958	1964
Federal aid to education	.01	.21	—.17	.47
Government-enforced school integration	.01	.27	—.16	.47
Government-enforced equal job opportunity	.05	.25	—.25	.36

Source: Adapted from Joel D. Aberbach, "Alienation and Political Behavior," *American Political Science Review*, Vol. 63 (March 1969), 97.

Thus it does appear that political distrust can have some interesting implications for voting. Clearly, when an extremist candidate, particularly one who expresses strong estrangement from the prevailing political norms and directions, offers himself to the public, the emotions of the politically distrustful are engaged. It also appears that distrust surfaces as protest voting when certain other attitudinal states are present. In the contemporary United States, opposition to active government initiative in domestic affairs, a bone of contention for years, appears to have this effect. Thus distrust, an internalized mental characteristic, has an effect whose occurrence is dependent upon additional variables, some of which are themselves internalized mental characteristics. Surface personality, it appears, is a major determinant of political behavior.

Research on alienation is part of a larger tradition of concern about the attitudinal requisites of democracy. Supposedly, citizens must behave in certain ways if a democratic political system is to survive —including actively participating in the political decision-making process, obeying laws, and providing "diffuse support" for the institutional arrangements of the regime. Undoubtedly one reason for the considerable interest in anomie, or alienation, is that some of the behavior that results from it—particularly nonparticipation and political deviancy —may not be consistent with the functioning of a democratic system.

One of the most well-known investigations of a complex of attitudes (called the *civic culture*) believed to be necessary to democracy was conducted by Almond and Verba.[14] They argue that "subjective competence" is of critical importance in many kinds of political participation and also in determining whether citizens will regard a political system as legitimate and accord it loyalty. *Subjective competence*, as we might guess, refers to whether an individual *feels* that he can influence the government.

The fact that an individual feels that his actions have an important bearing on public policy does not necessarily mean that they in fact do. People can be completely mistaken in this regard; officials may foster the belief that they are responsive to citizens, while really taking their cues from altogether different sources. On the other hand, it is not beyond our power to imagine a situation in which citizens are fully cynical about their own input to government decisions while the political elites in fact faithfully implement the perceived desires of their publics. That is, one's sense of political competence and one's actual competence are not the same thing; nor is one necessarily dependent upon the other. In discussing democracy, there is probably a tendency to regard actual competence as the more critical variable. The policies of a democracy, after all, depend on who influences whom, and not on who *feels* influential.

Why, then, should we study subjective competence? The answer is the same as that which justified our examination of other attitudinal variables. This internalized mental characteristic may affect significant political behavior. Perhaps—and this is a point we have touched on before—people who feel that citizen actions are effective are more likely to perform these actions. We have noted time and again that if people are withdrawn and nonparticipatory because they believe activity is futile democratic forms are unlikely to survive. Although it is not logically necessary that actual competence and subjective competence be related, the former is unlikely to exist without the latter. The study of the antecedents of participation hardly needs further justification. There is also another reason for political behaviorists to be interested in subjective competence. We know that political participation is significant quite apart from the fact that it may take the form of influential acts. Participation in public affairs can be gratifying in and of itself, irrespective of its results. Indeed, all governments try to involve their citizens in public actions of some kind in order to produce a sense of gratification that leads to commitment to and enthusiasm for the regime. Totalitarian governments in particular seem to use this technique. It is thus quite possible that not only participation, but belief in the efficacy of participation, affects an individual's allegiance to a regime. A sense of subjective competence, then, may lead not only to participation, but regardless of whether actual influence is attempted, to increased commitment to the political order.

Almond and Verba's research involved surveys of the citizens of five democratic nations: the United States, Great Britain, Germany, Italy, and Mexico. Subjective competence was measured by a standard procedure. Five parallel questions, dealing with (1) whether the respondent believed he could understand local politics, (2) whether he felt he could and (3) would act to influence the local government, (4) whether he had any expectations of success in influencing the local government, and (5) whether he had ever attempted to influence it, were asked. Every

TABLE 5-5

The Relationship Between National Pride and Subjective Political Competence in Five Nations

SUBJECTIVE POLITICAL COMPETENCE

What Respondents Are Proud of About Their Country	U.S.			Great Britain			Germany			Italy			Mexico		
	H*	M	L	H	M	L	H	M	L	H	M	L	H	M	L
Government	92%	87%	67%	50%	49%	36%	9%	5%	6%	3%	8%	2%	38%	31%	26%
Other	7	12	20	46	44	43	81	85	70	80	76	61	60	60	48
Nothing	0	0	4	2	4	8	5	3	9	8	4	11	0	2	5
Don't Know	0	0	9	3	4	13	5	6	15	9	12	26	2	7	21
Total †	99%	99%	100%	101%	101%	100%	100%	99%	100%	100%	100%	100%	100%	100%	100%

* H, M, and L refer to high, medium, and low levels of subjective competence.

† Totals may not add to 100% because of rounding.

Source: Part of Table 5, "Pride in Nation Among Three Groups of Subjective Competents, by Nation and Education," in Gabriel A. Almond and Sidney Verba, The Civic Culture: Political Attitudes and Democracy in Five Nations, p. 248. Copyright © 1963 by Princeton University Press. Reprinted by permission of Princeton University Press.

positive answer resulted in the addition of one point to the individual's score. Accordingly, scores for any individual could range from 0 (no positive answers and least competent) to 5 (all positive answers and most competent).

Not surprisingly, the data clearly showed that in each of the five nations studied this internalized mental characteristic was important in determining the extent of citizen involvement or political participation. Perhaps more interesting, however, are the data in Table 5-5, where the effect of subjective political competence on pride in the governmental system of one's country is displayed. Such pride could easily be considered an important kind of political allegiance. In three of the five countries, it is clear that the subjectively competent express more pride in their government than those who do not feel competent. Similar results were found for other allegiance variables. As Almond and Verba comment, "the democratic government that fosters a sense of ability to participate in decisions does appear to reap the benefit of this participation."[15] Of course, like most generalizations, this must be qualified. What is there about the citizens of Germany and Italy which makes them have little pride in their governmental system regardless of the degree of competence they feel? Could this lack of pride stem from the fact that their current governments were in some sense imposed by those who defeated them in World War II? If so, it would be accurate to say that another internalized mental characteristic, an attitude toward a political object, accounted for the difference between the citizens of these countries and those of the other countries examined.

Democratic political attitudes that are even more specific than these have also received considerable academic attention. Belief in the right of a majority to have its opinion prevail, acceptance of political opposition, approval of civil liberties and civil rights, and support for political institutions such as elections and competitive political parties have all been investigated at some length. Of course, these are often investigated as dependent variables, as we saw in Chapter 4. They constitute a kind of diffuse support that is surely well worth explaining. However, there is some question as to what difference the holding of such attitudes makes. Their possible macro-level impact is truly intriguing. Do countries whose citizens hold such attitudes have materially different kinds of government from those whose citizens have different internalized mental characteristics? The difficulties of conducting mas-

175

sive, cross-national research on this question are obvious; but until it is done, we must admit that though such macro-level differences are likely we are not really sure they exist. Similarly, there is considerable doubt about how much effect such variables have on the political behavior of individuals. Although it seems logical that a person who supports civil liberties will take some action when those liberties are threatened, we are not really sure that this will happen. The behavioral implications of such attitudes as support for the institution of elections seem obvious, but they have not really been thoroughly investigated. Unlike anomie, political trust, and subjective political competence, these more particular democratic attitudes remain shrouded in considerable mystery.

A nagging suspicion that such attitudes may—contrary to what seems logical—be fully consistent with behavioral passivity is supported by an interesting piece of research. Dennis surveyed a sample of Wisconsin adults in order to investigate a number of aspects of support for American institutions.[16] He devised measures of approval of the electoral process and of support for the party system using such items as "It is impossible for most voters to make informed decisions when they go to the polls" and "More often than not, the political parties create conflicts when none really exists." Although support for both institutions was found to be very widespread, it is perhaps significant that neither attitude contributed very strongly to an important kind of democratic political behavior, participation in elections. The partial Pearson correlation coefficient between approval of the electoral process and turnout, with other independent variables controlled, is only .05. The corresponding partial for support of the party system and turnout is .08. Of course, this discussion and these negligible correlations should not be interpreted to mean that attitudes such as we have been discussing are unimportant. Such an interpretation would be a very grave error. Rather, we should keep in mind the important point that attitudes are not the same as behavior. A verbally expressed attitude of support for a democratic norm does not insure democratic behavior. The connection between internalized mental characteristics and political behavior is not always obvious. Indeed, some scholars eschew the study of attitudes altogether on the ground that they are removed from behavior, the object of ultimate importance. Though most people would regard this as an extreme position, it should nonetheless serve as a word of caution.

176

(The relation between attitudes and behavior will be considered in more detail in Chapter 8.)

There is an area of political science in which speculation about and empirical research on surface-personality characteristics has played a very large role. This is the study of voting behavior. Internalized mental characteristics play a very large role in normative democratic theory. Citizens are supposed to be able to identify their own interests in the political world and behave in a way that will further those interests. They are supposed to have a consistent and relatively complete view of what the good life is like and to pursue it whenever possible. In short, they are supposed to have an ideology. Consistent "conservatives" or "liberals," therefore, are expected to be very well equipped to decide where they stand on all the current issues of the day and to vote in a rational fashion.

The ideologically motivated rational voter obviously depends upon a very sophisticated set of internalized mental characteristics for his orientations to politics. Ideology is a surface-personality characteristic well worth investigating. However, in the American electorate, anything like an ideology is quite rare. Few people have a comprehensive view of the world that guides their choice of alternate public policies. Even the very vague notions of what is liberal or conservative do not appear to structure the political thinking of many people. This of course does not imply that opinions on issues (also a kind of internalized mental characteristic) are irrelevant to voting decisions. Indeed, in most samples of voters one can find relationships between expressed views on issues (independent variables) and voting choice (the dependent variable). But such relationships are not typically pervasive. To be sure, as we have suggested before, there are times of crisis, such as during the Depression of the 1930s, when a central set of issues seems to dominate all political decisions. It is not even unreasonable to think that a major crisis caused by conflicting policy goals and priorities is developing at this very moment. But we do not live in a constant crisis, and voters do not behave as if we did.

Citizens' orientations to the non-issue-related features of candidates are also important determinants of how they vote. There is no question but that previous military heroism, perceived personal morality, religion, and general appearance have all influenced citizen be-

177

havior in recent elections. The whole question of candidate "images" revolves around this point. Though the argument that advertising techniques can make a candidate appear irresistible on the basis of characteristics that are ultimately irrelevant has been vastly exaggerated, there is a certain validity to it. Public-relations men cannot always "sell" an office-seeker to the voting public by improving his image. On the other hand, as we move further into an age dominated by a mass medium (television) that emphasizes personal characteristics, the candidates who are recruited seem increasingly to possess the kind of image that is required. More than ever before, they appear youthful, vigorous, and physically attractive, and to be skilled in speaking and interacting with people. But again, the connections between orientations to candidates and voting are not pervasive. For one thing, a great variety of candidates have come and gone over the years, but many aspects of American political life have remained stable. The existence of a two-party system involving the same protagonists for well over a century is a case in point.

The stability of certain political patterns over time suggests that voting behavior is based on some criterion more persistent than specific issues or candidates. The latter two are, after all, relatively transient. As we might guess, given the fact that so many of our persistent political patterns are related to party ("the solid South,'" for example), this criterion is explicitly partisan. People generally consider themselves either Democrats or Republicans. That is, they identify with a party in much in the same way that they identify with a religious denomination. This prevalent psychological partisanship is called, logically enough, *party identification.* It is not surprising that people readily adopt such an identification. Americans are confronted with a tremendous array of political choices. Many go to the polls at least twice a year and vote for large numbers of offices each time. The magnitude of the task of dealing sensibly with all these options is imposing—as evidenced by the fact that many citizens decline to participate at all. For those who have not the time to inform themselves about the detailed implications of all these choices—or who lack the necessary mental capacity—the tendency to grasp at a relatively durable principle that imparts some order to things is understandable. People also need something to love and trust at election time. How much easier everything appears if the alternatives are defined in terms of party, as they often are, and if one considers oneself a member of one of those parties. Indeed, all classes of citizens, not only the busy and the relatively less able, find party identification congenial. The salience of this mental characteristic is so great that it may well influence how a person feels about issues and candidates. It may not be the issues and candidates that determine a voter's preference for a particular party, but his preference for a particular party that determines his stance on candidates and issues. Party identification is in fact much more closely related to the vote in most elections than voter orientations toward issues or candidates. Figure 5-1 shows the role of

FIGURE 5–1

How Partisans and Independents Voted in Five Presidential Elections from 1952 to 1968

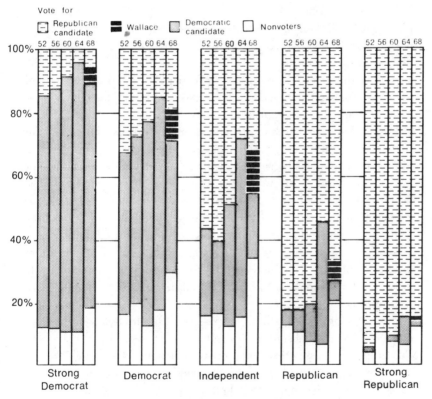

Source: Survey Research Center, University of Michigan. Reported in William H. Flanigan, *Political Behavior of the American Electorate* (Boston: Allyn & Bacon, 1972), p. 40. Copyright © 1972 by Allyn & Bacon, Inc., Boston. Reprinted by permission.

179

party identification in five recent Presidential elections. The voting behavior of five categories of voters, ranging from "strong Democrats" to "strong Republicans," is compared. It is evident that party identification is and has been a very significant factor, though not of course a totally determinative one. (Comparing the graphs also gives us some interesting insights into the source of Wallace votes in 1968 and the widespread unpopularity of the Republican candidate in 1964.)

As we have already suggested, party identification is not necessarily rationally determined. It may be related to policy considerations, or it may be related to quite different factors. For example, we know that there is a high degree of transference of party identification from parent to child. How distressing it must be to the normative democratic theorist to contemplate a situation in which children, quite without reference to public policy, acquire a party identification from their parents and, all their life long, use it, again without reference to public policy alternatives, as a basis for voting decisions. We must acknowledge that, regardless of whether we contemplate the ideal world of the normative theorist or the empirical world of politics, it is indeed helpful to use internalized mental characteristics—such as an ideology or party identification—to help explain things.

As we have tried to show in this analysis, the processes by which the surface personality affects behavior are not always simple. Diverse internalized mental characteristics may conflict with one another or interact in complex patterns. This is even true of party-related attitudes, despite the great importance of party identification. Kirkpatrick was especially concerned with the consistency or inconsistency of partisan attitudes.[17] Since few people develop attitudes as a consequence of ideology, there is no guarantee that their attitudes will be consistent with one another. They may well be the product of interactions with various groups, and the groups may emphasize different, if not inconsistent, norms.

Surely, one would think, there are different behavioral consequences of attitudinal consistency and inconsistency. Kirkpatrick tested this proposition using three measures of partisan consistency. His data on an extensive national sample contained a number of responses to party-related questions. The first measure was called AIP, for *affect-identification-preference.* It had three components. *Total partisan affect* was assessed by amalgamating the number of pro-Democratic or pro-Republican responses to a series of very broad, open-ended questions such as "What do you like about the Democratic Party?" It was then classified as pro-Republican, pro-Democratic, or neutral. *Party identification* was determined by a now standard series of questions dealing with what a person considered to be his affiliation. The categories Democratic, Republican, and Independent were used. *Political preference* was determined simply by asking whether the respondent preferred the Democratic or Republican candidate (or neither) in the upcoming Presidential election. If a subject gave two or more responses consistent with a given partisan alternative (i.e., Democratic or Republican) and none that were inconsistent, he was classified as totally consistent on AIP. If he had a pro-Republican and a pro-Democratic attitude he was classified as not totally consistent on AIP.

Partisan attitudinal consistency was also measured by a *conceptualization index* (CON). This was derived from a series of questions that permitted an assessment of partisan thinking along several dimensions. The questions treated the two candidates in the Presidential election, parties with respect to groups, domestic issues, and foreign issues, and parties as managers of government. For each of these six areas a Republican, Democratic, or neutral affect was assigned. If all the non-neutral affects (six or fewer) in a given individual's configuration were Republican, he was regarded as attitudinally consistent. He was also regarded as attitudinally consistent if all the non-neutral affects were Democratic. Of course, any combination of Democratic and Republican affects indicated a state of inconsistency.

Kirkpatrick's third index of consistency was based on the congruence between voters' *expectations* about who would win the Presidential election and their *preference* for a particular candidate. Subjects were scored as consistent on this expectation-preference (EP) index if the two elements were congruent and inconsistent if they were not congruent.

From what we know about the effects of inconsistent *social* cross-pressures, we might be inclined to posit that attitudinal inconsistency induces withdrawal and apathy. A person who feels a conflict may well respond by backing away from the situation altogether. However, as we can see from Table 5-6, this is not entirely the case. Kirkpatrick examined the relationship between his three measures of attitudinal inconsistency and several indicators of political interest and participa-

TABLE 5–6

Attitudinal and Behavioral Consequences of Partisan Consistency-Inconsistency

Consequences	LEVEL OF SIGNIFICANCE AND DIRECTION OF RELATIONSHIP					
	AIP		CON		EP	
ISSUE INTENSITY						
General power of the federal government	.89	0	.00*	—	.00*	—
Aid to education	.34	—	.00*	—	.00*	—
Medicare	.84	0	.06	0	.14	—
Government responsibility for living standards	.24	—	.63	0	.00*	—
Government ownership of power plants	.30	—	.00*	—	.00*	—
Equal job opportunities	.52	—	.20	—	.81	0
School integration	.53	—	.23	0	.45	—
Integrated public accommodations	.21	—	.38	—	.90	0
INTENSITY OF PARTISAN IDENTIFICATION	.00*	+	.00*	+	.25	+
DECISION TIME FOR MAKING UP MIND ABOUT VOTE DIRECTION	.00*	+	.00*	+	.00*	+
POLITICAL INTEREST AND PARTICIPATION						
Interest in the campaign (asked before election)	.90	0	.00*	—	.00*	—
Attention paid to the campaign (post-election)	.64	+	.16	—	.00*	—
Expect to vote	.95	0	.05*	—	.20	—
Turnout	.91	0	.27	—	.11	—
Mass media usage	.47	0	.00*	—	.06	—
Talking to others to influence them	.68	0	.03*	—	.00*	—
Attending political meetings	.60	0	.37	0	.01*	—
Political club membership	.53	0	.66	0	.02*	—
Using a button or bumper sticker	.00*	+	.02*	+	.03*	—
Giving money	.30	+	.22	—	.00*	—
Political involvement index	.01*	+	.28	0	.13	—
POLITICAL EFFICACY	.88	0	.06	—	.02*	—

* Significant relationship.

Note: Entries are significance levels (p) followed by a +, 0, or — which indicate, respectively, a positive, substantially nonexistent, or negative relationship.

Source: Adapted from Samuel A. Kirkpatrick, "Political Attitudes and Behavior: Some Consequences of Attitudinal Ordering," *Midwest Journal of Political Science,* Vol. 14 (February 1970), 14.

tion, as well as intensity. The data in Table 5-6 provide no information about the magnitude of these relationships, but only the direction (indicated by a +, 0, or −) and the level of significance (p values) of each. The smaller the p value, of course, the smaller the probability that the relationship appears by chance. All the p values of .05 or less are marked by an asterisk. The first entry in the AIP column is a p value of .89 followed by a 0. This means that the relationship between AIP consistency and intensity of feeling on the issue of power of the federal government is substantially nonexistent and that the miniscule relationship which does appear has an 89% probability of being a function of chance alone. The second entry in this column is a p value of .34 followed by a −. This means that a negative relationship was indicated between the two variables, but that we cannot have much confidence in it; a 34% chance of error is too much. On the other hand, both the first and second entries in the CON column are .00* followed by a −. This means that both these relationships were negative and that the p values approached zero. We can thus have great confidence in the relationship, a fact which is emphasized by the asterisk.

Substantively, the interesting thing about Table 5-6 is that, except for the intensity of party identification and the decision time, the overwhelming majority of the significant relationships that do appear are negative. In this study, a consistent person, almost by definition, is more intensely partisan; and a person who is consistent no doubt has no difficulty reaching a voting decision and therefore makes up his mind early. But why should consistent persons be *less* intense about issues and *less* participatory? Unlike group cross-pressures, attitudinal inconsistency seems to motivate people to do something about the state of imbalance it implies. For example, EP inconsistency may motivate people to attempt to bring their expectations in line with their preferences. If a person believes that his candidate will lose, he may become much more intense about and involved in politics in hopes of improving his candidate's chances. He may deal with the tension generated by inconsistency not by withdrawal, but by substantive attempts to change objective political circumstances. Similarly, the negative relationships between consistency and communications behavior (usage of mass media, talking to others, etc.) may indicate that additional information is being sought to provide a basis for resolving an unbalanced state of affairs. More knowledge may make choice possible. Perhaps, too, feel-

183

ing very intensely about an issue makes any incongruity of one's stance with partisan leanings less important. Partisan incongruity may therefore stimulate a strong orientation toward the issue. In any event, attitudinal inconsistency has discernible and significant effects on political behavior, as well as on other attitudes.

The dynamics by which internalized mental characteristics operate, though sometimes direct, are often very subtle. Nevertheless, there seems little doubt that surface personality plays a large role in many kinds of political behavior. In general, surface-personality characteristics are relatively straightforward in their operation. We expect behavior to be consistent with these feelings, and it often is. Of course, the great problem is knowing when congruent behavior may be expected and when it may not. The extent of the correspondence between internalized mental characteristics and parallel actual behavior has been a matter of scholarly dispute over the years, and a great deal more research will have to be done before a very clear or complete picture emerges. The question of the consistency of various elements of surface personality also complicates matters. It may be that inconsistency creates a series of "needs" not unlike those we discussed in relation to the more deep-seated aspects of the personality. Here too behavior may be a response to a set of private motives in the personality; even surface-personality characteristics may create tensions that can only be relieved through external behavior.

Internalized Characteristics
and Behavior: A Recapitulation

Personal characteristics, whether they be physiological features, emotional needs parallel if not identical to those treated as mental disease, or mere beliefs profoundly influence our behavior. The examples presented in this chapter by no means cover the entire range of possible personal influences. Our goals in this chapter have been modest. Basically, we have sought to communicate some appreciation for the tradition of research that stresses deep psychological needs. This type of research has long been important in the social sciences, and only the most naive political scientist would be unaware of the possibility that people have inner needs which are expressed by various types of mass and

184

elite behavior. We have also sought to show that not all the personality is composed of such deep needs. There are much more proximate and accessible mental characteristics of a very ordinary nature. They too must not be ignored, for it is demonstrable that people have attitudes and identifications upon which they rely for guidance in political matters. Finally, we have attempted to consider personality in the context of other variables that we know affect political behavior. The study of personality supplements the study of social factors discussed in Chapter 4. Group variables and personal variables are linked. Understanding the possible intervening role of personality may help us to understand how groups influence behavior.

The explanation of political behavior involves a complex mosaic of variables. Undoubtedly, some of the most important elements in that mosaic are personal variables, perhaps caused by environmental variables, and surely determinative of some of their effects, but essential to a complete understanding of our subject nonetheless. Having communicated, we hope, some appreciation of the great insight that attention to internal variables can provide, we shall now turn to another aspect of our environment, and a very politically relevant one.

Notes

1. Fred I. Greenstein, *Personality and Politics* (Chicago: Markham, 1969), pp. 3-12.
2. Harold D. Lasswell, *Psychopathology and Politics* (New York: Viking Press, 1960). Originally published in 1930.
3. Herbert McCloskey, "Conservatism and Personality," *American Political Science Review*, Vol. 52 (March 1958), 37-38.
4. Giuseppe DiPalma and Herbert McCloskey, "Personality and Conformity: The Learning of Political Attitudes," *American Political Science Review*, Vol. 64 (December 1970), 1054-1073.
5. *Ibid.*, 1064-1065.
6. *Ibid.*, 1066.
7. Paul M. Sniderman and Jack Citrin, "Psychological Sources of Political Belief: Self-Esteem and Isolationist Attitudes," *American Political Science Review*, Vol. 65 (June 1971), 401-417.
8. Ira S. Rohter, "Social and Psychological Determinants of Radical Rightism," in Robert A. Schoenberger (ed.), *The American Right Wing* (New York: Holt, Rinehart & Winston, 1969), p. 229.
9. *Ibid.*
10. Rufus P. Browning and Herbert Jacob, "Power Motivation and the Political Personality," *Public Opinion Quarterly*, Vol. 28 (Spring 1964), 75-90.
11. Brent M. Rutherford, "Psychopathology, Decision Making, and Political Involvement," *Journal of Conflict*

Resolution, Vol. 10 (December 1966, 387-407.

12. *Ibid.*, 407.

13. Joel D. Aberbach, "Alienation and Political Behavior," *American Political Science Review*, Vol. 63 (March 1969), 86-99.

14. Gabriel Almond and Sidney Verba, *The Civic Culture* (Princeton: Princeton University Press, 1963; Boston: Little, Brown, 1965), Chapters 5, 8.

15. *Ibid.* (Little, Brown edition), p. 198.

16. Jack Dennis, "Support for the Institution of Elections in the Mass Public," *American Political Science Review*, Vol. 64 (September 1970), 819-835.

17. Samuel A. Kirkpatrick, "Political Attitudes and Behavior: Some Consequences of Attitudinal Ordering," *Midwest Journal of Political Science*, Vol. 14 (February 1970), 1-24.

6

Individual
Behavior:
Political
Factors

In a sense, the preceding two chapters may leave the reader feeling that the explanation of individual political behavior is mysterious and obscure. To some observers, attributing phenomena to social or psychological variables takes the "politics" out of political inquiry. It may appear foolish to seek the reasons for political behavior in early family life or a desire to protect the ego when our lives are immediately, deeply, and massively affected by such dramatic events as "Watergate" or conditions like urban poverty. Somehow, Watergate and poverty seem real and important, while concern for family and ego pressures seems artificial, "academic," and contrived. This view is easy to understand, for there is an element of wisdom in it.

It should be very clear to the student of political behavior at the individual level that the "group" and "personality" factors alone cannot explain all the political things people do. There are many other kinds of independent variables that may be important. The critical views just discussed suggest another category of explanatory variables. It is true that people do live in a political world and that specifically political events and influences impinge upon them. There is no reason why the effects of these *political factors* cannot be systematically investigated. They are no less a part of the environment of the behaving organism than groups. The impact of policy, propaganda, and political persuasion should certainly be closely examined. Fortunately, political behaviorists have realized this. They have contributed to the understanding of political behavior through research on a considerable variety of influences that stem directly from political events.

There are a great many ways in which political factors can be classified, depending on what one wishes to include in the category of political. Indeed, since there are no "natural" boundaries to this concept, there is perhaps some risk of thinking of it as a residual category into which one places anything that cannot be located elsewhere. To complicate matters, the processes by which political factors may operate are equally diverse. Nonetheless, it is clear that we must grapple with this notion, so we will present some of the more important areas of concern, keeping in mind that our treatment is a very partial one indeed.

Section A
The Policy Process and Mass Behavior

It seems obvious that people are greatly affected by the public policies to which they are exposed. Government, in the most philosophic sense of the word, probably exists because people feel a need for some device that will, in certain circumstances, exert influence on their behavior. Politics is a device for the achievement of collective goals—such as defense of the nation or construction of bridges—which individuals could not realize by themselves. If legislation provides for the construction and operation of a university (a collective goal), it implies the organization of many people's behavior along very predictable lines. The behavior of construction workers, material suppliers, instructors, students, taxpayers, and many others is likely to be affected by this act of public policy. Government is also a device for the settlement of conflicts among individuals.[1] Virtually all court decisions, as well as many executive decisions and pieces of legislation, are made essentially to settle disputes. If an electric-power company and a

188

conservation organization disagree about the construction and place-
ment of a dam, the matter will very probably be settled, ultimately, by a
suit in a court of law. Legislation funding a welfare program represents a
solution to a conflict between less affluent classes and those who believe
that wealth should not be shared in this way. In each case, we expect that
the losers of the dispute will be stopped from behaving in a certain way
and that the winners will be able to perform actions they would otherwise have had to forego.

However, the connection between public policy and behavior,
though it seems obvious, is not necessarily clear or direct. Particularly in
the case of policies designed to cure particular social problems, no one
knows whether some efforts are effective or not. Antipoverty programs
may generate great debate; but often, because they have not been
effectively evaluated, we cannot say whether they modify behavior in
the way they are intended to. Does investment in vocational education
programs really produce more people prepared to enter skilled trades?
Many policies are legislated, funded, and applied in great ignorance of
their actual effects.[2] Though political theologians, political engineers,
and political anecdotalists may discuss policy with an air of great certainty, it seems that there is still a role for systematic investigation by
political behaviorists.

Not only does public policy promote or discourage certain kinds of
substantive behavior (such as the choice of a career or the acquisition of
an education), but it sometimes aims at securing compliance to specific
directives. A law or decree specifying criminal penalties is a clear
example of this type of policy. Actions interfering with the achievement
of some collective goal are often declared criminal, as are the acts losing
parties to disputes would prefer to perform. In both cases, the role of
policy in securing compliance seems straightforward—people comply or
they are punished. But in most societies, compliance is not entirely a
matter of official enforcement. If there is to be compliance, it must come
because people are *willing* to be constrained by policy. It is too costly to
try to insure compliance by force or the threat of force alone. In the
absence of comprehensive enforcement mechanisms, behavior is thus
sometimes explained by policy imperatives and sometimes not. It would
be an interesting and important task for a political behaviorist to determine when policy is effective (that is, when voluntary compliance is
secured) and when other variables are more important.

189

Another aspect of the problem of policy and substantive behavior involves a question that has long been at the heart of democratic theory and the subject of much commentary in democratic political systems. According to standard conceptions of what democracy is all about, citizens make decisions about supporting a particular administration or candidate on the basis of promised or actual policy outcomes. If the government's policy is gratifying, citizens vote to retain or otherwise support those in power. If the government's policy output is not gratifying, then citizens are supposed to elect a new slate of officeholders. A sort of exchange process is presumed—with citizens offering support in return for gratifying policies. Supposedly, support decisions rest upon how well the administration achieves collective goals or the extent to which policy confers victory in disputes.

The idea that electoral behavior is motivated by policy has not been limited to philosophers. The American educational system has almost universally urged students to base political decisions on a consideration of the issues involved, and newspaper analyses frequently suggest that issues have an overpowering effect on voting behavior. Yet many early political behavior studies, as we noted in Chapter 5, showed that the rational, informed, issue-oriented citizen envisioned by political philosophers is a rare bird. In fact, they demonstrated that the independent variables which explain voting may have nothing to do with issues; they may be group variables or internalized dispositions like party identification. The classic paradigm was tested and found wanting. This had the unfortunate effect of creating the impression that the political behavior approach somehow involved a positive denial of rationality and of the role of issues in electoral decisions. Though this is clearly not true, much emotional controversy has ensued as a result.[3] The import of such research, of course, is not to deny that issues explain behavior. The evidence of day-to-day observation on this point is overwhelming. But political behavior research has raised a question, and one that only more research can answer: How great, actually, is the role of issues in electoral behavior?

Thus, as far as policy is concerned, there are three questions of particular import: Do public policies promote the substantive behavioral modifications they are intended to promote, do they generate compliance with their imperatives, and do preferences with respect to policies motivate the political behavior of citizens? Needless to say, these simple statements are capable of considerable elaboration. At once, we can ask under which conditions behavioral modification, compliance, or issue motivation occurs. There are many other worthy related questions as well.

By its nature, public policy seeks to influence behavior. And some kinds of behavior literally all governments attempt to modify. Perhaps the chief example involves political socialization. All architects of public policy have a program for building political support among the masses or increasing their political knowledge. All regimes encourage the "right kind" of citizens. Thus they often make a tremendous investment in the civic education of youth. It has often been assumed that governments determine their own destinies by regulating civic education. Particularly in authoritarian countries, where control of education is especially stringent, socialization is thought to be highly effective. Even in the United States, as the continuing concern for civic education at both the elementary and secondary levels shows, there is a great belief in the efficacy of this kind of public policy.

Langton and Jennings[4] sought to determine whether these assumptions were justified by conducting a survey of a national sample of highschool seniors. A total of 1,669 students in 97 schools were interviewed, and their political knowledge and beliefs along a variety of dimensions (with respect to a variety of dependent variables) were measured. The extent of the students' civic education (an independent variable) was determined by noting the number of civics courses they took during their highschool careers. More than 90% had taken either no courses at all or only one course. Although one would expect substantial relationships to emerge from the data if such courses mean anything to the political development of highschool students, Langton and Jennings found only extremely small ones regardless of which dependent variable was used. The greatest relationship was between the number of civics courses and political knowledge, where the partial beta coefficient (a statement of the relationship between two ordinal scales with other relevant variables controlled) was .11. Civics courses had almost no impact on political orientations. How can these results, which "raise serious questions about the utility of investing in government courses in the senior high school, at least as those courses are presently constituted,"[5] be interpreted? Why does civic education have no impact on political behavior? Langton and Jennings feel that the lack of impact

191

is due to redundancy, that is, that civics courses in general fail to teach anything that is not learned elsewhere.

Some interesting data reinforce this interpretation. Langton and Jennings found that civics courses consistently produced quite different results for black students than for white students. Typically, white students were not at all affected by the courses, but black students apparently changed considerably under their influence. A representative pattern appears in Table 6-1, which shows the relationship between the number of civics courses taken and the students' ability to distinguish the Democratic and Republican parties on a "liberal-conservative" dimension when race is controlled. Whites who have had civics courses are scarcely different from their counterparts who have not. Of course, since whites made up the overwhelming proportion of the sample, this accounts for the fact that the overall data showed courses to have little effect. This racial difference is also consistent with Langton and Jennings' interpretation of the results as indicating the redundancy of civic education. For many reasons, active discrimination among them, blacks are more likely to have an inferior education prior to arriving in highschool. Other forms of cultural deprivation are also typically experienced by blacks. Thus, while highschool civics materials may be relatively redundant for whites, they are likely to be new to blacks. Accordingly, there should be some impact among blacks, but little among whites.

The redundancy hypothesis is confirmed by a further look at black

TABLE 6–1

The Relationship Between the Number of Civics Courses Taken and Knowledge of "Ideological" Differences Between Parties, by Race of Student

Number of Courses Taken	PERCENTAGE OF RESPONSES CORRECT	
	Blacks	Whites
None	0	29
One or more	19	31

Source: Adapted from Kenneth Langton and M. Kent Jennings, "Political Socialization and the High-School Civics Curriculum in the United States," *American Political Science Review*, Vol. 62 (September 1968), 860.

students. Civics courses traditionally try to implant the idea of political efficacy in youngsters; good democratic citizens are supposed to believe that they can influence the government. Such efforts are least likely to be redundant among blacks, for reasons we have already discussed. We thus expect that blacks who have taken civics courses will feel more efficacious than those who have not. This turns out to be only partially true, but even this confirms the redundancy interpretation. Among black students whose parents had only a primary education, the Gamma coefficient between the number of civics courses taken and political efficacy measured by a traditional scale is .56; among those at least one of whose parents had a secondary education it is .36; and the comparable measure for those with a college-educated parent is but .02. It is very easy to see why the teaching of citizen effectiveness in a democracy would be quite new to the child of very poorly educated parents, for government and the role of a citizen in it are not likely to be frequent topics of discussion in the home. On the other hand, well-educated parents are likely to provide a milieu in which this kind of problem receives some attention; such parents thus preempt the impact of schooling.

Of course, the implication of these findings is twofold. First, this variety of public policy does not have the widespread effect that it is commonly thought to have. (One can imagine how meaningless many debates over the political orthodoxy of textbooks have been.) Second, one of the conditions of effective civic education is nonredundancy. These, it seems, are results of some importance.

That behavior does not automatically conform to the imperatives of policy is nothing new to anyone who has studied compliance with the law. We are all aware that some laws just do not work. In some cases, people disregard laws even though they may be risking prosecution. Though some people can be expected to react this way to most public enactments (all societies have criminals), it becomes a matter of political interest when large numbers of people refuse to comply with government decrees. Probably the most obvious case of widespread noncompliance occurred during "prohibition" in the United States. Public policy simply could not regulate people's consumption of alcohol. Though this was clearly an exceptional case, we can easily imagine many other, less spectacular instances of noncompliance.

Consider, for example, the problem of compliance to court edicts.

193

Recent years have seen a great upsurge in litigation as many have sought court settlement of disputes. The courts have responded to this demand by actively issuing decisions on a great variety of matters. From the standpoint of public policy, we are perhaps living in the age of the court. Yet, though court decisions on civil liberties, free speech, and race relations, to name but a few issues, supposedly have sweeping implications, and though they are vigorously (and bitterly) debated, their intent is not always realized. Witness the state of racial segregation in public education, even though the key Supreme Court decision on this matter was handed down in 1954. Levine[6] was interested in a currently prominent topic—the sale of allegedly obscene literature. Matters of "public morals" have always been in the domain of state law under American federalism, and thus have been adjudicated in state courts. However, because the question of free speech is involved in the sale of allegedly obscene materials, the U.S. Constitution is frequently invoked and cases find their way into federal courts and the Supreme Court in particular. Supreme Court decisions are supposed to provide guidelines for state courts. However, the guidelines have been sufficiently ambiguous so that state courts could pursue quite divergent policies, with the result that some states have had a relatively lenient approach to obscenity while others have had a more restrictive policy.

Levine expected that booksellers who operated in lenient states would offer more sexually oriented literature for sale than their counterparts constrained by more restrictive judicial policies. He therefore sent mail questionnaires to a random sample of 250 booksellers in twelve states whose judicial policies on obscenity covered a great range, from strict to permissive. The booksellers were then categorized according to the stringency of judicial policy-making in their state (which was termed restrictive, fluctuating, or permissive). The booksellers were asked which of ten "sexually oriented" books prominent at the time of the research they stocked, and the number was recorded. Several other variables relating to the booksellers were also measured. The results of the questionnaire are reported in Table 6-2. Though booksellers in the restrictive states offered slightly fewer of the ten books for sale than those in permissive judicial climates, the differences are small and the overall pattern is not what we would expect. The relationship is not significant. Clearly, judicial policy on obscenity does not govern bookseller behavior in offering materials for sale.

194

TABLE 6–2

**The Relationship of State Appellate Court Policy to the Number
of Sex Books Stocked by Booksellers**

	LOCAL JUDICIAL POLICY		
Number of Sex Books Stocked	*Restrictive* (N = 55)	*Fluctuating* (N = 40)	*Permissive* (N = 47)
0–3	25%	35%	17%
4–7	22	40	21
8–10	53	25	61
Total	100%	100%	99%*
Gamma = .10, not significant.			

* Total does not equal 100% because of rounding.

Source: Adapted from James P. Levine, "Constitutional Law and Obscene Literature: An Investigation of Bookseller Censorship Practices," in Theodore L. Becker
(ed.), *The Impact of Supreme Court Decisions* (New York: Oxford University Press,
1969), p. 141.

If it is not policy that explains what these merchants sell, what, we
may ask, is it? It is perfectly reasonable to think public demand would be
a prominent factor (economists would predict this) or perhaps other
manifestations of community expectations. Arguing that demand for this
kind of material, as well as other kinds of community expectations,
would vary with urbanism, Levine examined the impact of the size and
population density of the community on the number of sex books offered
for sale. As it turned out, the booksellers from larger, more densely
populated communities offered more sex books for sale: in the case of
size, Gamma = .27 ($p < .01$); in the case of density, Gamma = .24 ($p <
.05$). It is interesting that these environmental factors (group) explained
behavior, whereas policy could not. Perhaps even more interesting is
the fact that an internalized mental characteristic, the booksellers' own
attitides toward sexual material (measured by a series of questions on
censorship), explained more than any other factor: the Gamma relationship between attitude and the number of sex books offered for sale was
.80 ($p < .001$). An adequate explanation of these attitudes would no
doubt require inquiries into the booksellers' past associations and possibly their personal makeup as well.

Of course, as is always the case, there are some difficulties with this

195

study. Most notably, the 65% of the subjects who returned the mail questionnaire may have been quite different from those who did not respond, and thus the responses may not be truly representative. Similarly, though the procedures used were responsible, the ten books selected may not have tapped the dimension of obscenity very well. Finally, and in a different vein, it must be admitted that not all policy in this area is a function of the courts; police and prosecutors make policy also. Perhaps some of these other aspects of policy—unmeasured in this study—impinge heavily on bookseller behavior. But even given these qualifications, findings such as these cannot but give us pause. Only so much can be accomplished by the implementation of public policy. It does modify behavior some of the time, but there is hardly an automatic, one-to-one relationship between policy and behavior.

Policy may not only induce substantive modifications in behavior, as we have noted, but it may also produce an evaluative response that may in turn be a motive for political behavior. In the classic democratic paradigm, citizens are supposed to evaluate policy (actual or promised) and proffer or withhold support from would-be officeholders on the basis of that evaluation. Considerable research has been devoted to determining the extent to which real-world behavior conforms to this paradigm. It is perhaps not surprising that much of this research should have shown the voter to be not up to the demands of this scheme. We saw in Chapter 5 that party identification has been shown to explain more variance in voting behavior than a concern with issues. The relative ease with which the idea of party may be grasped makes relying on this label a very convenient way of organizing one's political world. Citizens who have other things on their minds, such as making money, sporting events, or their family lives, perhaps cannot be expected to spend too much time assessing political events.[7] The role of party identification is sometimes thought to be so great as to distort voters' perceptions of issues completely. In order to avoid "cognitive dissonance," voters may selectively perceive issues, noting only those on which their party takes a stand congruent with their own. Alternately, they may view their party as taking an issue stance congruent with their own when in fact the party advances just the opposite position. This kind of psychological distortion suggests that issues play a very small role indeed in political behavior.

Independents, whom we might think of as having commendably avoided the easy route of party identification, have been shown not to

196

conform to the stereotyped image of enlightened citizens either. Instead of evaluating issues on their merits and making decisions free of any consideration of party, independents have often been found to be politically lethargic. They are independents because they have no political interests or preferences of any kind. They are less issue oriented than Republicans or Democrats, have less political information, and participate less.[8] Independents, like their partisan counterparts, do not seem to meet the requirements of the classic democratic paradigm.

Though the evidence makes it impossible to believe in the issue-oriented, informed, rational voter, it is also true that issues cannot be ignored entirely. For one thing, it is clear that party loyalties break down in times of crisis; indeed, parties themselves may cease to exist and be replaced by other organizations. Behavior in times of great upheaval cannot be governed by long-standing identifications; it must in part be governed by immediate events, that is, by issues. Civil wars, revolutions, depressions, and the like can and do involve large numbers of people who are surely, in very large part, responding to issues. Some elections have the character of crises too. Many less severe but nonetheless momentous changes have involved elections as either the stimulus or the response to action. During such elections, issues rather than party identifications are certain to play a major role. Campbell calls such contests *realigning elections.*[9] The criteria for decision in such elections indeed involve the critical issues of the day. But in addition, believes Campbell, because of the involvement of parties in these conflicts, new patterns of party identification are established. In short, as a consequence of going through the critical election, there is a realignment of party identifications. These new patterns are likely to last for long periods. The results of elections following the crisis are likely to be heavily a function of the new patterns of party identification. Thus, though issues as such are relatively rarely involved in electoral choices, when they are it is in a massive and critical way. The last American realigning election occurred in the Great Depression, establishing patterns of party identification that persist to the present day. Whether we are on the verge of another realigning election is, of course, a fascinating question.

It is also true that at least some voters at least some of the time are issue oriented between times of crisis. As we have seen, much of the evidence suggests that such voters are few. There is some concern, however, that this evidence may in part be an artifact of the way in which measurements have been taken. Much of the evidence has been compiled by the Survey Research Center at the University of Michigan. RePass suggests that earlier analyses may have understated the importance of issues because of the use of "closed-ended" questions (those requiring an "agree-disagree" response to some substantive remark provided by the interviewer).[10] Furthermore, many of these questions, he argues, were aimed at the evaluation of parties in terms of the issues rather than at the evaluation of issues themselves. Perhaps voters care about issues that the interviewer does not mention, or perhaps they do not always regard them in party terms. RePass therefore undertook an analysis that relied on "open-ended" questions (those which allowed the subject to provide any response he wished) and items that did not initially require any coupling of issue and party. In this way, he hoped to uncover an issue sensitivity that would not have been revealed by previous investigations.

Fortunately for RePass, the Survey Research Center began to include open-ended issue questions in its periodic election surveys in 1964. He examined the 1964 national sample of adults for the number of issues mentioned as important, the party regarded as best able to implement preferences on those issues, party identification, and several other variables. If his basic notion was correct, there should have been considerably more issue concern than that manifested in response to previous questions. And, indeed, this turned out to be very much the case. Far from being devoid of a concern for issues, the subjects mentioned an average of 2.5 issues. Moreover, as Table 6-3 shows, concern for issues was not lacking even among Independents. This finding is rather new and fails to support the notion that those who are not partisan are political dropouts. Indeed, Independents could name more issues than voters in any other category except strong Republicans. Though this should not be taken to mean that Independents are involved, "ideal" citizens (RePass too reports that they are less involved and less politically participatory), it forces us to modify our view about the incidence and extent of concern over issues.

More interesting than these descriptive data, however, is the question of the extent to which concern with issues explains voting decisions. Since RePass was dealing with a partisan election (the 1964 Presidential election), he found it necessary to construct an additional measure called

TABLE 6–3

**The Relationship of Party Identification to the Number
of Issues Mentioned**

PARTY IDENTIFICATION

Number of Issues	Strong Dem. (N = 394)	Weak Dem. (N = 363)	Inde- pendent (N = 314)	Weak Rep. (N = 194)	Strong Rep. (N = 156)
0 or 1	33%	35%	26%	28%	13%
2 or 3	52	47	44	46	42
4 to 6	15	18	30	26	45
Total	100%	100%	100%	100%	100%

Source: David E. RePass, "Issue Salience and Party Choice," *American Political Science Review*, Vol. 64 (June 1971), 398.

issue partisanship. For each issue mentioned as important, respondents were asked which party, the Democrats or the Republicans, was most likely to do what the respondents wanted done. The Democratic, Republican, and "no difference" responses were summed to yield a net score for each subject that indicated which party (if either) was, on balance, perceived as preferable for dealing with the (considered to be important) issues of the day. Issue partisanship scores were classified along a continuum from strong Democratic to strong Republican.

Given the other data we have examined, we would expect issue partisanship and party identification to be related; that is, we would expect more Democrats to perceive the Democratic Party as a preferable instrument for dealing with important issues. This turned out to be the case, but the relationship was not overpowering. Perhaps particularly in 1964, many Democrats believed the Republicans to be preferable from an issue standpoint, and vice versa. The critical question was the effect of this feeling on voting behavior. In the face of a conflict between party identification and issue partisanship, how was the vote ultimately cast? RePass's answer is reported in Table 6-4, which shows the relationship between issue partisanship and the Presidential vote controlling for party identification. Each cell shows the percentage of respondents in that cell voting Republican and (in parentheses) the number of respondents involved. That is, the upper-left cell tells us that of the 55 respondents who were both strong Democrats and had highly

199

TABLE 6—4

The Direction of the Vote in the 1964 Presidential Election, by the Strength of Issue Partisanship, Controlling for Party Identification

PARTY IDENTIFICATION

Strength of Issue Partisanship	Strong Dem.	Weak Dem.	Ind.	Weak Rep.	Strong Rep.
High Dem.	2% (55)	4% (22)	9% (11)	0% (3)	—
Med. Dem.	1% (77)	2% (41)	4% (28)	20% (10)	40% (5)
Low Dem.	0% (83)	11% (63)	8% (40)	18% (28)	33% (6)
No difference	10% (37)	21% (57)	22% (45)	56% (39)	94% (16)
Low Rep.	20% (10)	45% (20)	58% (33)	77% (31)	83% (17)
Med. Rep.	33% (3)	62% (13)	81% (16)	93% (14)	96% (27)
High Rep.	100% (5)	89% (9)	93% (27)	90% (20)	99% (71)

Note: Entries are the proportion and (in parentheses) the number voting Republican.

Source: David E. RePass, "Issue Salience and Party Choice," *American Political Science Review*, Vol. 64 (June 1971), 399.

Democratic issue partisanship scores, only 2% voted Republican. On the other hand, of the 5 respondents who were strong Democrats but had highly Republican issue partisanship scores, 100% voted Republican. The implications of the table are clear. Partisans in 1964 were often prepared to defect from their party if their concern for issues indicated the superiority of the opposite party. Party identification does not, apparently, have the overpowering influence often attributed to it. Voters are perhaps a bit more "rational" than has been recently thought.

Of course RePass's data do not imply a complete revision of earlier findings about the importance of party identification. It is clear that in many instances party triumphed over issues; and it is even more clear (from examining the numbers involved) that the great majority of voters, perhaps for psychological reasons, never allowed themselves to perceive a conflict between party identification and issue partisanship. Nonetheless, the role of issues is impressive. A multivariate analysis of the same data showed that the "standardized regression coefficient" (an indicator of the impact of a variable with all other relevant factors controlled) between party identification and the vote was .27, but that for issue partisanship and the vote it was nearly as high, .23.

Though earlier studies of voting clearly deserve a great deal of credit for demonstrating that citizens do not rationally calculate the wisdom of their vote as far as issues are concerned, the conventional wisdom that has emerged from this research also appears to be in need of some revision. This is hardly surprising, for it is by the modification of conclusions in the face of new knowledge that science grows.

We might note in passing that the classic democratic paradigm assumes not only that the masses are influenced by and respond to public policy, but also that the makers of public policy (an elite) are influenced by common citizens. In a democracy, it is argued, one of the chief determinants of elite behavior is "public opinion," or the will of the masses. Indeed, all modern governments, regardless of whether they conform to the prevailing Western image of democracy, claim that official action is somehow a consequence of popular demand. But philosophies and passionate claims aside, it is an empirical question how much official behavior can be explained by constituent demands, and by whom and how such demands are put forward.

Not only masses, but persons of all kinds function in a specifically political environment. We may thus invoke political factors to explain a great variety of behavior. Though there has indeed been a great deal of research on the impact of various political factors on elite behavior, little of it has sought to explain variance in the sense emphasized in this book. Though we shall not go into the problem here, it is clear—especially given the dramatic significance of these questions for the understanding of democratic government—that there is here an unmatched opportunity for the imaginative behavioral researcher.

Section B
The Manipulation of the Masses

Although it is almost diametrically opposite in principle to the classic notion of the democratic process, there is a second kind of thinking about how masses respond to their political environment that enjoys just as much popularity. This stand suggests that democratic citizens—or for that matter citizens of any modern government—are heavily influenced by, if not totally controlled through, mass-mediated messages, campaign techniques, or political propaganda. Often, in the press or popular literature, we get a picture of the individual whose will crumbles before the machinations of those who control the mass media, or whose vote is totally at the mercy of clever advertising men. This picture is clearly overdrawn, many such discussions being presented to provoke a dramatic response rather than to communicate accurate information. However, it is nonetheless true that mass media are widely used in attempts to politically influence the masses, and it is true that modern advertising techniques are employed to manufacture candidate images. Any modern campaign bears testimony to the fact that large sums are invested in just such efforts to sway the American public.

In a similar vein, the entire world is often viewed as being subjected to a "communications explosion" with manifold political consequences. Though the effects of this explosion are asserted to be many and varied, perhaps the most intriguing suggestions along these lines have to do with the ability of mass communications to produce feelings of national unity in the "developing" nations of the world. Many of these nations, often former colonial areas, are composed of peoples of diverse heritages with rather local and parochial orientations. The task of creating a national consciousness and integrating these people into the life of a modern nation is not easy. Supposedly, a centrally operated mass communications system can contribute importantly to this end.

Thus, ordinary observation of the modern world makes it seem as if political, and often mass-mediated, manipulation of the masses is common. Though it is clear that the attempt is made, it is less clear what the impact of such efforts is. Perhaps systematic political behavior research can help us find out.

Although the belief that all democratic citizens are in the clutches of political manipulators is exaggerated, there is no doubt that at least some overtly political efforts have measurable effects on mass publics. There is considerable literature, based on macro-level research, on the impact of certain types of campaign activity. Most of this research, it might be noted, does not deal specifically with the mass media. A recent study showed that the level of political party activity within North Carolina counties (measured by the money spent by county chairmen, the completeness of voter records, the amount of time put in by party officials, etc.) contributed significantly to the distribution of the vote by party. That is, over and above the usual demographic variables (e.g., wealth, urbanism) that predict vote distribution, party activity explained variance in the party vote for all officials from the President to the sheriff, with the effect concentrated at the lower political levels.[11] In one interesting study, a researcher was actually able to convince competing candidates for the county legislature to employ different types of campaign techniques (e.g., door-to-door canvassing or telephone calls) in different districts according to a plan devised to facilitate the investigation. By comparing the election returns in the different districts, the researcher was able to demonstrate that canvassing did in fact both increase the turnout and affect the distribution of votes between the candidates.[12] Though it might be possible to argue that most of the observed effect was due to the fact that mass media pay little attention to lower offices, thus abandoning the field to other persuasive forces, it is extremely interesting that such traditional campaign techniques continue to be important in the modern, electronic world.

The research on mass communications itself is less convincing than we might expect. To be sure, there is a great deal of highly suggestive evidence that the media are extremely potent. There are any number of examples of successful political candidates who used the latest in mass media techniques. Eisenhower's election to the Presidency is supposed to have been partly due to his employment of a large advertising agency to obtain public exposure. Television is supposed to have been instrumental in converting Ronald Reagan from an actor to a governor, and professional advertising skills were liberally applied in Nelson Rockefeller's gubernatorial campaigns and Robert Kennedy's Presidential primary campaigns. The primary campaign of Republican candidate Don Tabbert of Indiana in 1964, which was managed by an advertising agency, relied exclusively on television and radio. Tabbert was victorious over an opponent who did not use such techniques.[13] The association between such campaigning and success *seems* evident. However, there are also examples of candidates who have waged sophisticated, modern media campaigns and lost. Media use does not inevitably mean victory, and it remains for systematic research to determine how great a relationship, if any, exists between this kind of campaign and electoral success.

Moving to specifically micro-level investigations, we find that survey research on general populations often reports a relationship between the frequency or rate of mass media consumption and the level of conventional political participation. This is not at all surprising, for mass media convey information that may act as a stimulus; the more stimuli one receives, the more likely one is to act. In this way, mass media appear to have a considerable effect on behavior. However, this relationship probably results, at least in part, from the fact that people who are already involved, interested, and active in politics choose to expose themselves to many political communications. In short, it may make more sense to think of involvement as the independent variable and media use as the dependent variable.

This relationship between involvement and media use leads to some interesting and almost paradoxical results. The most politically involved people, that is, those who are likely to expose themselves to the campaign media, are also the most partisan and the most politically knowledgeable. Thus they are more likely to have made up their minds about voting well before a campaign gets under way. They are more likely to have stable political attitudes and less likely to change their minds. Their uninvolved, unpartisan counterparts have less stored information and are thus more likely to be influenced by campaign communications; but at the same time they are less likely to receive them.

A fascinating piece of descriptive information bears directly on this problem. Using survey data on a national sample, Converse plotted the number of media (television, newspapers, etc.) citizens used during a Presidential campaign against "stability" of attitude.[14] The latter variable was defined in two ways. People were asked, at a point well before the election, for whom they intended to vote. Later, their actual voting behavior was determined. The extent to which a respondent's actual vote reflected his earlier intention (rather than a change) was regarded as a measure of stability. Similarly, congruence between party identification and a partisan vote was also taken to indicate stability. Can the media induce change, that is, produce instability? Converse reasoned, as did we in the discussion above, that involved voters will pay attention to the media but will, because of existing commitments and stored knowledge, continue to show stability. Uninvolved voters, though potentially vulnerable to the media's persuasive impact, will also demonstrate stability because of nonexposure. But if *some* information does get through to them, perhaps through minimal media usage, they should demonstrate considerable instability in response to the stimuli. Converse thus anticipated a U-shaped curve in his plot. People who use no media (are very uninvolved) would, he thought, be stable because of a lack of any information input. People who use very few media (who are also uninvolved and thus very susceptible) should be moved to instability. And people who use many media (are very involved) should already have commitments and knowledge that make them resistant to new information inputs; thus they also should demonstrate stability. Figure 6-1 demonstrates that Converse was right.

On the vertical axis of the graph are tau-b ordinal correlation coefficients. Remember that the *relationship* between two variables is taken as the measure of stability. Though the curves are not dramatic, the anticipated effect is present. Slight media exposure can produce an effect in the uninvolved.

The import of these data is not primarily in their demonstration of mass media effects, but rather in their seeming confirmation of the formidable obstacles that communication stimuli must overcome to affect human political behavior. On the one hand, persuasive stimuli bounce off the media's most avid consumers because these people have internalized characteristics that render them resilient; on the other hand, the most susceptible types of people appear to avoid contact with the media. No doubt because of this fact, few mass media studies demonstrate much in the way of conversion effects. (A theoretical discussion of this problem is presented in Chapter 11.)

If these observations are accurate, we would suspect that some of the fears about unfortunate consequences of political use of the media are at least partly unfounded. For example, it is often suggested that pre-election polls and election-night projections of results, though not specifically designed to be persuasive, have important persuasive effects

FIGURE 6–1

Attitude Stability, by Number of Mass Media Used

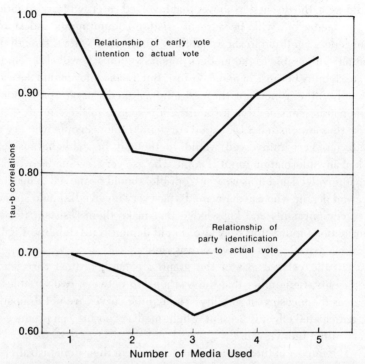

Source: Philip E. Converse, "Information Flow and the Stability of Partisan Attitudes," in Angus Campbell *et al.* (eds.), *Elections and the Political Order* (New York: Wiley, 1966), p. 146.

upon voters. Citizens supposedly either jump on the bandwagon of a predicted winner or lapse into apathy when the chances of their preferred candidate look poor. In either case, it is argued, the election returns are altered and the process of democracy is distorted. What is the evidence that such effects occur? In a word, such evidence is extremely limited, if it exists at all. Both survey data (from questions about voting intentions and awareness of poll results) and distributions of preferences across time may be construed as slight positive evidence of a bandwagon effect, but the interpretations of such data are often ambiguous[15] Several studies have investigated the effect of television networks' election-night projections of results. Because of time-zone difference, many voters in the western United States have access to these projections (and early returns) before they cast their votes. The question of whether those votes are affected by this information has always been answered in the negative.

A recent study[16] seems to offer fairly definitive results. Samples of eligible voters in both the Eastern time zone and the Pacific time zone were surveyed just before the 1968 Presidential election and again immediately after it. Prior to the election, subjects were asked whether they planned to vote and, if so, for whom. Following the election, the same people were contacted and asked if they had in fact voted and, if so, for whom. In addition, those in the Pacific time zone (since they were the only ones who had access to projected results before voting) were asked whether they had seen the projections on television before going to the polls. The extent to which the actual voting behavior of each group was different from its previously declared intent (with respect to both intention to vote and the choice of a candidate) was determined. The results are displayed in Table 6-5. If the broadcasts had any effect on actual voting choice, some difference between the exposed and unexposed Pacific zone respondents should appear. In fact, there is no significant difference in the extent to which voters changed their minds. There was also no significant difference observed when changes in the intention to vote and in the direction of the vote were considered separately. The insignificance of the broadcasts is underscored by the

TABLE 6–5

The Total Change in Voting Plans Among Voters Exposed and Unexposed to Election-Night Broadcasts Before Voting

	Percentage Who Changed Voting Plans or Switched Candidates
PACIFIC TIME ZONE	
Unexposed voters (N = 1,361)	8.9*
Exposed voters (N = 94)	10.6*
EASTERN TIME ZONE	
(N = 513)	12.1

* $p = .58$

Source: Adapted from Sam Tuchman and Thomas E. Coffin, "The Influence of Election Night Broadcasts in a Close Election," *Public Opinion Quarterly*, Vol. 35 (Fall 1971), 322.

TABLE 6-6

Changes in the Commitment of Viewers and Nonviewers of the Kennedy-Nixon Debates

	FIRST DEBATE		SECOND DEBATE		THIRD DEBATE		FOURTH DEBATE	
	Viewers	Non-viewers	Viewers	Non-viewers	Viewers	Non-viewers	Viewers	Non-viewers
Unchanged	58%	52%	65%	66%	73%	69%	70%	67%
Changed to Kennedy	25	25	17	17	14	15	16	16
Changed to Nixon	17	23	18	17	13	16	14	17
Net gain for Kennedy	+8	+2	−1	0	+1	−1	+2	−1

Source: Adapted from Elihu Katz and Jacob J. Feldman, "The Kennedy-Nixon Debates: A Survey of Surveys," in William J. Crotty (ed.), *Public Opinion and Politics* (New York: Holt, Rinehart & Winston, 1970), p. 428. Published earlier in Sidney Kraus (ed.), *The Great Debates: Background—Perspective—Effects* (Bloomington: Indiana University Press, 1962). Copyright 1962 by Indiana University Press. Used by permission.

difference between the behavior of the unexposed Pacific zone voters and the Eastern zone voters. This relatively large difference (though still small in an absolute sense) is obviously not due to media projections. It is a function of the Easterners' greater tendency to change their turnout plans. But what regionally related variables produce this effect are unknown. Whatever their nature, they are more important than the mass media in causing change.

Perhaps the most dramatic mass-mediated campaign events ever were the Kennedy-Nixon debates in the 1960 Presidential race. In that year, the two candidates, neither of whom was an incumbent, held four face-to-face debates that were televised nationally during prime time. These discussions of public issues were unique and, for this reason, attracted a truly huge audience. Research indicates that upwards of 80% of the population watched one or more of these debates. "Surely," as one study notes, "this is one of the great political assemblages of all time."[17] Any number of surveys of voters were made in an attempt to assess the effect of these presentations. Although many voters claim that the debates influenced their decision, and although there is evidence that people learned a great deal about the issues and candidates from them, these events apparently induced only very small changes in voting behavior.

Table 6-6 compares attitudinal changes in viewers and nonviewers of the debates. The data are based on a survey of a national sample of 2,672 voters interviewed both before and after the debates. The critical variable reported here is the degree of "commitment" to vote for one or the other of the candidates, measured on a nine-point continuum ranging from "strongly committed to Nixon" to "strongly committed to Kennedy." Thus, a change does not always imply a reversal of a voting decision; even an alteration in the degree of support for a given candidate is regarded as a change. It is at once clear that a moderate amount of change occurred among both viewers and nonviewers and over the entire period during which the debates took place. It is further clear that most of this change appears to have had nothing to do with the debates. Only in the case of the first debate, one which Kennedy is widely agreed to have "won," was there any appreciable difference between the behavior of viewers and nonviewers. Even the most generous interpretation of these data could not accord the debates more than a miniscule impact on the predisposition to vote.

It would almost seem that we are confronted with something of a paradox. We know that people spend a great deal of time attending to mass media. We know that people claim to get most of their political information from television. We know that vast sums are spent on mass media campaigns by candidates. And despite all this, the overt impact of the media on voting seems to be very slight. How can these apparent inconsistencies be resolved?

First of all, it may be that mass-mediated campaigns are effective in ways that are not measurable in terms of converts from one political opinion to another. A much less overt process of shaping people's political perceptions and expectations may be taking place. Though little change may be observed during one election campaign, continuous, year-after-year exposure may create strong impressions of what the political world is like and what good candidates are like. The media repeatedly tell us how we should evaluate candidates, and perhaps, after many campaigns, we accept their criteria as correct. It is probably true that physical attractiveness, personal style, a talent for articulation, and the ability to "project a good image" in general are now expected of any candidate for high office. And candidates who exhibit these qualities are selected above those who do not. A harsh and not very personable individual like Harry S Truman would almost certainly not be a Presidential nominee today. Our modern perceptions of what candidates should be like are almost certainly due to the impact of the mass media, especially television. And such massive alterations in our political expectations over the years could have occurred without a single person's preferences being altered in any given campaign. Undoubtedly, perceptions are being altered along a number of different dimensions. Moreover, these changes are probably of tremendous importance.

Second, it is clear that there is a great deal of dynamism in electoral politics. People's voting preferences do change considerably from election to election and even, as Table 6-6 shows us, from time to time within the period of one campaign. A relatively stable party identification does not always govern behavior. What produces these changes? The studies in Chapter 4 and the evidence presented earlier in this chapter make it likely that the answer is *other people*, whether in the guise of friends or other "significant others" or as campaign workers making personal contacts. But, and this is significant, the mass media may be *indirectly* involved in this process. In short, it may be interpersonal

210

communication that directly induces most voting changes. Persons whom we could designate as "opinion leaders" may be the source of a most important flow of persuasive political communications. But what is the source of change among opinion leaders? Very possibly it is the mass media. This "two-step flow" of influence has been envisioned for some time.

Finally, we should keep in mind that the political role of the mass media extends far beyond contemporary election campaigns. For the last several pages, we have been discussing an extremely narrow, albeit traditionally interesting andtopical, area of concern. Especially in the United States, it is exactly in this area that people are likely to have predispositions at any given moment—most notably of course, with respect to party identification. These dispositions make people resistant to the persuasive efforts of the mass media. But, worldwide, there are a great many politically important dimensions on which people do not possess such predispositions. In these areas we would expect attempts at influence through the mass media to be much more effective. New nations seeking to create feelings of national identity might face just such a situation. Often, as we have noted, the people at whom such efforts are aimed are quite parochial, having no experience with the kinds of ideas that are important for twentieth-century nationhood. Unlike U.S. citizens experiencing a campaign, they may have few internalized defenses against the urgings of the media.

An interesting study by Harik presents some data which bear on this point.[18] Harik had access to a sample (N = 135) of the population of a rural village in Egypt. Three mass media were available in the village: newspapers, radio, and, to a more limited degree, television. The critical dependent variable in this study was political awareness rather than political preferences or overt behavior. Obviously, making citizens aware of national goals is a necessary step in securing their participation in political life. Though this represents a separate problem from shaping political preferences, it is very much related. National and international awareness was assessed by determining knowledge of, among other items, new policy enactments in the area of economic saving, family planning, and nationalization of sectors of the economy. Parallel items allowed the measurement of provincial political awareness. The respondents' exposure to the various media available was also assessed. (An index was constructed taking into account both the number of media attended to and the frequency of use.) Finally, the survey determined if respondents had received whatever political information they had through interpersonal communication rather than via the mass media.

The results are impressive testimony to the impact of the media. The overall national and international awareness index was related to media exposure to the extent that $r = .58$. Unquestionably, those exposed to media were more knowledgeable. All other indicators of media exposure—for example, radio ownership—were also related to awareness. Moreover, only one variable other than exposure was able to account for awareness and that, not surprisingly, was literacy. The more literate were more aware. However, controlling the exposure-awareness relationship for literacy by no means washed it out. Both among literates and illiterates, exposure produced an effect.

Harik was also interested in whether the "two-step flow" hypothesis held in this context, so he examined the differences between those who received their political information from the media and those who depended on opinion leaders. Not surprisingly, given the results we have discussed, he found much evidence of a direct flow of political information. Moreover, as we can see from Table 6-7, the direct media flow seemed to be more effective. On both measures of awareness, those

TABLE 6–7

The Relationship Between Political Awareness and Sources of Political Information

	SOURCE OF INFORMATION		
Level of Awareness	Mass Media*	Opinion Leaders*	p †
Provincial affairs	60	51	$< .05$
National and inter- national affairs	57	42	$< .05$

* Entries are mean awareness index scores.

† Difference of means test.

Source: Adapted from Iliya F. Harik, "Opinion Leaders and the Mass Media in Rural Egypt: A Reconsideration of the Two-Step Flow of Communication Hypothesis," *American Political Science Review*, Vol. 65 (September 1971), 738.

who depended on opinion leaders scored lower than those who were directly exposed to the media. Apparently, the current efforts of less developed countries to get radios into the hands of all citizens and televisions into public places in every village and town are not likely to be in vain. Quite literally, the mass media may be the chief instruments in one of the great political revolutions of the world.

Clearly, the masses of the world are politically manipulable through conscious effort. Party efforts, we have seen, do produce measurable effects, but the great modern campaign device of the mass media is not the pervasive, irresistible instrument it is sometimes portrayed as in the press or popular literature. The mass media's effects on the voting public are probably much more subtle. Their efforts may be counteracted by internalized characteristics of their audience which make it resilient or inattentive. Yet though we are well advised not to accept crude estimates of the omnipotence of the media in campaigns, we should not go to the other extreme of attributing to them no influence at all. As we have seen, there are conditions—notably in less developed countries—that are probably conducive to their having a very profound influence. Mass media must be reckoned with, though perhaps not in the typical sense of campaign vehicles, by any serious student of politics in the late twentieth century.

Political Factors and
Behavior: A Recapitulation

The systematic investigation of individual political behavior need not be restricted to questions of background or personality; indeed, it should not be. We have seen that some of the causes of individual political behavior lie in the political process itself. Basically, we have investigated two possible processes by which political factors may affect mass behavior. On the one hand, we sought to determine whether citizens responded to the variables prominent in traditional democratic theory. Apparently, there are some occasions when citizen behavior is constrained by the dictates of policy and some when it is not. There are some circumstances in which an evaluation of policy motivates citizens' responses to government (primarily their voting behavior) and some in which it does not. Analyzing these political factors allows us to begin the task of specifying when and how the classical theory of democracy really operates. Perhaps with a great deal more research we will be able to understand the relationship of citizens to government in the modern world, to know the extent to which the precepts of classical democratic theory describe the real world and the extent to which they describe merely a traditional ideal.

We have also investigated a set of political factors that assert almost the opposite of classical democratic theory—that citizens do not evaluate political alternatives rationally but instead are easily manipulated by campaigning and by the mass media. We found that such political factors are important, but not all the time and not overwhelmingly so. Exaggerated views of omnipotent media are unjustified, but the fact that their effects may be subtle only underscores the importance of understanding them.

It is tempting at this point to speculate on the implications for democracy of what we have discussed here and in previous chapters. Can man govern himself? Can he remain "free" in the modern world? To what extent is there "distortion" in the representative process? These and similar questions are truly fascinating, but we will resist the urge to discuss them directly—primarily because we can offer no definitive answers. We can say with some confidence that many simplistic views of the sources of human behavior are inaccurate. People are not totally products of their backgrounds, they are not totally policy oriented, and they are not totally manipulable. But these findings are only a beginning. The total volume of research available—and we have discussed only a tiny fraction of it—does not allow us to reach cosmic conclusions. We are still unsure, for example, of the implications of the fact that mass communications can apparently be effectively used to implant political orientations among the citizens of developing nations. Does it bode ill for democracy that conscious manipulation is succeeding? Or does it suggest the possibility that relatively isolated and parochial peoples can learn the norms and skills necessary to participate in a modern, perhaps democratic, state? The number of relevant puzzles like this one is very large. And our ability to arrive at conclusive answers to them is still very limited. However, their great importance ought to encourage us to try to build up that ability.

The task, of course, is prodigious. And looking back on the general knowledge we do possess, which is partial, qualified, and subject to all sorts of reservations, we may come away somewhat discouraged. We need some guidance. What do we do with what we have, and where do we go from here? If we are determined to push on—and there is no way to avoid the fact that there are important questions to be answered despite the difficulty of dealing with them—we may well find some aid and comfort in *empirical theory*, the major concern of the remainder of this book.

Notes

1. William A. Gamson, *Power and Discontent* (Homewood, Ill.: Dorsey Press, 1968), Chapter 1.
2. Donald T. Campbell, "Reforms as Experiments," *Urban Affairs Quarterly*, Vol. 7 (December 1971), 133-136.
3. V. O. Key, *The Responsible Electorate* (Cambridge, Mass.: Belknap Press, 1966).
4. Kenneth Langton and M. Kent Jennings, "Political Socialization and the High-School Civics Curriculum in the United States," *American Political Science Review*, Vol. 62 (September 1968).
5. *Ibid.*, 858.
6. James P. Levine, "Constitutional Law and Obscene Literature: An Investigation of Bookseller Censorship Practices," in Theodore L. Becker (ed.), *The Impact of Supreme Court Decisions* (New York: Oxford University Press, 1969), pp. 129-148.
7. For a discussion of basic findings in this area, see William H. Flanigan, *Political Behavior of the American Electorate* (Boston: Allyn & Bacon, 1972), Chapter 2.
8. *Ibid.*
9. Angus Campbell, "A Classification of the Presidential Elections," in Angus Campbell *et al.* (eds.), *Elections and the Political Order* (New York: Wiley, 1966), pp. 63-77.
10. David E. RePass, "Issue Salience and Party Choice," *American Political Science Review*, Vol. 64 (June 1971), 389-400.
11. William J. Crotty, "Party Effort and Its Impact on the Vote," *American Political Science Review*, Vol. 65 (June 1971), 439-450.
12. John C. Blydenburgh, "A Controlled Experiment to Measure the Effects of Personal Contact Campaigning," *Midwest Journal of Political Science*, Vol. 15 (May 1971), 365-381.
13. For these and other examples, see Dan Nimmo, *The Political Persuaders* (Englewood Cliffs, N.J.: Prentice-Hall, 1970), pp. 112-113, 137-149.
14. Philip E. Converse, "Information Flow and the Stability of Partisan Attitudes," in Angus Campbell *et al.* (eds.), *Elections and the Political Order* (New York: Wiley, 1966), pp. 136-157.
15. Harold Mendelsohn and Irving Crespi, *Polls, Television, and the New Politics* (Scranton, Pa.: Chandler, 1970), pp. 17-25.
16. Sam Tuchman and Thomas E. Coffin, "The Influence of Election Night Broadcasts in a Close Election," *Public Opinion Quarterly*, Vol. 35 (Fall 1971), 315-326.
17. Elihu Katz and Jacob J. Feldman, "The Kennedy-Nixon Debates: A Survey of Surveys," in William J. Crotty (ed.), *Public Opinion and Poli-*

Research in Political Behavior

tics (New York: Holt, Rinehart & Winston, 1970), pp. 409-431.

18. Iliya F. Harik, "Opinion Leaders and the Mass Media in Rural Egypt: A Reconsideration of the Two-Step Flow of Communication Hypothesis," *American Political Science Review*, Vol. 65 (September 1971), 731-740.

PART III

Purpose and Direction Among the Behaviorists: The Imposition of Order on Eclecticism

PROLOGUE

Conceptual
Choices

Political behaviorists are interested in many different phenomena and try to explain them in many different ways. Their research covers so many topics and uses so many approaches that the total picture perhaps represents a bit of hodgepodge. It is well to realize this and not shrink from it. Indeed, we should appreciate the opportunity for choice and breadth of interest it provides.

However, we cannot applaud this condition without reservation, for taken to its logical extreme, it suggests diffuseness and confusing disorder. Although it is not logically necessary, most political behaviorists—and especially researchers—respond by trying to organize generalizations in some fashion. The great desirability of this is discussed in Chapter 7. The tool for this process is empirical theory. To be sure, the employment of theory imposes constraints. But in return we enjoy guidance and direction; we are able to comprehend more information, including items that might otherwise appear unrelated.

Despite its constraining effects, theory is a tool in the hands of the behaviorist, not his master. Theory is imposed on empirical data and generalizations. It is the behaviorist who does the imposing, and he enjoys several choices in doing so. That is, he may choose any of several theories to organize the generalizations he finds of interest. Of course, as we shall see, there are some strong criteria that should be employed in making a selection. Simple individual interest or preference will not entirely suffice. But the field of political behaviorism is nonetheless a very open one, and choosing theoretical models can be among the most creative and interesting work a behaviorist does.

The treatment of political behavior offered in Part III differs substantially from that in Part II. Whereas in the previous section it was possible to go into actual behavioral research in some detail to illustrate important points, it will not be possible to do so in this section. Although political behaviorists take many different theoretical perspectives on the study of political behavior, it is still only rarely that a theory is explicitly developed and hypotheses critical to it are tested. Theoretical and empirical research tend to be quite disjoint. Moreover, there is no dominant theoretical perspective in the study of political behavior; thus it would make no sense to go into great detail on one theory, observing all its implications and applications. Instead, we shall try to indicate how theory may be, at some future time, used to guide empirical research.

We have selected four relatively general theoretical perspectives that political behaviorists have attempted to use. Though each is developed systematically, only a brief sketch can be presented here. Hopefully, this will give the reader a sound understanding of the basic concepts and relationships involved. We would like, eventually, to see theoretical and empirical research in our discipline become closely allied. Perhaps these tastes of theory will whet some future political behaviorists' appetites for this union and encourage them to make a contribution toward it.

Chapter 7 discusses the logic of empirical theory, describes its organizing functions, and specifies the criteria for choosing among theories. Chapters 8-11, the order of which is arbitrary, discuss particular theoretical approaches that have been used by political behaviorists to organize empirical data. They provide examples of theories that have been found particularly useful or are capable of being made so. Of course, these examples do not exhaust the list of usable theories, but they are a good sample.

Since choice was involved in the selection of theories to be discussed, and since there is no unfolding order in the arrangements of Chapters 8-11, it is again appropriate that students have some leeway in deciding what to read. Certainly, Chapter 7 should be read in its entirety, and more than one of Chapters 8-11 should also be read from beginning to end. But some chapters can easily be omitted if the reader does not think that they offer good organizational paradigms, if he feels the approach to be uncongenial, or if they are incongruent with the approach and emphases of his instructor. On the other hand, we do feel that, once the contribution of empirical theory is understood, most readers will want to examine several examples of it. A reasonably wide sampling will, after all, help to answer two very important questions: "What can theory do for me?" and "How can I decide which theory will be most helpful in achieving my goals?"

7

Political
Behaviorism
and the
Uses of
Theory

Some Features of Scientific Theory

In some ways, it may seem strange to talk about political behaviorism and political theory in the same context. To many, political behaviorism and political theory represent not only *different* ways of approaching the study of politics, but incompatible ones. According to many political behaviorists, however, theory is indispensable to empirical scholarship. The difference in viewpoints is due to the fact that the word "theory" is used in many different senses, both in political science and elsewhere.

One way in which the word "theory" may be used is to signify something that is not known. For example, we may say "It is my theory that Teddy Kennedy will be elected President in 1976" or "It is my theory that there is life on Jupiter." Unproven general hypotheses, such as "No nation can survive in the modern world by means of force alone," may also be called theories. These usages of the word are not consistent with the usage political behaviorists find helpful, but one feature is common to both: Neither regards theory as factual; it is clearly something other than fact.

We sometimes hear of a dichotomy between theory and practice. In theory, ornithopters (airplanes which are propelled by the flapping of their wings) should fly; in practice, they don't. In theory, courts of law merely interpret statutes; in fact, they make law. Theory in this sense apparently refers to formal or prescribed arrangements that are somehow impracticable or unrealizable. It describes an ideal dichotomous with what can actually be observed. Again, this is not the way in which the behaviorist uses the term "theory." However, the idea of comparing what one actually observes with some sort of standard is, as we shall see, a notion that behaviorists' share.

A frequent conception of theory, and one which is very important for studies of politics, involves the notion of *ethical imperatives*, or *normative judgments*. A theory in this sense tells how things ought to be. According to Thoreau's theory, man should eschew certain features of modern technology and return to a more natural lifestyle. Communist theory asserts the desirability of a working-class revolution. Platonic theory extolls the virtues of a state in which all classes of people know their place and have no ambition to change it. Courses in "ancient" or "modern" political theory are likely to be devoted to the moral prescriptions of prominent thinkers. This kind of theory seeks to provide normative standards that transcend any particular situation. It provides a method of evaluating real-world happenings. In this sense, normative theorists are trying to contribute to *general wisdom*. Of course, behaviorists do not use theory to make moral judgments, but they too seek an increase in general wisdom. It is empirical rather than ethical wisdom, but it is wisdom nonetheless.

What, then, is empirical theory? Thus far, judging from the features it shares with other kinds of theory, we can say that it is not mere factual description, that it entails standards to which real-world events can be compared, and that it involves a search for general wisdom. Empirical theory, however, has some features that make it very different from other kinds of theory. Let us examine it at closer range.

We have seen that it is possible to discover many partially true generalizations about the behavior of people or collectivities in politics

224

and that there is a fair amount of knowledge about various causes of political actions and events. For example, political scientists can demonstrate that the level of literacy in nations is related to the degree of democratic political practice they experience, or that certain political norms of children are explained by parental views. The same can be said, of course, of all sciences. Chemists have accumulated a great series of chemical equations that are nothing more than generalizations about certain kinds of chemical reactions. They are logically equivalent to the generalizations of political science. $Na + Cl \rightarrow NaCl$ is a generalization about the formation of salt. It refers to all situations in which salt is formed, not just a single instance in a particular test tube in a particular laboratory. There are thousands of other chemical equations, each expressing a small bit of the general, explanatory knowledge of that discipline.

However, as anyone who has taken a good chemistry course knows, there is more to learning the discipline than committing to memory long lists of chemical equations, prodigious as that feat would be. Unfortunately, many beginning chemistry students approach the subject in just this way. As a result, they soon come to regard it as very taxing and dull. Treating the science of chemistry as nothing more than a collection of generalizations has other liabilities as well. For one thing, it leaves one with no guidelines for solving new problems. Suppose a chemist of this persuasion wishes to develop a new process for removing certain industrial pollutants, say oils, from the water of streams or lakes. How can he proceed, having at his disposal only a huge list of valid chemical equations? He knows the chemical composition of the oils and the chemical composition of water and that the two do not react together chemically. So he begins the long, long task of looking up all the known equations involving these elements. Let us imagine that none of these equations have a solution that separates the oils from the water. The only course of action remaining is to discover a new chemical equation that does have such a solution—perhaps one in which the components of the oil combine with a new chemical to form a removable precipitate. But how can he make such a discovery? About the only method open to him is trial and error. He can attempt one process after another in the hope of chancing upon a practical solution. This, of course, may be terribly time-consuming and inefficient. He may spend a fortune and a lifetime on this work and still not happen on a solution. Occasionally research does proceed in approximately this way. There are strictly fortuitous discoveries in science. For example, some sprays for the treatment of plant diseases were developed after desperate researchers decided to throw everything they had together and see what happened. However, such discoveries are relatively rare and tend to have relatively unimportant applications.

Of course, even the crudest scientific investigation does not consist entirely of trial and error. In point of fact, no one who was trying to remove oils from water would proceed by adding, say, milk to the mixture. Nor would he introduce gasoline or any of a great number of "unlikely" substances. Of course, eliminating "unlikely" solutions makes the process of discovery considerably more efficient and less like looking for a needle in a haystack. But how is it that certain options can be eliminated as unlikely? What directs us away from these unlikely alternatives?

The answer lies in conceptualization. Somehow, we organize the knowledge we possess. That is, we organize the generalizations we know to be true. In the case of chemistry, we think in terms of *categories* of chemicals rather than of individual substances as such. We thus think in terms of *categories* of chemical reactions and *categories* of chemical equations. We may suspect, for example, that the category of chemical reactions which produce precipitates is particularly likely to permit the separation of oil and water, since other kinds of reactions have not been satisfactory in this regard. The known reactions involving the components of milk and the organic substances in oils do not appear to produce separable precipitates. Thus, there is little ground for expecting any positive results if milk is mixed in. Similarly, what we know about the components of gasoline and oils does not reveal any evidence of the formation of such precipitates.

In a way, we are generalizing about generalizations. We are saying that reactions that produce precipitates are somehow similar. We are saying that reactions which involve the components of milk are somehow similar. We are saying that the various reactions involving gasoline are similar. And, we are saying that the reactions involving milk and the reactions involving gasoline are, for our present purposes, similar to each other. In other words, we are making *general statements that relate generalizations*. In doing this, we are really forming a view of what the chemical world is like and then eliminating the reactions that are unlikely in terms of that view. This is a very low level of empirical theorizing. Empirical theory is indeed a series of statements that relate generalizations according to some view or concept or standard of what the world is like. In this case, we have a view of the chemical world which asserts that substances can be removed from solutions by a process called precipitation and that certain components participate in certain kinds of reactions. This has led us to general statements about generalizations, the generalizations being chemical equations about the components of milk, gasoline, oils, and other substances.

In a sense, the relation between theory and generalization is like that between generalizations and individual facts. Generalizations relate facts and theories relate generalizations. However, the two linkages are different. We have seen in previous chapters that the relationship between specific facts and generalizations is empirical. A generalization is established by a body of evidence; it is induced from a body of specific facts. There is a very tight link between generalizations and specific observations. The generalization that silver dissolves in nitric acid is based on the observation of uncounted instances of silver being dissolved in this way. The generalization that a mental state of alienation is associated with political withdrawal is based on many observations of individuals who displayed both alienation and withdrawal. If the observations had been different, the generalization would not have been made.

Theory, however, is not merely a supergeneralization, dependent for its validity solely on the empirical truth of the generalizations it subsumes. The link between theory and the generalizations it relates is *conceptual.* Theory relates generalizations by appealing to some similarity that makes them appear to be special cases of a broader principle. That similarity and that broader principle, however, are not empirical or factual. They do not emerge from facts, but are conceived in the mind of the theorist. The theorist *imputes* similarities which occur as concepts in his imagination. Theories are thus creatures of the mind; they need not be observable at all. They are, in a sense, artificial, or "made up."

Let us consider some further examples from the science of chemistry. All the various chemical equations (generalizations) look similar if we posit that elements have such properties as atomic weight, atomic number, and valence. That is, they look similar if we invoke a certain principle embodied in the periodic table of elements and the rules of chemical reaction it implies. All the equations supposedly follow certain "rules" implied by their atomic weight, atomic number, and valence. For example, because of the posited character of the electron shells of their atoms, hydrogen has a valence of +1 while oxygen has a valence of −2. Thus, according to the rules, a compound of the two elements must involve two hydrogen atoms for every one oxygen atom. This, as we know, turns out to be the case. These principles and rules, these similarities, of chemical reactions are very well known. Their logic is impressive, and they clearly constitute the first key to understanding chemistry. They are, of course, part of the *atomic theory of matter*.

Despite its fame, logic, and clear relevance to science, this theory, like all others, is *conceptual* rather than factual. Valence is an invention of the human mind, as is atomic weight, atomic number, and the idea of an electron shell. No one has ever seen an element's valence, and atomic number is clearly something that chemists have assigned to elements rather than an observable property they possess. To be sure, chemical reactions take place in accordance with the "rules" of atomic theory; but these events would take place whether the theory had been thought of or not. All sorts of chemical reactions were occurring in nature long before the atomic theory of matter was articulated—or for that matter long before there were men to articulate it. Moreover, though we can observe phenomena that may be interpreted in terms of a theory, the concept and elements of the theory itself may be unobservable. No physicist can observe *gravity*, and no social scientist can observe a role; but we can see objects falling or humans performing certain acts, and these phenomena make sense if we use the theoretical notions of gravity or role to explain them.

An implication of this nonobservable property of theories is that they can never be shown to be true or false in the sense that a generalization can. Since they are conceptual, data cannot "prove" or "disprove" them. The validity of a theory does not rest in its empirical truth.

On what, then, does the validity of a theory depend? In order to answer this question, we must consider the purposes of empirical theory. These purposes have already been touched upon. Early in this chapter we argued that a person who tried to comprehend the science of chemistry by arbitrarily committing to memory thousands of chemical generalizations would find himself in great difficulties. He would have severe problems in organizing and comprehending the existing body of chemical knowledge, and he would have few guidelines for making new discoveries. In order to get around these problems, we argued, some conceptualization, or theorizing, at least of a primitive sort, was necessary.

Theory, whether primitive or sophisticated, is used *to organize or account for what is already known* and *to stimulate the discovery of new knowledge* (i.e., new generalizations). Thus, in the physical sciences, the atomic theory of matter is used not because it is true (in fact, it is inappropriate to discuss theories in terms of their truth or falsity), but because it makes sense out of the knowledge accumulated thus far and because it leads researchers to new discoveries. Almost all physical knowledge is consistent with this theory, and we can be sure that researchers seeking to solve the problem of energy through nuclear fusion do not proceed on a hit-or-miss basis. They may reason that if the "rules" of the atomic theory are true then fusion should take place when hydrogen is exposed to certain conditions. New hypotheses are deduced from existing rules.

Of course, since theories are conceptual, more than one theory can be employed in dealing with given scientific phenomena. Different kinds of similarities may be imputed to generalizations, or different principles may be invoked. For example, for many years there was some controversy over rival theories of light. Some physicists argued that light should be considered a type of energy that traveled in waves, whereas others felt that light should be regarded as moving particles called *quanta*. How should the physicist think of light, as waves or as quanta? The issue is not whether light *actually* moves as waves or as quanta. Rather, it is which of these two *conceptions* best comprehends what we know about light and which does the best job of suggesting new generalizations about light. A scientist chooses the theory that works the best for his purposes according to the criteria above.

In general, the more that is known in a scientific field the smaller the number of viable theories is. The "hard" or natural sciences tend to have few or even one; the social sciences, especially political science, tend to have several. Particularly in the social sciences, one may have directly competing theories, and there may not be enough knowledge available to make an intelligent choice between them. For example, someone interested in how children acquire political beliefs may wonder whether to base his approach on psychoanalytic theory or learning theory. Psychoanalytic theory involves the notion of conflict between instinctual, sensual, or sexual urges on the one hand and socially imposed constraints on the other; learning theory depends on the concept of reinforcement, the idea that behavior which is rewarded by significant others is repeated. Both theories seem, on the surface, relevant to childhood. Should children's high regard for political figures be regarded as resulting from a psychoanalytic conflict or from some kind of learning experience? Either conception may help the investigator. There is usually no definitive basis for choice.

It is also typical of the less well-developed sciences to have several partial theories, each capable of comprehending a limited set of generalizations in a given area. In effect, several theories may exist side by side. For example, *role theory*, involving the notion that people behave according to expectations about how people in their position in life should behave, seems to have found some favor among those studying behavior of legislators. However, it has rarely been invoked to explain the behavior of the mass of citizens. Voting, being patriotic, rioting, demonstrating, and other mass behaviors seem more explicable in terms of some sort of communications theory in which behavior is conceived of as a response to the receipt of information. Of course, a more useful theory would not be so parochial. It might apply to all political behavior. And indeed a more general theory that relates the generalizations about both legislative and mass behavior may well be developed. But until such time as there is enough knowledge to do this kind of thing, the less developed sciences will have to be content with partial theories.

It is fairly easy to understand how theories, by providing a standard set of rules, can help to organize the accumulated knowledge of a science. All chemical reactions fit the atomic theory of matter as it is presently articulated. The idea of being able to figure out new generalizations that fit existing rules is also, at least on the surface, fairly easy to understand. However, exactly how this fit is determined is not always clear. Ideally, the rule of correspondence is one of logical deduction. That is, if the known generalizations in a field are logically deducible from the principles of a theory, it does a fine job of organizing existing knowledge. In the case of the atomic theory of matter, one can deduce from looking at the periodic table that hydrogen and oxygen will normally combine in a ratio of two to one to form a compound. Given the valences ascribed to these elements, no other configuration can be expected. In an analogous fashion, it should be possible by starting with what we know of atomic theory to deduce other, possibly new chemical reactions that have perhaps not yet been observed. Given the rules, only certain reactions are possible. It is up to the research chemist to determine whether the reactions the theory predicts in fact occur in the real world.

An interesting example of how theory "spills over" into yet unexplored areas involves the discovery of the more distant planets. The observation of the planets nearer to the earth has been going on for centuries. Some are even visible to the naked eye. In an attempt to understand the behavior of these heavenly bodies, scientists over the years evolved a theory of planetary motion. Deducible from the theory were generalizations about how planets should behave. However, astronomers in the early twentieth century found that the outermost known planets, most particularly Neptune, were exhibiting behavior that was not in accord with these generalizations. Assuming that measurement of the planets' behavior was not in error, this situation could mean one of two things: either the theory was of limited value because it suggested generalizations that were not true, or there were additional, unknown planets beyond Neptune responsible for the deviant behavior of that planet. In effect, the theory of planetary motion foretold the existence of planets that no one had ever seen. Indeed, scientists could predict quite precisely the location and size of these planets. Guided by theory, they knew exactly where in the night sky to look for the farther planets, and they found them. Without the guidance of the theory of planetary motion, these planets would not have been discovered. Finding these bodies essentially by accident would have been absolutely impossible, given their great distance from the earth and the great expanse of the heavens to be examined. Even with the guidance provided by the theory, it took painstaking celestial observation to find them. The role of theory in discovery is absolutely unmistakable in this case.

Unfortunately, all theories are not so unambiguous in the way they relate to generalizations. Especially in the social sciences—where the fund of accumulated knowledge is vastly less than in either chemistry or astronomy—logical deduction is simply impossible. Sometimes the principles of a theory or the linkages to generalizations seem a bit vague.

Sometimes all that can be said is that the principles are sensible and that through the employment of some reasonable procedure they lead to generalizations. Often, the end result seems somewhat fraudulent and contrived. Often, there is a certain sloppiness in social science theories that is somewhat unsatisfying. However, despite this vagueness, despite the fact that the mental operations involved in relating a theory to a generalization may seem a bit obscure to some observers, the theory may still do its job; if it fulfills the two functions described above, its elegance, or lack of elegance, doesn't really matter too much.

Thus we can see that empirical theory such as the student of political behavior would use is a strange animal indeed. Like normative or value-oriented theory, it is a device employed in seeking general wisdom; indeed it is crucial in the seeking of generalizations. Like the theory that is viewed as dichotomous with reality, empirical theory provides standards for judging reality; it makes predictions about the real world. Like all theory, it is a creature of the mind. But despite these and other strange characteristics, it is a very useful tool to the empirical scientist, natural or social. How limited we would be without it.

Some Objects of Empirical Political Science Theory

It should be obvious that there can be theories about anything that behaves, from atomic particles, through rocks, clouds, bugs, trees, and human beings, to planets and other heavenly bodies. Since theories are conceptual, their bases are limited only by the scope of human imagination. For empirical political science, the ultimate object of course is the behavior of the human being or collectivities of human beings. However, human behavior is also the ultimate object of several other social sciences—sociology, psychology, anthropology, and economics, to mention just a few. Logically, there should be just one theory of human behavior, encompassing the concerns not only of political science but of all other social sciences as well. Unfortunately, such a monumental achievement appears to be beyond the capability of social scientists in the foreseeable future. What an incredible number of generalizations would be involved!

Though a universal behavioral theory is still clearly impossible, the

232

ultimate theoretical similarity of the social sciences is revealed by the fact that they often share theoretical perspectives. In fact, political science really has little theory that is peculiar to itself. The several theories that are discussed in Chapters 8-11 do indeed have applications in political science, but they have applications—usually dating from an earlier period—in other sciences as well. Political scientists are great theoretical borrowers.

Theories exist at several levels of generality. That is, they may comprehend a few very similar generalizations about the same phenomena, some larger number, or conceivably, but probably not actually, all the generalizations about everything in the world. Most theories are in fact of relatively limited scope. Indeed, there are few scholarly disciplines characterized by a theory that attempts to account for all empirical generalizations or to explain everything of interest within the discipline. We have already seen how political science may be characterized by different theories about the same phenomenon. Distinct substantive areas may have theories that apply to a particular type of behavior but to little else, such as the theories of legislative and mass behavior cited.

This kind of fragmentation of theoretical application can perhaps be seen by examining Figure 7-1. This is merely a chart that very roughly and very partially represents the organization of empirical political science. Some topics fit logically under general areas of study, which are in turn classified under still broader areas of investigation. Though this diagram is illustrative only—and leaves out entirely some very important areas of political science—its logic should be quite clear. A person may be interested in judicial behavior and have very little interest in legislatures. Another may find legislators fascinating but care nothing about judges. Still a third may have a more general interest in political elites and be curious about both judges and legislators as well as many other kinds of individuals. The diagram also illustrates an important distinction we have noted before, between empirical studies that focus on individuals and those that focus on collectivities of individuals. Though it is possible to confine one's interests to one or the other of these broad areas, there are many ways in which interesting problems creep over the "boundary" between them. Of course, all the possible bridges from one area to another are not shown in our diagram. Nor does the diagram depict all the possible levels of study. The six levels

233

FIGURE 7–1

Levels of Study in Some Areas of Political Behavior

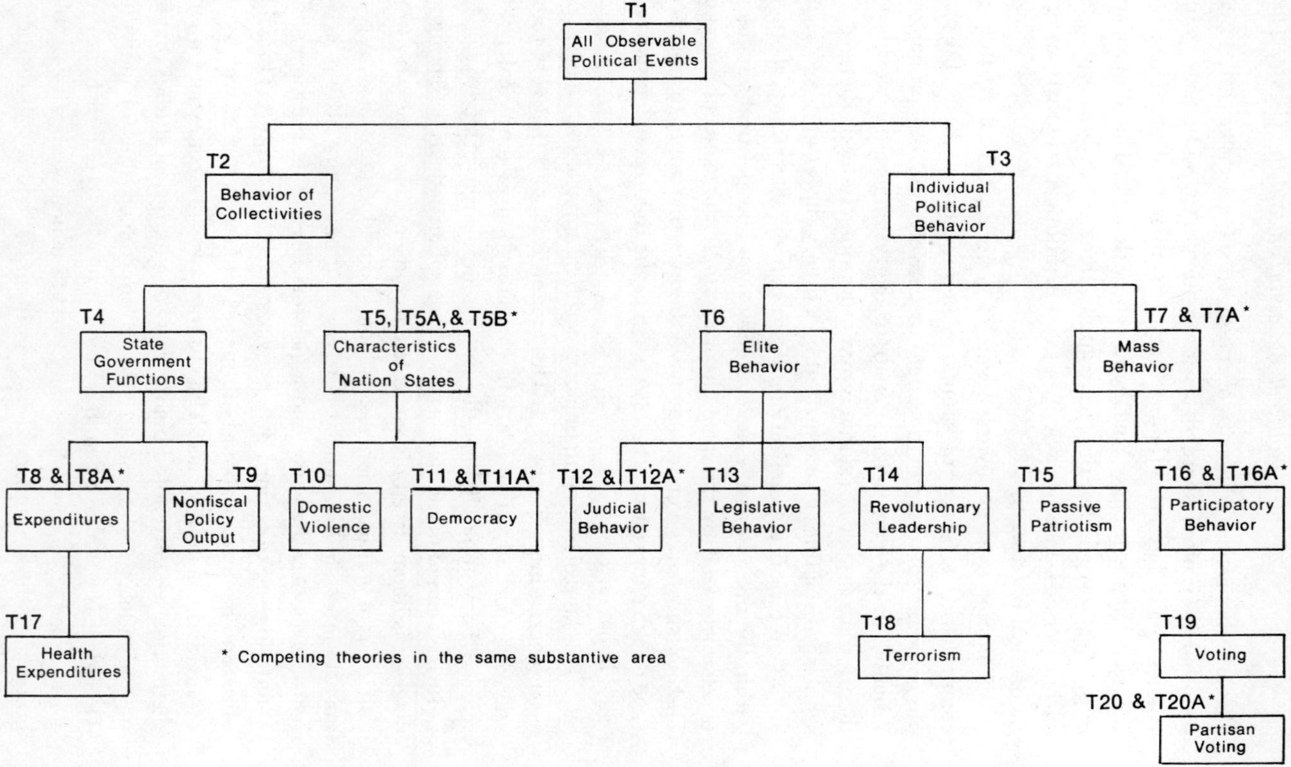

* Competing theories in the same substantive area

shown should not be taken to mean that political behavior has only six levels of generality. Nor should it be inferred that any two areas of study appearing on the same level in the figure are in fact identical in quality or degree of generality. Figure 7-1 is symbolic only. Nonetheless, it is probably not an unfair representation of the kind and level of activity behaviorists study.

Research in any of the substantive areas indicated by boxes may be greatly aided by the application of theory. Numbers prefixed by a "T" represent possible theories in each substantive area; T15, for example, refers to a possible theory of patriotism. There are many opportunities for competing theories such as we have previously discussed. And, as we can easily see, theories can refer to any of the several levels of generality that characterize the empirical study of political behavior. In Figure 7-1, theories T20 and T20A are the least general. That is, relative to the theories above them, they are concerned with the narrowest subject area and therefore comprehend the fewest generalizations. Theories T17, T18, and T19 would be slightly more general. Theory T19 would presumably account for the same generalizations as T20 and T20A, plus many more from substantive areas not shown in the diagram.

Of course, it may be that the only relationship between theories T20 and T20A on the one hand and theory T19 on the other is that the latter is more general than the former. Their basic characters may be quite different and the theories may stand alone on their merits. Sometimes, however, a more general theory, such as T19, *includes* the features of less general theories such as T20 or T20A. In this case, the connection between the theories on different levels is quite explicit and logical. The less general theories are comprehended by, or become part of, the more general ones.

Of course, the more general a theory is, the more potentially useful it is and the more potential it has for increasing our knowledge. This is true regardless of whether it is logically connected to broader and narrower theories or whether it stands alone. Thus, everything else being equal, one should try to apply one's theories as broadly as possible. But of course everything else is not equal. As we have already said, superwide, multidisciplinary theories comprehending vast numbers of generalizations are presently impossible. Not enough knowledge has accumulated to permit them. Even within the discipline of political

235

science, it is often very difficult to formulate theories applicable at what are represented as the higher levels of the diagram. Attempts at high levels of generality sometimes result in theories that are so vague, and so sloppy, that they cannot be related to the observable world in any way. Accordingly, the most useful theoretical effort is often at lower levels of generality. It generally makes more sense to work with theories of democracy in nations than theories of the behavior of all political collectivities in all circumstances, just as it generally makes more sense to seek theories of voting than theories that account for all forms of mass political behavior. We find in the literature of political science that theories often have a very specific focus. At this stage in the development of the discipline, this is altogether sensible. Perhaps at later times such theories will be supplemented by or subsumed under broader ones.

We should point out, in this regard, that people sometimes attempt to find relatively specific applications of broad theories. For example, Marxism is a comprehensive theory of human behavior. It is even broader than the T1-type theory in Figure 7-1. According to Marx, all social behavior and institutions are a function of the ownership of the means of production in a society. Ownership arrangements create classes, and these classes have interests. All behavior can be interpreted in terms of these interests. Many scholars have attempted to apply these principles to fairly narrowly defined areas, including such unlikely ones as sex and the composition of music. Of course, since the conflicts between classes that Marx posits often lead to revolution or less violent attempts to control public policy, there are many political applications of this theory whose validity may be the focus of research. It is possible, for example, to posit that American judges must be agents of the dominant, exploiting class since all government is alleged to be but an instrument of that class. Their decisions, one might deduce, must be exploitative of the working class for the benefit of the dominant class, which owns the means of production. No doubt specific hypotheses could be formulated that would indicate exactly what an exploitative decision would be like. Research could be done on whether the actual pattern of judicial decisions conformed to that deduced from Marxist theory. The end product would be a theoretical effort of rather limited scope, focused on American judges and equivalent in generality to T12 or T12A in Figure 7-1. However, it would test an application of a much broader theory which, if it were found to be valid, would fit into that larger theory.

236

As a practical matter, then, even when one works with very broad theories, the phenomena under consideration are often very circumscribed indeed. In the chapters that follow, the discussion will center on broader types of theory that perhaps have more specific applications in many areas of political science and also in the other social sciences. Though these theories may be applicable to many phenomena in many fields, they are probably most useful when they are applied to a concise problem area.

A Theoretical Parable

Although the idea of empirical theory is relatively complex, our presentation of it was necessarily brief and somewhat abstract. Hopefully the discussion in the following chapters will convert the reader's understanding of this abstract construct into an appreciation of the problems and possibilities of empirical political research. However, before beginning a detailed review of the features of politically relevant theories, let us examine a hypothetical (and somewhat contrived), but still instructive, example of theoretical reasoning and theoretically informed research involving most of the points that have been made so far in this chapter. It is not a political example; it is designed to be more clear-cut than political examples could be.

Let us imagine the case of the commander of a British military garrison stationed at some remote tropical outpost in the 1870s. We choose this time period because important knowledge in many fields was then lacking; we in the 1970s possess a great deal of data that was not available a century ago, and yet we can appreciate the difficulties that the absence of knowledge created. Our commander is responsible, let us imagine, for maintaining military patrols throughout his area in order to secure the transportation and communications networks and generally facilitate the colonial administration. To accomplish this, he has, let us say, 200 troops at his command. As it turns out, his patrol responsibilities stretch his human and material resources nearly to the breaking point. The problems of tropical operations are manifold. The single most taxing difficulty is the fever. A certain number of troops are always contracting this debilitating disease. Those who catch it are bedridden or must be sent home. There are even some fatalities, and replacements are few and far between. Our commander correctly perceives that if the fever could be controlled or even substantially reduced, the efficiency of his garrison would increase dramatically. However, doctors know nothing about how to control the fever, merely that it strikes certain people.

Being of a scientific bent, our commander decides to make a study of the fever, not only to determine whether his military effectiveness can be improved but to satisfy his own curiosity. He begins to examine the personnel records of the garrison. He begins with a number of facts: Jones contracted fever on June 5, Smith contracted fever on July 12, and so on. Of course, as we learned in Chapter 2, specific facts are often not terribly useful scientifically. To be sure, Jones himself found the first specific fact reported above very relevant, but without further elaboration and juxtaposition with other facts it is not going to help the commander in his search for the causes of, and a preventative for, the fever. What he needs are generalizations. He must find a cause-and-effect relationship. Obviously, the fever is the effect of something. It is a dependent variable; and if he can find an explanatory relationship with another, independent variable (that is, isolate a cause), he may be able to do something about it.

The search for generalizations involving fever entails searching for similarities in each of the cases of fever among the soldiers—for something that is true about all these cases. Perhaps Jones, Green, and the others all experienced the same cause. The commander may painstakingly study case records. But he has no idea what to look for, since so little is known about the fever and there is no theory about it. Thus, if he does hit upon a causative agent, it will be essentially by accident. Perhaps he samples the records of the fever victims for the last ten years, selecting 10% for extensive scrutiny. In his random search, he notices that most of the fever victims were on night patrol shortly before becoming ill. He wonders if there is some connection. He then surveys *all* the soldiers' records for only two items of information: whether they contracted the fever and whether they were assigned to night patrol. His data for any given month look something like the table on page 239. Similar data emerge for each month, and the commander is overjoyed. He has discovered a generalization about the fever. Moreover, the independent variable in the generalization—day or night patrol—is subject to his control. He cancels the night patrols and, as he expects,

	NIGHT PATROL ASSIGNMENT	DAY PATROL ASSIGNMENT
Contracts fever	17%	2%
Does not contract fever	83	98
Total	100%	100%

the incidence of fever drops dramatically. He writes an enthusiastic report to his superiors telling of his success in lowering the incidence of fever, fully expecting to be promoted. His superiors, who are totally lacking in scientific curiosity, instead of promoting him, reprimand him for endangering the security of the area by cancelling night patrols and order them resumed at once. Crestfallen, the commander does as he is told and watches the incidence of fever climb back to previous levels.

However, our commander is a true scientist; his success at finding one generalization only whets his appetite for more discoveries. Unfortunately, no more accidental discoveries are forthcoming. So, although he does not recognize it by this name, he begins to search for a theory of the fever. He does this by reading the journals of the pioneering medical researchers of the day. One articulates what may be called the "foul nocturnal humor" theory of disease. This theory conceives of disease as a response to mysterious vapors that float on damp, night air. It reasons that man is by nature a daytime animal and is somewhat out of his natural element if he is about at night; the humors of the night air are inconsistent with the normal functioning of the human body. Our commander is impressed with this theory. It can be used to predict that soldiers who go out on night patrol are more likely to become ill than those who do not, precisely what is occurring. The commander further reflects that in his experience the onset of most other disease occurs at night. People rarely suffer the initial attack of a disease during the day; it usually occurs during sleep. Thus, the humor theory successfully relates at least two generalizations he knows to be true. It appears to be consistent with his existing knowledge. (Notice that it performs these functions despite the fact that it is rather imprecise, more than a little vague, and totally unobservable.)

The commander finds that the theory not only relates existing generalizations about disease, but guides him toward new and possibly helpful conclusions. In a moment of creative genius, he deduces that if

239

humors are mysterious nocturnal substances that thrive on dampness, then *fire*, which both sheds light and evaporates dampness, ought to drive these noxious agents away. The theory has now led him to a new generalization (still really a hypothesis, since it is completely untested) about an inverse relationship between the presence of fire and contraction of the fever at night. Greatly excited, he orders all his night patrols to build roaring fires at their camps, a practice not previously followed because of the heat.

Imagine his gratification when he discovers that the fires do indeed reduce the incidence of fever once again. He writes another report to his superiors, detailing his accomplishments. This time he is promoted. Moreover, he publishes an article in the *Colonial Commanders' Quarterly* in which he not only urges the adoption of the new fire technique in tropical areas, but also praises the foul nocturnal humor theory very highly. It has done an excellent job, and given what was known at the time, was fully deserving of the praise that it received. Many persons who might otherwise have been fever victims owe their health if not their lives to it.

However, our poor commander's troubles are not over, despite the fact that he has deduced a valid and helpful generalization from the humor theory. Unfortunately, the damp forest in the area of his garrison produces very little usable firewood. What there is is soon burned up, and with no more fires the incidence of fever among the night patrols again rises. Disappointed for both humanitarian and professional reasons, our commander is scientifically undaunted. He tries to deduce another valid, usable generalization from the humor theory, but to no avail. Deducing that protection of all parts of the body from the humors will reduce the incidence of fever, he orders some night patrol troops to swathe themselves from head to toe in heavy clothes. This indeed reduces the incidence of fever (our commander had deduced another true generalization from the humor theory), but it is impractical, as the clothes are terribly uncomfortable and interfere with the troops' ability to work.

This discouraging set of circumstances causes the commander to have doubts about the humor theory he once praised so highly. These doubts, it should be noted, are not based on a judgment that the theory is no longer true, but rather on the fact that it is no longer performing one of the two important functions of empirical theory: It is not generating any new, useful hypotheses. His confidence in the theory is further shaken by an encounter with a naval captain. While on vacation in a nearby seaport, our commander calls on the captain to inquire what is being done about the fever in the navy. On the basis of the humor theory, the commander would predict a very high incidence of the fever on ships at sea. Sailors have to man watches around the clock and are therefore out at night, unprotected from humors, as a matter of course. Moreover, the dampness at sea is surely highly congenial to humors —certainly more so than the climate at any place on land. The commander is therefore utterly astonished to find that the incidence of fever among sailors at sea is virtually zero, and this in spite of the fact that no protective measures whatever are taken. The only time sailors get the fever, reports the naval captain, is in port.

The humor theory now seems very suspect. Not only is it failing to suggest new generalizations, but it is not capable of accounting for all the commander's existing knowledge. The information about the incidence of fever among sailors is completely incompatible with the humor theory. Accordingly, the commander begins to read again in hopes of finding a new and more useful theory of disease. Among his new sources are the writings of a man who thinks of disease as a consequence of the actual invasion of the body by tiny foreign organisms. If certain organisms get into the circulatory system, he argues, the process of sustaining their life is so taxing that the host human being shows symptoms of disease. This theory of disease gives the commander renewed hope. He deduces from it that persons who suffer lesions (through which the foreign organisms can enter the circulatory system) are more likely to contract an illness than those who have no wounds. He knows from his own military experience that breaking the skin is terribly dangerous, for infections and other complications can set in. Here, then, is a generalization fully consistent with the new invading-organism theory of disease. Is it possible that the fever also can be explained by the new theory? The commander now has a new hypothesis: Soldiers who have suffered a cut, puncture, or other wound are more likely to contract the fever than those who have not. It may be, he muses, that lack of visibility at night causes men on patrol to stumble about and receive more small wounds through which invading organisms can enter the body. Accordingly, he searches his records on his troops once again to see if those who contracted the fever reported lesions shortly before becoming ill. The

241

data, however, fail to support his hypothesis. Few of the soldiers ill with fever had lesions. Perhaps, thinks the commander, the wounds through which the organisms entered were so slight that they were not reported. If so, there would be no valid data for testing the hypothesis. He continues to ponder the problem. How could fever-causing organisms have entered the soldiers' circulatory systems?

While deep in such thought, the commander is stung by a mosquito which draws a quantity of blood before he swats it. The sight of the small amount of blood on his arm brings a flash of inspiration. The circulatory system can be invaded by mosquitoes! Disease-causing organisms can enter at the same time as the proboscis of the insect. The commander has now deduced a new generalization from the invading-organism theory: Soldiers who experience many mosquito stings are more likely to contract the fever than those who do not experience such stings. Since the stings are in and of themselves minor, they are rarely reported by the victim, and thus such information is rarely part of a soldier's record. This, of course, would make accidental discovery of this generalization extremely unlikely. Only the guidance of theory could bring this obscure and yet tremendously significant hypothesis to light. Our commander now orders protective gear made of fine netting for his troops on night patrol. Such netting, already used by some people for comfort, is easily available. Imagine the gratification he feels when the incidence of fever among net-wearing soldiers goes down dramatically. His knowledge of the fever's real source leads to other preventative techniques also. For example, our commander discovers through reading that mosquitoes breed in stagnant water and orders patrols to avoid camping in the vicinity of swamps or ponds. Again, the incidence of the disease falls.

When these results are reported to his superiors, our commander is again promoted and transferred to a new position at the Institute of Military Medicine. His essay on techniques of mosquito control and in praise of the invading-organism theory of disease is accepted as the lead article in the next issue of *Colonial Commanders' Quarterly*, and because of it he acquires fame, fortune, and rectitude. He lives happily ever after.

The superiority of the invading-organism theory to the humor theory is obvious. But why is it so superior? It is surely not because the invading-organism theory is true while the humor theory is false. Truth or falsity, remember, is not a criterion applicable to theory. There was a time early in our parable when great advances were made using the humor theory; it would hardly be fair, therefore, to denounce it as false. Given the circumstances that initially prevailed, it was a great theory. It was replaced only when it failed to generate new hypotheses and to account for new data in the field. And it was replaced by a theory that could do everything it could plus more. The invading-organism theory is consistent with the same hypotheses as the humor theory. The humor theory predicts contraction of the fever at night; so does the invading-organism theory, because more mosquitoes are abroad at night. The humor theory predicts that fires will inhibit the contraction of fever; so does the invading-organism theory, for smoke irritates mosquitoes and drives them away. But the invading-organism theory does more. It is consistent with the data on sailors, for there are no mosquitoes on the high seas; the humor theory is not consistent with these data. The invading-organism theory suggests new and important generalizations, as we have just seen, which the humor theory cannot. Though at one time these two theories might have been said to be competing, it soon became clear which theory was preferable.

Though this parable is a bit oversimplified and indeed something of a distortion of actual discoveries made in the conquest of malaria, it does represent how useful theories are in scientific research and how they enable us to improve upon the process of essentially accidental discovery. It also indicates how more than one theory may operate in a given substantive area and how one decides whether a theory is a good one. Though the parable might be continued to show how the invading-organism theory is also applicable to other diseases—how it might be subsumed under a broader theory—it is not essential to do so. At this point it is enough to indicate how theoretical reasoning about a narrowly defined substantive area proceeds and aids the researcher in the acquisition of knowledge.

Theory and Political Knowledge: A Recapitulation

Whether one is interested in the fever or in political behavior, the uses of empirical theory are essentially the same. Theory is clearly *not* factual; valence is not a fact, and neither are conceptions of disease as humor-induced or organism-induced. In contrast to facts, which rest on evidence, theory is strictly a creature of the mind. But despite its nonfactual character, its utility in helping us to understand the factual world is great indeed. In a sense, theory provides a standard to which we can compare the real world. Does the real world reflect the atomic theory of matter or does it not? Does what we see about the fever comport with the humor theory or does it not? We have seen what happens both when the real world squares with theory and when it does not.

Theory is most valuable, perhaps, for its contribution to general wisdom. Atomic theory makes us think beyond individual chemistry experiments to the behavior of the physical substance of the world in general. In our parable, the commander saw fit to publish the findings he had unearthed with the aid of theory because they were relevant beyond the particular garrison he happened to command. He had discovered general wisdom. Fires or mosquito control would work anywhere to reduce the incidence of fever.

To be sure, the scientist could proceed without theory. Sometimes, as we have noted, discoveries occur essentially by accident. Trial and error, however, is a grossly inefficient process. Especially in a field like political science, where the objects of research are complex, the guidance of theory should be eagerly sought. We shall now turn to a more detailed examination of some of the notions that may provide that guidance.

8

Attitudes:
Belief
Systems and
Political
Behavior

In this chapter, we will look first at how attitude theory fits into the behaviorist approach to political science and then examine two relatively distinct traditions in the study of attitudes: the view of attitudes as discrete objects and the view of attitudes as a structure. Our next step will be to examine several related theories of attitude change in order to (1) understand attitude as a dynamic concept and (2) show how different theoretical perspectives can be applied to the same phenomena and thereby influence the process of inquiry. We will then return to the role of attitudes in understanding political behavior.

The Behaviorist View

Though some may think it strange for political scientists to study attitudes, others will be immediately aware of attitudes as the most publicly visible object of political behavior studies. The public opinion survey, has, in the last twenty years, become so common that we scarcely think of it as a product of behavioral research. Of course, not all public opinion surveys are run according to the canons of sound scientific practice, nor are they all designed to answer theoretically significant questions.

Typically, what we observe about a public opinion survey is the fact that someone has asked various individuals certain questions such as "Do you think that up to this time the President of the United States is doing his job well?" or "Which of the following candidates in the upcoming election do you think you will vote for?" or "Would a merger of the city and county governments make it easier to solve pressing local problems?" The distribution of individual responses to each of these questions is reported, and we are expected to believe that it is in some sense typical, or representative, of the distribution of responses that would result if the entire population was questioned. The ostensible purpose of surveys or polls is to inform the researchers, or the readers of newspapers, what the general population *thinks* about certain past, present, or possible future states of affairs.

Naturally, the kinds of questions asked about opinions in a survey by a behavioral researcher would be expected to be more theoretically significant than the examples given above. But why is it of value to know what people are thinking—particularly if one is a behavioral researcher? It may well seem ironic (and definitely is to some behavioral scientists) that political behaviorists should invest so much time and effort in studying a mental phenomenon—precisely the kind of thing that the radical behaviorist (especially in psychology) has been trying to get away from. Of course, one could argue that statements of opinion are in fact behavior—verbal behavior; nevertheless, on the surface at least, the purpose of such research is clearly to find out what people think rather than what they do.

In order to understand why scientists who emphasize the study of behavior are so concerned with something as mentalistic as attitude, it is necessary to know something about basic behavioral psychology. Strictly behavioral psychology regards only directly observable variables as theoretically significant. The major classes of variables are observable stimuli that affect an organism and the behavioral responses the organism makes to each stimulus. Behavioral psychologists have

246

found that, in a given situation, certain kinds of stimuli are related to an increased probability of a specific behavioral response; such stimuli are said to be *reinforcing*. Given a situation "similar" to a situation encountered before, an organism is more likely to exhibit a behavior that has been reinforced than one that has not. The behavioral psychologist argues, therefore, that the laws which relate stimuli to behavioral responses determine the pattern of an organism's behavior. In other words, an organism learns behavior patterns through reinforcement. In principle, any behavior of an organism that has the capacity to learn can be completely explained by the specific reinforcing stimuli to which it has been subjected. Thus it is not at all necessary to refer to the mental states (attitudes) of an organism in order to explain behavior.

Most behavioral scientists accept this view; namely, that varying behavior patterns can be accounted for by varying histories of exposure to reinforcing stimuli, or reinforcement; that is, by different patterns of learning. Therefore, to explain why a given individual votes, say, for a Democratic candidate and another votes Republican, we need *only* show how their histories of learning were different. With respect to human beings, however, this is an impossible task. Because we cannot obtain access to a complete learning history for any given human being, many behavioral scientists argue that it is necessary to presume that *because of varying histories of reinforcement* individuals are *predisposed* to respond to specific stimuli in certain ways. Thus the political behaviorist may argue that the individual who votes for the Democratic candidate has a different set of predispositions with respect to the act of voting than the person who votes Republican. Of course it was precisely this point of view that underlay the discussion in Chapter 4.

These predispositions to respond we call *attitudes*. It is important to understand that attitude is a *theoretical construct*; that is, it is a concept which does not refer to any "thing" in the real world—it is not something that can be observed. The behaviorist is not interested in attitudes because there is something *in the mind* to which the notion of attitude corresponds. The concept of attitude is included in behavioral theories because it is *useful* in explaining human behavior. In some ways, the concept of attitude is similar to the concept of potential energy in certain physical theories. An object that is supported at some distance above the earth will, barring the interposition of other objects, fall and

247

strike the earth when the thing that supports it is removed. The force of its fall will depend upon the potential energy associated with its original position, which is a result of the object's history (how it came to be where it is). Thus the concept of potential energy enables us to explain the object's disposition to respond to a particular stimulus—the removal of support. Attitudes serve substantially the same function in behavioral theories. They describe mental dispositions which are due to the history (learning experience) of the individual.

Thus theories of attitudes are attempts to contribute to general theories of behavior by adding a new set of variables useful in explaining the relations between stimuli and behavioral responses. The behaviorist makes two fundamental points about attitude theories. First, if attitude theories are to be considered useful in behavioral inquiry, they must contribute to the understanding—that is, the prediction and explanation—of actual behavior. Second, if we are to explain the behavior of individuals we must have information as to the specific stimuli (the physical environment or *situation*) in which the behavior is elicited, and we must know the predispositions (attitudes) the individual brings to the situation. After we have examined some basic properties of attitudes, we will return to the discussion of the ways in which attitudes affect behavior.

Attitudes as Discrete Objects

One perspective from which we might wish to view attitudes is as objects, as entities that we can separate from other objects for purposes of analysis. If attitudes are viewed as entities, they are also viewed as having characteristic properties, just as other entities, be they rocks, trees, or human beings, have characteristic properties.

Attitudes, as objects, are seen as having an evaluative component and a belief component. The evaluative component consists of an individual's likes or dislikes concerning the subject of his attitude. These evaluations have two fundamental properties—direction and intensity. The *direction* of an attitude may be "positive" (an "approach" response), "negative" (an "avoidance" response), or neutral. An individual's "likes" are said to be expressed by positive attitudes; his dislikes, by negative attitudes. The *intensity* of an attitude has to do with the strength with which the evaluative component is felt by a given individual. Individuals are described as having likes and dislikes that are more or less intense.

The belief component of an attitude has to do with the kind and degree of information that underlies the evaluative component. "Single" attitudes can be very complex and abstract; that is, they may be generalized predispositions which are made up of simpler or more elemental attitudes, each with a different belief component. For example, we may have a general like or dislike of a particular individual that is actually an amalgamation of more particular feelings about various aspects of his person or behavior. We may like his ability to cope with problems that affect his family and the kindly way he disciplines his children, but heartily dislike his political views or the way he speaks of some of our friends. In general, we say that attitudes are more or less *inclusive*. Attitudes toward fathers, mothers, girl and boy friends, or university education are likely to be more inclusive than our attitudes toward brussel sprouts, a stranger in a raincoat standing at a bus stop, or the librarian who checks out books for us.

The kind or quality of informational support for an attitude is also important. This is a function of the extent of the interrelationships within the supporting information for a given complex attitude. For example, an individual's attitude toward labor unions may be a very inclusive one. Yet the information on which this attitude is based may be merely individual bits and pieces of data, such as the total number of a union's members, the length of time it has been in existence, and the names of the officers. Or, it may be based on a complex world view, in which labor unions have a certain function. A Marxist's feelings about labor unions, for example, are likely to be related to the unions' contribution to the evolution of class consciousness, their attitude toward the ownership of the means of production, and their value as a tool in the ever-present conflict between the proletariat and the bourgeoisie.

A third aspect of the belief component of attitudes is their *salience*—their relative importance to a given individual at a given time. For example, a mother's attitudes toward her children, a photographer's attitudes toward his camera equipment, and a miser's attitudes toward spending are highly salient. An automobile racer's attitudes toward horses, an adolescent boy's attitudes toward sewing, and a chemistry major's attitudes toward political science are likely to be less so.

The more traditional view of attitudes is that we can explain differences in attitudes among different individuals by understanding the various properties of attitudes. Furthermore, from a knowledge of the properties of specific attitudes we can make important steps in explaining actual behavior. Thus we find various polling agencies asking such questions as, "How do you feel about the way the President is currently performing his job?" or "Will the President's trip to China influence your decision in the upcoming election?" Both questions may give us information on the direction of the respondent's attitudes, as well as some information on what he feels to be important in evaluating candidates for political office.

There are problems with this perspective on attitudes, however. In the first place we find that, even though individuals tell us that they like a particular candidate, they will not necessarily vote for him at election time. Even though they say they do not support racism, they will behave as racists. Even though they claim to support such basic constitutional liberties as freedom of speech, they are not willing to allow radical organizers to speak at public meetings. In other words, attitudes as specific entities are not particularly well related to actual behavior. Perhaps even more important, many of the attitudes political scientists are interested in demonstrate a surprising degree of inconsistency. For example, if we ask an individual at two-year intervals whether he supports the nationalization of railroads in the United States, it is not at all unlikely that the second time we ask the question he will change his response. Four years later he may change it again. In fact, one researcher has estimated that perhaps as many as 60% of the respondents to such attitude questions behave as if their answers depended upon the flip of a coin rather than upon some basic, learned predisposition.

This is particularly disappointing if it is true that we cannot hope to understand individual behavior without some means of understanding individual predispositions associated with learning histories—that is, attitudes. However, giving up the study of attitudes is not necessarily the answer. Though it is probably true that treating them as discrete phonomena is not theoretically rewarding, modern political psychologists and social psychologists are finding that if they study the interrelations among attitudes—that is, the total structure of attitudes an individual has—they are likely to come closer to the theoretical and practical goals of behavioral prediction and explanation. This is hardly surprising. It is only natural, in the face of inconsistent attitudes and attitudes that are inconsistent with behavior, to ask how important those attitudes are to the individual who holds them. If they are not important, as, for example, a tool and die maker's attitudes toward the United States' coastal fishing policy, we can hardly expect that they will play an important part in determining behavior. It also makes sense, in the face of such inconsistencies, to investigate the other attitudes an individual holds. For example, an individual who believes in freedom of speech in the abstract, but seemingly not in practice, may hold other beliefs that explain his behavior. He may feel, for example, that "anti-American propaganda" or treasonous speech is not the kind of speech the Constitution refers to. If this is the case his behavior is not so inconsistent with his attitudes after all. In the next section we will examine attitudes as related phenomena, as part of a cognitive structure.

Attitudes and Cognitive Structure

Some outstanding behavioral research on attitudes was carried out at the University of California in the late 1940s and early 1950s. The result of this research, which began as an investigation into the nature of antisemitism, particularly that which underlay the treatment of Jews in Germany from 1934 to 1945, were published under the title *The Authoritarian Personality*.[1] In general the researchers hypothesized that antisemitism was not an isolated attitude; rather, it was related to (and perhaps symptomatic of) other attitudes of prejudice and to general personality traits. In other words, antisemites could be classed as a definite personality type characterized by many other attitudes in addition to antisemitism. The methods and results of this investigation have often been challenged by behavioral scientists, but it did stimulate a good deal of research on personality which in large part confirmed many of their basic hypotheses.

The *Authoritarian Personality* researchers generally found that people who demonstrated a definite predisposition to antisemitism were also likely to be "rigid" and "intolerant of ambiguity." Possession of these attitudes was, moreover, characteristic of a certain type of personality, an "authoritarian" personality. An authoritarian individual would tend to agree with the following statements:

The most important thing to teach children is absolute obedience to
    their parents.
There are two kinds of people in the world: the weak and the strong.
No decent man can respect a woman who has had sex relations before
    marriage.
Any good leader should be strict with people under him in order to gain
    their respect.

The most important lesson of this research, and of personality
research in general, is that if we are to completely understand the
predispositions of humans to behave in certain ways, we must be prepared to consider the whole structure of predispositions an individual
has developed. Thus the emphasis in attitude theory has shifted from a
concern for specific attitudes toward an emphasis on understanding the
entire *belief system* of a human being.[2]

The basic components of belief systems are the attitudes we hold
toward all the things we are aware of, all the things that impinge upon
our consciousness. These "things," generally referred to as *idea
elements*, may be persons, mental constructs, or material objects—in
short, they may be any "things" at all. Attitudes toward particular idea
elements may vary from individual to individual. For example, for a
given individual, the idea element "President of the United States" may
have a positive, negative, or neutral "valence." In everyday language,
we would say that the person "likes," "dislikes," or is "neutral" toward
the President. This view of attitudes as having "valence" is really no
different from our earlier approach to the properties of attitudes. To a
behaviorist interested in understanding belief systems, however, the
most important property of an attitude is its "location" in a system of
attitudes; that is, the emphasis is on which attitudes of a given individual
or group of individuals are related. The structure of any particular belief
system depends on the interrelations among attitudes—the *psycho-
logic*[3] of the belief system.

To get an idea of this notion of psycho-logic, consider the following
hypothetical conversation:

Retch: I'm thinking about taking a trip down to Mexico over the Spring
    vacation. Care to come along?
Letch: (Adamantly) Not at all.

R: Why not?

L: Mexico is communist, and I don't want to get involved in that.

R: (Somewhat taken aback) Since when is Mexico communist?

L: Well, a couple of days ago I read that the Mexican government said it
was opposed to our policy in Indo-China.

R: (Still a bit mystified) So?

R: Well our policy there is anticommunist, isn't it?

R: That's what they say.

L: Then Mexico is communist, isn't it?

R: (Shaking his head) Oy.

In a logic class, Letch's argument wouldn't get him very far, but it is
not unreasonable to believe that there are people who would actually
argue in this way. The logic that is implicit in this conversation is a
psycho-logic; that is, it is based on a specific way of organizing beliefs. In
this example, there are roughly three idea elements: "Mexico," "U.S.
policy in Indo-China," and "communism." What is important, for our
purposes, is the way in which Letch interrelates them. For example,
"Mexico" is "dissociatively" related to "U.S. Indo-China policy"; that is,
there is a negative relationship between the two. "U.S. Indo-China
policy" is also dissociatively related to "communism." "Mexico," on the
other hand, is associated with the idea element "communism." There is
a positive relationship between these two elements. None of these
relations is *logically* necessary. An individual who has not read that
Mexico opposes U.S. Indo-China policy may not associate or dissociate
the two idea elements at all. Moreover, he may also believe that Mexico
is not communist, or that U.S. policy in Indo-China is not in any way
connected with communism. The interrelations between these particular idea elements are characteristic of Letch's belief system, but not
necessarily of anyone else's.

Properties of Belief Systems

It should be clear by this point that if we are to understand the
predispositions that affect behavioral responses to a given situation, we
must be able to deal with different systems of beliefs. Belief systems, as
one might well imagine, are likely to be very complex. However, they

253

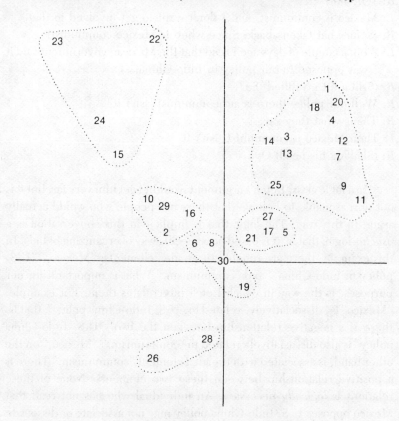

FIGURE 8–1

A Segment of the Belief System of a Christian Activist Group

1. Bible	11. Sex	21. Knowledge
2. Socialism	12. Heaven	22. Hell
3. Life	13. Freedom	23. Race conflict
4. Prayer	14. Revolution	24. Communism
5. Flag	15. Sin	25. Soul
6. Chile	16. Poor people	26. Atheist
7. Peace	17. Nixon	27. Democracy
8. Capitalism	18. God	28. Buddhism
9. Father	19. Republican	29. Vietnam
10. World	20. Jesus Christ	30. Neutral (A relative point of "no evaluation")

appear to have a few basic properties in common, which make at least certain generalizations possible.

The first and most general property of belief systems is the *variety* of the idea elements included. The notion of variety simply refers to the number of idea elements an individual or class of individuals incorporates into its belief system. An individual who has attitudes about a large number of different subjects is said to have more variety in his belief system than an individual who has attitudes on relatively few subjects.

An understanding of the organization of idea elements within a belief system is crucial in attitude studies. This organization is generally described in terms of the amount of *constraint* in the system. In general, the amount of constraint in a given belief system depends upon the interrelationships among idea elements. In a highly constrained system, idea elements tend to be richly interconnected, or to occur in clusters. In a less constrained belief system, idea elements tend to be more isolated from and independent of other elements in the system. An important kind of constraint is *centrality*. Centrality is a relational property of idea elements. An element is highly central to a given belief system if it is closely related to a large number of other elements.

Many of the concepts we have been discussing are very abstract, and it may be useful to see how they are applied to concrete research. The purpose of one study was to examine a small subset of the belief systems of two different groups. One group consisted of five individuals who were members of an activist Christian student organization. The other group consisted of five generally left-wing activist students. Figures 8-1 and 8-2 are simple two-dimensional maps of segments of the belief systems of these two groups. Figure 8-1 describes a segment of the belief system of the Christian activists. Figure 8-2 describes the relations among the same idea elements for the left-wing activists. The distance between two idea elements represents the relative similarity or difference in their meaning. This similarity or difference is assumed to be a function of the beliefs an individual holds concerning these idea elements. Thus the distances between various concepts represent the degree of association between them in the minds of the students in the two groups.

What is important, for our purposes, are the differences between the two belief systems. By virtue of the research design, both have the same number of elements. In terms of the definition of variety given

FIGURE 8–2

A Segment of the Belief System of Left-wing Student Activists

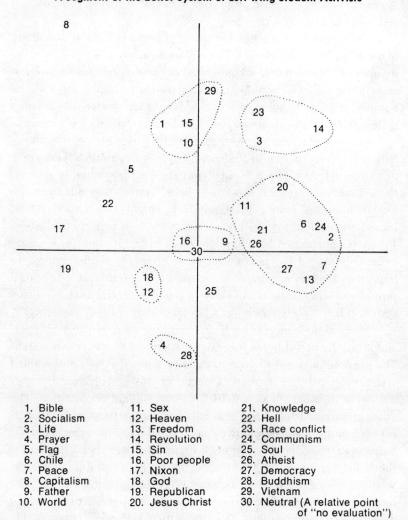

1. Bible	11. Sex	21. Knowledge
2. Socialism	12. Heaven	22. Hell
3. Life	13. Freedom	23. Race conflict
4. Prayer	14. Revolution	24. Communism
5. Flag	15. Sin	25. Soul
6. Chile	16. Poor people	26. Atheist
7. Peace	17. Nixon	27. Democracy
8. Capitalism	18. God	28. Buddhism
9. Father	19. Republican	29. Vietnam
10. World	20. Jesus Christ	30. Neutral (A relative point of "no evaluation")

earlier, then, they are alike. However, the idea of variety entails more than just the scope or range of the idea elements. It is also a measure of the amount of *disorganization* in a belief system. In Figures 8-1 and 8-2, the belief systems are divided into relatively specific clusters encircled by dotted lines. It is theoretically possible to have a belief system with no clusters; that is, a system in which each idea element is essentially independent of all the others. Such a system would be totally disorganized.

We can define the *relative variety* of a system as the amount of disorganization that exists relative to the maximum amount of disorganization possible. One way to measure relative variety is by comparing the number of clusters in the system to the number of elements. It should be relatively obvious from even a cursory examination of Figures 8-1 and 8-2 that the belief system of the Christian activists is less disorganized than that of the left-wing activists. We can obtain a measure of this difference by calculating the relative variety for each group, using the following formula:

$$\text{Relative variety} = \frac{\text{number of clusters}}{\text{number of elements}}$$

Generally speaking, the amount of constraint in a belief system is essentially the complement of the relative variety. If we define a perfectly constrained belief system as one that contains a single tightly knit cluster and represent perfect constraint by unity (i.e., 1.0), we can obtain a rough measure of the constraint in a belief system by the following formula:

$$\text{Constraint} = 1.0 - \text{relative variety}$$

Of course, there are obvious inadequacies in the procedures described here. For example, in Figure 8-1, the idea elements "Father" and "Sex" are in the same cluster as "Bible," "Jesus Christ," "God," and "Prayer." To the researcher, this "made sense"; but there are no objective criteria for making such a choice. It is easy to see that the way idea elements are grouped affects our measures of variety and constraint. However, for our purposes here, which are illustrative, the precise configuration of idea elements is not important. We are not interested in learning how to describe belief systems quantitatively or in applying the simple formulas presented. We need only, at this point, to get some notion of the meaning of the concepts of variety and constraint as they apply to the analysis of belief systems.

The idea of centrality is not obviously illustrated by this example. However, it is possible to comment on the relative centrality of certain idea elements on the basis of the theory underlying this research. It was hypothesized that the idea elements directly related to Christian theology, such as "God," "Jesus Christ," "Bible," "Heaven," and "Soul," would be central to the belief system of the Christian activist group. This seems to be borne out by Figure 8-1. The largest single cluster of beliefs is clearly oriented around these idea elements. Similarly, it was hypothesized that left-wing political beliefs would be central to the belief system of the left-wing activists. The validity of this hypothesis is not nearly so clear, but the location of the concepts "Socialism" and "Communism" does appear to conform to the research expectations.

The organization of beliefs has been of considerable interest to political scientists in recent years.[4] A belief system that is characteristic of a particular group of people is, in a sense, an ideology. An *ideology* is, generally speaking, a set of central beliefs that allows the individual to interrelate and find meaning in a wide range of events. Thus the Marxist ideology is a set of beliefs that allows the individual to understand current events in terms of the general development of history. In the example above, we can easily observe at least the kernel of an ideology, especially among the individuals represented in Figure 8-1. We have already noted the close association of some of the major elements of Christian theology in one of the clusters. But notice also the cluster containing "Race conflict," "Hell," "Communism," and "Sin." How can we account for the clustering of these idea elements? Note especially the difference in the location of these idea elements in the belief system of the left-wing activists (that is, their position with respect to other elements). Is there an "ideological" reason for the proximity of the elements "Bible," "Sin," "World," and "Vietnam"?

These considerations lead us directly to the idea of *political ideologies*. Popular accounts of mass political behavior often refer to the supposedly prevailing political ideologies to explain events such as the outcome of elections or student protests. There have been many chal-

258

lenges to this way of explaining the behavior of individuals, or this way of characterizing "political movements."[5] For example, support for George Wallace as a Presidential candidate has often been explained by the general conservatism and, some would say, the related racism of his followers. The election of Nixon in 1968 has been explained as the result of a "shift to the right" in the American electorate. Such explanations presume a certain amount of ideological organization on the part of individuals that might be characterized as a *political belief system.* Some students of political behavior have argued that, for all intents and purposes, political belief systems do not seem to exist within the mass public. In other words, the belief system of the average individual is not necessarily characterized by a relatively constrained organization of political idea elements.[6] The example given above is certainly not conclusive on this point, but consider the location of the "political" idea elements in the two belief systems represented. Do they appear to form a highly constrained independent subsystem of beliefs? Are they interspersed within various belief clusters? Or do they appear to cluster around the "neutral" reference point, indicating a lack of any strong feelings?

Other investigators appear to reject the notion of a clear difference in the degree of constraint in the belief systems of elites and mass publics.[7] They find only inconsequential differences that could have little effect on behavior and argue that what is important is the actual nature of the constraint for a given group or individual. For example, Luttbeg found that patterns of constraint (that is, which specific idea elements actually go together) do indeed differ for elites and mass publics. Thus what is important in relating attitudes to behavior is what specific patterns of beliefs are found.[8] From this point of view, what is important in the example given above is the differences in the relationships among idea elements for the two groups, rather than the quantitative properties of constraint.

Attitudinal Dynamics

We have now examined the descriptive properties of belief systems in some detail. However, what is probably of more interest to the student of political behavior is the kinds of changes belief systems undergo. In this section we will look at three different but related theories of attitude change.

BALANCE THEORY[9]

One of the simplest theories of attitude change is *balance theory*. It is assumed in balance theory that we are interested in changes in the evaluative components of specific attitudes considered as discrete entities. Such changes can only be the result of new cognitive information; that is, of new information concerning the relations among the subjects of attitudes.

To see how balance theory works, let us consider an individual, X, who has a favorable disposition toward a particular political candidate. Let us say that X also has an unfavorable disposition toward the editor of the local newspaper and that he has always assumed that the editor would not favor his candidate. Using balance theory, we would represent this situation as in Figure 8-3. In general, balance theory assumes that attitudes have only direction, which is positive (+), negative (−), or neutral (0), and that relations between attitude elements can only be associative (*p*), dissociative (*n*), or null (0).

FIGURE 8–3

**A Simple, Balanced Belief
System of Two Idea Elements**

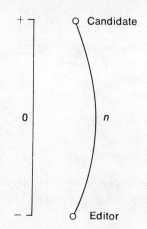

Balance theory further assumes that a belief system must be balanced, or "in equilibrium." A belief system is assumed to be in equilibrium as long as idea elements with the same sign are linked by positive or null relations and those with different signs are linked by negative or null relations. Any other condition changes the system from a state of equilibrium, and the system is supposed to effect changes which will bring about a new equilibrial state. To see how this might work, let us consider what would happen in our example if X read an editorial in the local newspaper endorsing his candidate. We would now have the situation depicted in Figure 8-4. This, according to the theory, is an imbalanced situation; and there is, therefore, an impetus for X to change his attitudes (or beliefs) to bring the system back into balance. There are a number of ways in which this might be accomplished. X might change his attitude toward the editor, producing the situation shown in Figure 8-5. Or he might change his attitude toward the candidate, producing the situation shown in Figure 8-6.

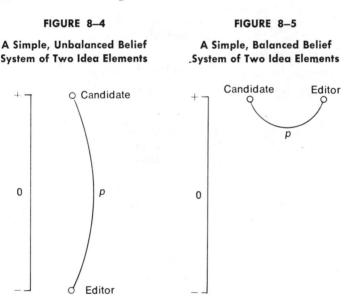

FIGURE 8–4

A Simple, Unbalanced Belief System of Two Idea Elements

FIGURE 8–5

A Simple, Balanced Belief System of Two Idea Elements

Another relatively common way of resolving X's dilemma would be to *differentiate* among the idea elements concerned. For example, X might simply choose to believe that it was not the regular editor who wrote the column supportive of his candidate, or that the editor was clearly "not himself" when he wrote it. This would produce the solution

261

FIGURE 8–6

**A Simple, Balanced Belief
System of Two Idea Elements**

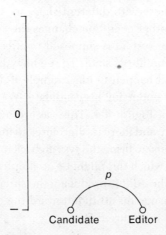

in Figure 8-7. Here, X has simply added a "new" element to his belief system to balance it. He could also do this by simply refusing to believe that the editorial had actually been written (a somewhat pathological, but not totally impossible, response), or that it was a satire or had some other nefarious purpose.

FIGURE 8–7

**A Simple Belief System
Showing the Result
of Differentiation**

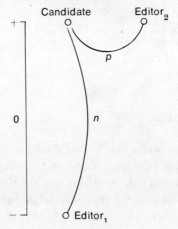

There are several problems with this simple version of balance theory as an explanation of attitudinal change. Though the propositions and assumptions make a good deal of intuitive sense, the theory can, in its present form, make no unique predictions about attitudinal changes. As we saw in the example above, any one of a number of possible changes could occur. This vagueness might be avoided if we were willing to make assumptions about the relative centrality of the various idea elements. We might regard the centrality of an idea element as a determinant of resistance to attitudinal change. That is, we might regard a relatively central idea element as more or less deeply imbedded in the belief system. If an element is related by beliefs to a great many other idea elements, any change in attitude toward it will probably require many additional changes throughout the belief system in order to maintain balance. Thus, we might with some justification assume that changes in belief systems will follow a path of least resistance. In the event of a conflict between attitudes, the one pertaining to the less central idea element would be the most likely to be changed. In the case of conflicting attitudes toward two (or more) relatively central idea elements, we might hypothesize that beliefs would change or be adapted to make them consistent with the central attitudes. However, there is no specific provision for this in the theory, and these possibilities can hardly be considered more than reasoned speculation at this point.

Another, and perhaps more serious problem with balance theory is that it is difficult to handle complex systems of beliefs. Balance theory is specifically designed to handle attitudes toward pairs (and sometimes triples) of idea elements. However, as we pointed out earlier, real belief systems can be incredibly complex. Thus, to the extent that it cannot handle the true complexity of belief systems, this theory serves little more than hueristic research purposes.

CONGRUITY THEORY

Congruity theory is similar to balance theory in that it too deals with the consistency of relations between pairs of idea elements. It differs, however, in that it takes into account differences in the intensity of attitudes, results in unique predictions, and hypothesizes that as a belief system moves to a state of equilibrium changes will occur in attitudes toward both idea elements.

263

For example, consider a hypothetical individual, *Y*, who feels positively about former President Kennedy, somewhat less positively about national health care insurance, and still less positively (but still positively) about Hubert Humphrey. She feels negatively about Richard Nixon, more negatively about the *National Review,* and still more negatively about George Wallace. This segment of her belief system is represented in Figure 8-8.

FIGURE 8–8

**Hypothetical Attitudes Toward
Several Idea Elements**

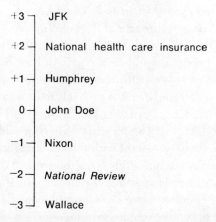

According to congruity theory, a belief system remains congruous (in equilibrium) only as long as (1) associative beliefs occur between idea elements that are the subject of attitudes having equal evaluative intensity and (2) dissociative beliefs occur between idea elements that are the subject of attitudes at opposite levels of evaluative intensity, or (3) no belief is held. Changes in belief systems can therefore come from two sources. The first source of attitudinal change is the emergence of an associative belief between two nonequilibrium idea elements (idea elements which a person evaluates differently). Let us say that Nixon makes some statements in support of a national health care insurance program. Congruity theory predicts that this will be a source of disequilibrium in *Y*'s belief system and that her attitudes will change to a congruous configuration. The evaluative component that is the least intense will change the most, and both evaluative components will change in inverse proportion to their intensity. Since Nixon and health care are three units apart on Y's evaluative scale, her evaluation of Nixon will "move" two units toward congruity (i.e., it will change proportionally to the intensity of her attitude toward national health insurance), and her evaluation of health care will move one unit toward congruity (i.e., it will change proportionally to the intensity of her attitude toward Nixon), as in Figure 8-9.

FIGURE 8–9

A Change to a Congruent Relation Between Two Idea Elements as the Result of an Associative Belief

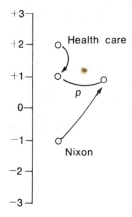

At first these predicted changes may appear a bit bizarre. However, they can be explained in commonsense terms by arguing that if national health insurance is linked to something we do not like, it is very possible that we will like it somewhat less. But if something we do not like —especially if our dislike is not particularly intense—is linked to something we have relatively strong positive feelings about, it is quite possible that we will feel more positively toward it. To take a more mundane example, suppose you went to a movie alone and came away thinking it really wasn't very good, and later, in talking with your best friend, found out that she thought it was tremendous. It is very likely that your estimation of the movie would rise; at the same time, your opinion of your friend's taste in movies might move down a notch.

The second source of attitudinal change in this theory is the incongruity produced by a dissociative belief linking two idea elements of unequal intensity. For example, let us say that the *National Review* ran an article attacking Humphrey. The theory hypothesizes that both evaluations must change toward their respective points of equilibrium. Y's feelings about Humphrey must move toward +2, since her initial attitude toward the *National Review* had an intensity of −2. Her attitude toward the *National Review* must move toward −1, since her initial feeling about Humphrey had an intensity of +1. This situation is depicted in Figure 8-10. Since each attitude must change in intensity in proportion to the intensity of the other attitude, her feeling about Humphrey must change twice as much (move twice as far along the evaluative scale in Figure 8-10) as her feeling about the *National Review*. Thus the new point of congruity for the idea element "Humphrey" is +1 2/3; for the idea element "*National Review*," it is −1 2/3.

FIGURE 8–10

A Change in the Relation of Two Idea Elements as the Result of Incongruity Produced by a Dissociative Belief

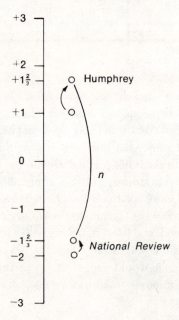

What should stand out in this example is the prediction that *Y*'s attitude toward the *National Review* will become less negative! This is certainly not likely to be a commonsense conclusion. But then does common sense tell us that a clock in motion runs slower than one "at rest," or that the mass of an object increases as it begins to move faster? Hardly! But the theories of relativity physics make these predictions quite plainly. Of course there must be many qualifications to these predictions on the individual level, but for the most part empirical research has not clearly denied support to them.

From the point of view of understanding the dynamics of belief systems, one deficiency of congruity theory is the relative difficulty of dealing with complex structures of beliefs. It is not an impossible problem, however.[10] A more serious deficiency of this theory is its inability to distinguish between intensity of evaluative disposition (that is, attitude) and centrality. For example, if our hypothetical individual, John Doe, were to criticize George Wallace, Doe would move to the position of +3. This does not seem very likely.

The important points of congruity theory are its major points of difference from simple balance theory, which attempts to treat the same subject. The actual methods of calculating changes in attitudes are relatively unimportant for our purposes. What should be grasped, however, are how the intensity of the evaluative component of attitudes is important, what the sources of attitudinal change are, and in general how incongruity is hypothesized to be resolved.

DISSONANCE THEORY

The theory of *cognitive dissonance* as a theory of attitude change, like congruity theory, contains some very interesting propositions that would probably not be considered common sense. Dissonance theory is also a theory of the consistency of beliefs. In this case, idea elements are said to have irrelevant, consonant, or dissonant associations with each other. If the idea elements have nothing whatsoever to do with each other (as, for example, the length of the President's hair and the price of tea in China), they are considered mutually *irrelevant*. If one idea element can be said to "follow from" another, the association between the two is said to be *consonant*. *Dissonance* between a pair of idea elements occurs when one implies the negation of the other.

267

A famous example of dissonance occurred in the mid-1950s when a woman in a midwestern city claimed that she was receiving messages from another planet predicting the destruction of the world by a flood.[11] She gathered around herself a number of followers who sincerely believed in the validity of this prediction. Many of the believers went so far as to give up their homes and jobs in the certainty that the end was near. Shortly before the flood was to occur, the believers received a message that a flying saucer would pick up the faithful and spare them from the flood. All packed and ready to go, they awaited the hour appointed for the rendezvous. Needless to say, the world was not destroyed by a flood and the flying saucer did not arrive. This is a classic dissonance-producing situation. What the believers had expected to occur did not; that is, the actual course of events did not logically follow from what was believed to be true.

Dissonance theory predicts that when dissonance occurs an individual may change his beliefs and/or attitudes; he may try to get others to change their beliefs and/or attitudes or he may perhaps decide that there is no real dissonance at all and that one idea element does logically (or perhaps psycho-logically) entail the other. The first hypothesis, that an individual will attempt to make his or her beliefs consonant with his or her actual behavior, is particularly interesting. A common example would be a person who smoked, rejecting information that smoking was injurious to health.

What would dissonance theory predict would happen to the faithful followers of Marion Keech, the lady who predicted the flood and the flying saucer that never appeared? Common sense tells us that they would give up their rather extraordinary beliefs and perhaps change their attitudes toward Mrs. Keech. Dissonance theory, on the other hand, would hypothesize that because of the followers' intense commitment to these beliefs, they would add new consonant elements to their belief systems and, furthermore, try to mobilize social support by getting others to "convert" to their views. In fact, a short time after the flood failed to come, the group "received" a new message which told them that, because of their extraordinary faith, God had delivered not only them but the rest of mankind as well. After that this group, which had previously avoided publicity and propagation of their beliefs, became active proselytizers for their views.

Another study, by Festinger and Carlsmith, also supports the dissonance theory hypothesis.[12] Subjects were required to complete a long and very tedious task, after which they were to tell other potential subjects that the task was a very interesting one, supposedly in order to get them to participate. The subjects were offered, in some cases, one dollar, and in others, twenty dollars to tell this obvious lie. Dissonance theory would predict that because those who were offered only a dollar could not fully compensate for the lie by saying that they did it "for the money," they would demonstrate more cognitive dissonance than those who were offered twenty dollars, or the control group who were asked only to report to the experimenters whether they found the task interesting. The effects of increased dissonance were hypothesized to be a change in attitude, toward a relatively positive evaluation of the experimental task. The results described in Figure 8-11 confirm the rather surprising predictions of dissonance theory.

The major contribution of dissonance theory is that, like congruity theory, its predictions—to the extent that they are borne out by facts —allow us to move considerably beyond what general common sense tells us about the dynamics of attitude change. The theory is not very rigorous, however, in that specific predictions are not logically deducible from it in every case. Like balance theory, dissonance theory is very difficult to disprove, because so many different kinds of results are considered to be possible. It is a theory of great richness and appears to be a move in the direction of being able, at least informally, to handle some of the complexities of belief systems.

Attitudes and Political Behavior:
A Recapitulation

At the outset, we argued that for the study of attitudes to be of any significance it would have to be useful in the explanation of behavior. Yet we have seen that attitude theories are in general somewhat remote from behavior. We have also seen that there is no single "attitude theory." There are, rather, a number of related but competing theoretical perspectives on attitudes. Whether any of these perspectives make any substantial contribution to understanding political behavior is not a question that can be finally answered here.

However, we have observed that these theories make us better-equipped to anticipate some aspects of behavior. In short, they suggest

FIGURE 8–11

Responses to Key Questions in a Study of Cognitive Dissonance

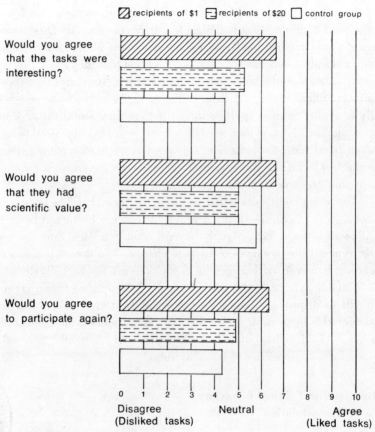

Source: Based on diagram in Henry C. Lindgren, *An Introduction to Social Psychology* (New York: John Wiley, 1969), p. 117.

apparently valid generalizations. One point which should be clear is that political behavior is not necessarily dependent on a political belief system, or ideology. Behavior in the political arena can be affected by attitudes and beliefs rather remote from what we would consider directly political. Basic personality traits, general attitudes toward the "self," and the relation of political beliefs to other aspects of an individual's total belief system are clearly significant.

In this chapter we have looked primarily at the structure and dynamics of behavioral predispositions. In the next, we will discuss some ideas about how these predispositions result in action.

Notes

1. T. W. Adorno *et al.*, *The Authoritarian Personality* (New York: Harper & Row, 1950). Other examples of the application of personality theories in political science can be found in Fred Greenstein, *Personality and Politics* (Chicago: Markham, 1969); J. N. Knutson, *The Human Basis of the Polity: A Psychological Study of Political Men* (Chicago: Aldine, 1972); R. Lane, *Political Ideology* (New York: Free Press, 1962); and H. D. Lasswell, *Power and Personality* (New York: Norton, 1948) and *Psychopathology and Politics* (New York: Viking Press, 1960).

2. See, for example, Milton Rokeach, *The Open and Closed Mind* (New York: Basic Books, 1960) and *Beliefs, Attitudes, and Values* (San Francisco: Jossey-Bass, 1968).

3. R. Abelson and M. Rosenberg, "Symbolic Psycho-logic: A Model of Attitudinal Cognition," *Behavioral Science*, Vol. 3 (1958), 1-13.

4. See, for example, N. Luttbeg, "The Structure of Belief Systems Among Leaders and the Public," *Public Opinion Quarterly*, Vol. 32 (1968), 398-410; S. R. Brown, "Consistency and the Persistency of Ideology: Some Experimental Results," *Public Opinion Quarterly*, Vol. 34 (1970), 60-68; R. Axelrod, "The Structure of Public Opinion on Policy Issues," *Public Opinion Quarterly*, Vol. 31 (1967), 51-60; Philip Converse, "The Nature

of Belief Systems in Mass Publics," in David Apter (ed.), *Ideology and Discontent* (New York: Free Press, 1964); and S. A. Kirkpatrick, "Political Attitudes and Behavior: Some Consequences of Attitudinal Ordering," *Midwest Journal of Political Science*, Vol. 14 (1970), 1-24.

5. Converse, *op. cit.*

6. Converse, *op. cit.*, and Axelrod, *op. cit.*

7. Luttbeg, *op. cit.*, and Brown, *op. cit.*

8. Luttbeg, *op. cit.* Kirkpatrick, *op. cit.*, tries to deal explicitly with a specific kind of structure (cognitive balance) and its potential relation to behavior. See also the section on "Balance Theory" below.

9. The use of "balance theory" follows that of Roger Brown, *Social Psychology* (New York: Free Press, 1965).

10. See Denis Sullivan, "Psychological Balance and Reactions to the Presidential Nominations in 1960," in M. Kent Jennings and H. Zeigler (eds.), *The Electoral Process* (Englewood Cliffs, N.J.: Prentice-Hall, 1966).

11. Leon Festinger, H. W. Riecken, Jr., and S. Schacter, *When Prophecy Fails* (Minneapolis: University of Minnesota Press, 1966).

12. Leon Festinger and J. M. Carlsmith, "Cognitive Consequences of Forced Compliance," *Journal of Abnormal and Social Psychology*, Vol. 58 (1959), 203-210.

9

Role
Theory

In the last chapter, we introduced the concept of "attitude" as a theoretical construct to account for the relationship between an individual's history of learning and his behavior. We observed how a person's belief system is determined by what he has learned to like and dislike and the relationships among his attitudes. In this chapter, we shall again be concerned with predispositions that result from learning; but in this case the predispositions will be more immediately related to behavior. We will discuss how the individual develops a repertoire of possible behavior patterns, and how certain behaviors are selected for use in given situations.

We often talk about political actors in terms of what it is we think they *ought* to do. Consider, for example, some common notions about representatives in legislative bodies. One theory of representation holds that the representative should act as the agent of the people directly responsible for his election. His job is to translate the preferences of his constituency into public policy. As a representative, he is expected to keep lines of communication to his constituents open and to be aware of their preferences; he is expected (in the United States, especially) to act as an intermediary between his constituents and the government bureaucracy; he is expected to serve on committees, in the legislative body, that deal with matters of direct interest to his constituents; he is

272

expected to vote on policy matters in line with the preferences of his constituency; and so on. Another theory of representation argues that a representative ought to act for the general good of "the people." It is not his function to serve slavishly the special interests and specific prejudices of the individuals or groups directly responsible for his election. He is expected, rather, to participate in the creation of public policy in the interest of reason and the good of all the members of society; he is expected to study the broader issues of the day and to use his judgment in deciding what actions are in the national interest, rather than to be a passive instrument of any single group.

Other examples of expectations with respect to political figures or institutions abound. For instance, we are frequently told that all citizens should vote, or accept jury duty. Certain behavior is *expected* of citizens, just as certain behavior is *expected* when a representative is elected to a parliament or legislature. A good deal of the behavior we observe in politics is prescribed as appropriate by other members of society. These expected or prescribed behaviors are called *roles*.

Position

From the perspective of role theory, a society or a group can be described in terms of the kinds and distribution of *positions* (sometimes called "statuses") in it. Also, an individual can be described, to a certain extent, by the various positions he or she holds in the society or in certain significant social groups. Thus a group can be described by noting that it has a presiding officer, a seniority structure, a budgeting office, and so on. An individual can be described as a female, a mother, a steelworker, a Protestant, a PTA member, and so on.

Certain positions, such as male or female, giant or midget, black or white, are *designative*, or ascribed to the individuals who occupy them. No action is required to achieve these positions. They are simply socially defined ways of describing various classes of people. Other positions, such as steelworker, college graduate, thief, or teacher, depend upon individual *achievement*. In other words, some kinds of positions are filled by individuals solely because of social assignments, irrespective of the individuals' private abilities or ambitions. Race, for example, is a matter of birth. Other positions are achieved by meeting certain

273

social standards of success (or failure). Thus an individual who develops his talent for playing football may achieve the position of "sports hero" or "champion"; if he fails to live up to certain social expectations, he may "achieve" the position of "thief."

Positions may be temporary or permanent. They may entail a good deal of social recognition or very little. They may be easy or difficult to change. And they may be clearly or loosely defined.

In general, positions are defined in terms of the kind of behavior society collectively expects of the individuals who occupy them. They are associated with particular rights and obligations, which are more or less well defined. When these rights and obligations are described in terms of specific behavior patterns, we say that positions are made up of sets of *roles*, which the holders of the positions are *expected* to perform.

Role Expectations

A few moments ago, we saw that the role (or roles) of a representative (a position) are often described in terms of expected patterns of behavior. These *role expectations* are, in effect, socially defined norms, or rules, for behavior. Some norms are *prescriptive*; that is, they define behaviors that must be exhibited by the individual who occupies a certain position. Thus a representative must take an oath of office, and he must relinquish his position if he loses an election. Some norms are *prohibitive*; they describe behaviors forbidden to holders of certain positions. A representative, for example, must not (in the United States) move out of the district that elected him. Other expectations (the largest share) are *permissive*; that is, they describe behaviors the individual in a certain position is permitted to perform. Thus a representative is permitted, and even encouraged to a certain extent, to associate with lobbyists from special interest groups. Of course, under certain conditions permissive expectations may become prohibitive or prescriptive. For example, a representative must not associate with lobbyists to the extent of taking direct payments for voting in specific ways. Similarly, he is permitted to avoid his constituents at times; but if he is directly confronted by them, he must make some effort to listen to them and show them that he is their servant.

Sanctions

The character of various role expectations—that is, whether they are prescribed, permitted, or prohibited—depends on the existence and degree of *sanctions* associated with them. A sanction is a behavior or set of behaviors that will be exhibited by an individual or group in response to the fulfillment or nonfulfillment of expectations. Sanctions increase the probability that prescribed behaviors will be performed and that prescribed behaviors will be avoided. Sanctions are, in effect, social rewards and punishments. The extent to which role expectations are binding is determined by the extent to which relevant members of society are willing to provide sanctions. Sanctions can be mild or severe, formal or informal, negative or positive. Imprisonment is a severe and formal negative sanction that discourages criminal behavior. The "silent treatment" is an informal negative sanction against behavior that, though not criminal, is considered undesirable by those who impose the sanction. Tax deductions for contributions to charity are positive, legal sanctions for what is considered worthy behavior. Public or private praise is a powerful informal sanction for many kinds of behavior. Expectations can be thought of as varying almost continuously between the extremes of prescribed and proscribed behavior, and the relative severity or subtlety of the attendant sanctions as varying in a similar fashion.

Significant Others

Behavior that is expected in one situation is not necessarily the same behavior that will be expected in another situation. For example, the behavior expected of a woman in the presence of a lover is quite different from that expected of her in the presence of some other individual, say a policeman. Social situations that determine which set of expectations is applicable in a given role are defined in terms of significant others. The concept of *significant others* was introduced in Part II. A significant other (or, more simply, an *other*) can be an individual, a group, or even a hypothetical composite "individual" sometimes called the *generalized other*. (A rather simple-minded, but useful, way to think

TABLE 9–1

Hypothetical Roles of a House Appropriations Committee Member

BEHAVIORAL EXPECTATIONS

Others	Hard Work	Specialization	Reciprocity	Subcommittee Unity	Compromise	Minimal Partisanship
Fellow committee members	0	0	+	+	+	0
Party workers	0	0	0	0	0	—
Constituents	+	—	—		0	0
Spouse	—					
Self (follower)	+	+	+	+	+	+
Self (idealistic rebel)	0	—	—	—	—	0

Note: Entries are interpreted as follows: a + indicates prescribed behavior, a — indicates prohibited behavior, a 0 indicates permitted behavior, a blank represents irrelevant behavior.

Source: Column headings are based on Richard Fenno, *The Power of the Purse: Appropriations Politics in Congress* (Boston: Little, Brown, 1966).

about the generalized other is as the person you talk to when you talk to yourself; that is, the "person" who sees you the way you think that other people in general see you.)

Others are defined in terms of roles or, more specifically, expectations. They are persons or groups whom we expect will, under certain conditions, exhibit specific behavior patterns. We expect a judge to behave one way in the courtroom and another way on the street. Others also have expectations about our own behavior. Just as we expect different behavior from lovers and policemen, so too we can be sure that they expect different behavior from us.

In addition to expectations about "others," role theory is concerned with our expectations about ourselves. All the expectations we as individuals have with respect to our own behavior, along with those expectations we have concerning the expectations of others, determine our image of what we ought to be. They determine our *self*.

In order to get a more concrete idea of how expectations and sanctions affect behavior, we shall examine, briefly, the roles of a hypothetical member of the Appropriations Committee of the U.S. House of Representatives.[1] Table 9-1 shows several general behavior expectations that may be exhibited by a person in this position, and the attitudes of various people (various "others"), including the congressman himself, toward such behavior. His colleagues on the committee view all the types of behavior described as either permitted or prescribed. They have no objections at all to his working hard, specializing in a particular area of committee work, or refraining from partisan rhetoric; and they expect him to accept the judgment of other members on matters related to their areas of specialization (reciprocity), to support the recommendations of his subcommittee, and to compromise his positions on issues so that the committee can function smoothly. Because reciprocity, subcommittee unity, and the ability to compromise are important to the functioning of the committee, positive sanctions are associated with these behaviors. These sanctions may include fairly substantial rewards such as subcommittee chairmanships with some public visibility, access to increased staff assistance, and special help from more senior members on bills. Negative sanctions such as assignment to dreary subcommittees, social isolation, and even removal from the committee, although they are not indicated in the table, may be presumed to be associated with the failure to behave properly.

Persons other than a committee member's colleagues may have a different conception of his roles. A loyal party member, for example, may view refraining from party rhetoric (minimal partisanship) as highly undesirable, while tolerating in various degrees the other behavior patterns indicated. The legislator's constituents may see no reason why "their representative" should specialize in one area and leave decisions in other areas to others. They may consider the committee member's behavior in this regard totally irrelevant. The congressman's spouse may view most of his colleagues' expectations as irrelevant, but disapprove of his working so hard that he has no time for his family or weakens his health.

The last two rows of Table 9-1 show how the legislator himself may feel with respect to various types of behavior. If he is a follower, he may take the expectations of his colleagues as absolute prescriptions, adding perhaps the very real sanction of his own guilt to the actual sanctions wielded by the committee. If he is an idealistic rebel, on the other hand, while approving of hard work and minimal partisanship, he may define his overall role as a committee member quite differently. Moreover, the negative sanctions associated with behavior disapproved of by this inner self, though of his own making, may be more potent than those of the committee. In avoiding such behavior he is not acting incongruously; he only marches to the tune of a different drummer.

The Acquisition of Social Roles

A natural question at this point is "Where do role expectations come from, and how does the individual find out about them?" The answer is that roles are learned. Certain patterns of behavior and patterns of expectations are acquired because an individual finds that members of his society—his significant others—reward his performance of certain actions and punish his failure to perform them. The process of learning through social rewards and punishments is called *socialization*; and, as we pointed out in an earlier chapter, the process of learning political behavior is called *political socialization*.

Through socialization, the individual discovers which patterns of behavior are expected of him in given social situations and which patterns of behavior he can expect from others. Social learning is a very

278

complex phenomenon, and from the perspective of role theory may be thought of as the learning of *contingent expectations*. We learn that *if* a certain situation arises, *then* we are expected to behave in a certain way. We also learn that *if* we behave in a certain way, *then* we can expect others around us to behave in particular ways. We learn role behavior as a way of dealing with social situations. These social situations have two elements: the others who are "present" and the sets of expectations they have about us and about themselves.

The primary agent of socialization in most societies is the family. From our families we learn most of the basic behavior patterns we will be called upon to follow for the rest of our lives. We learn, for example, how and what to eat, when and how to communicate, and, most importantly, how to reward and punish the behavior of others that we ourselves find rewarding or are averse to; that is, we learn the role of a socializing agent.

As we get older the main agent of socialization shifts from the family to other social groups—especially peer groups, those others whom we perceive as more or less like ourselves or whom we aspire to be like. As children we find peers among our playmates or classmates. As we get older, we often find peers among those who work with us. The early periods of socialization are generally periods of learning who we are; that is, what position or positions we hold in the larger society—to whom we are expected to defer and from whom we can expect deference. In later periods of socialization we learn more complex role expectations: the range of situations in which we may expect to find ourselves, the positions to which we may aspire and what new roles may be required there, and how to present to others specific concepts of our self—that is, how to create expectations in others which conform with what we would like to have expected of us. In general, we learn complex patterns of role relations.

Role Relations

In the previous section we spoke of roles as contingent expectations. Our behavior in a social situation is largely contingent upon the behavior of others, upon our expectations of their behavior, and even upon how we would like others to behave. In certain instances our behavior (or *role performance*) is a reaction to the behavior observed around us; roles in this sense can be thought of as *responses*. Our behavior is not necessarily contingent on the *actual* behavior of others. We can, and do, often select the roles we play on the basis of what behavior we *expect* from others, even though this behavior has not actually occurred. Our behavior may also be contingent upon the kind of behavior we would *like* to see exhibited by others. We choose our own roles in the expectation that others will take cues from us and perform the roles we would like them to.

In learning to interact with others (other individuals or groups) it is necessary to learn to play our roles according to their expectations. If we violate their expectations regarding our behavior, we risk sanctions. Perhaps more important, if we behave contrary to the expectations of others, no matter what our intentions are, we may fail to communicate; others may not understand our behavior. For example, if a political candidate wishes to make a good impression on, say, a group of teen-agers, he may think it necessary to make a few jokes to show them that he is a "regular guy." However, if the teenagers take politics very seriously and expect a serious discussion of policy issues, his jokes may offend them or give them the impression that he is a political buffoon. Such a start will make it exceedingly difficult for him to communicate his stands on important policy issues. In general, such violations of mutual role expectations confuse communications among people and make the process of interaction more difficult for all parties.

In order to be able to play appropriate roles ourselves, we must learn appropriate behavior; *and* we must learn the expectations of others. In role theory it is said that we must learn to *take* the role of the other in a situation. If we know what kind of behavior an other is likely to expect, it is possible to, in effect, rehearse an anticipated interaction. Thus we can select our own behavior on the basis of what we know the other expects of us. This is not to say that the expectations of others determine our behavior; in general, however, knowing what is expected of us, we frame our behavior accordingly. Consider, for example, a boy who rehearses what he will say to a girl when he asks her for a date, or a teenager who rehearses what he will tell his father in explaining how the family car was damaged while he was driving it. This process of rehearsal may involve a generalized other rather than a specific individual or individuals. For example, a person about to be interviewed by a news-

paper reporter may rehearse his statements keeping in mind the probable reactions of the public.

Looking back at Table 9-1 we can also see some possible examples of
contingent role behavior. If a member of the House Appropriations
Committee is discussing his activities with a fellow committee member,
he will certainly emphasize different aspects of his work than he would if
he were talking to a party worker or to one of his constituents. In talking
with his colleagues, he may discuss the output of the committee, how its
reports are likely to be received by the House as a whole, and so on. In a
conversation with a party worker, he may show more concern about how
the committee's actions will help or hinder the party's fortunes in the
coming elections.

Once the basic idea of roles as contingent behavior in a process of
interaction is understood, it is possible to move to a somewhat higher
plane of abstraction. Generally, rather than being concerned with
specific behavioral contingencies in relatively unique interactions, behavioral scientists are interested in the basic regularities in role relationships and in patterns of interaction in a social setting. Thus we are
interested in general classes of contingent behavior, or, more specifically, in general *role relations*.[2]

One way to understand role relations is to visualize a rather simple
experiment—a piece of research almost anyone could do with little
trouble. The basic hypothesis in this experiment is that patterns of role
relations are an important property of groups. For example, in any
group there is likely to be a relationship of liking or affection among
various individuals. Moreover, this relationship is likely to affect the
roles, or behavior, of those in the group, since people who like each
other expect different behavior from each other than they do from
people they do not like. The subjects of this experiment may be any
group of people in regular contact with one another—say, all those who
live in the same fraternity or sorority house or in the same dormitory. To
determine the patterns of affection within the group, we have simply to
ask each member of the group which of the other members he or she
particularly likes. When we have obtained data from everyone, we can
"map" the results by drawing an arrow from each individual (represented by a number or a letter of the alphabet) to all the other
individuals in the group the person likes. This map will show us the
general pattern of affections within the group. (Note that when we

consider all the members of a group in terms of specific relationships between pairs of individuals, we move from specific relationships to a general relation.)

Let us say that our group has nine members and that their feelings for one another are as described in Table 9-2. We can then map the pattern of affections for the group as a whole as in Figure 9-1. This map tells us a number of interesting things about the group. For one thing, it tells us whether the pattern of affections is symmetric. (If, in every case where X likes Y, Y likes X, then the relation is symmetric.) The map also tells us whether the affection relation is transitive. (It is if, in every case where X likes Y and Y likes Z, X likes Z.)

TABLE 9–2

Hypothetical Data on Affection Relations Within a Group

Group Member	Persons Member "Likes"			
A	C	D		
B	C	D		
C	A	B	D	E
D	A	B	C	
E	C	F		
F	E	H	I	
G	C			
H	F	I		
I	F	H		

FIGURE 9–1

Patterns of Affection in a Hypothetical Group

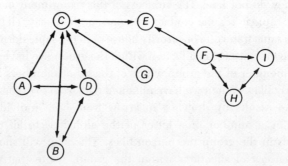

Suppose we actually decided to do this "experiment." What might we expect to find? For example, might we expect to find different sorts of patterns in different kinds of groups? Why? What would this tell us in general about such groups?

Another aspect of group behavior of interest to social scientists is communication within the group. We might continue our hypothetical experiment by asking each person whom they communicated with on a regular basis or simply by observing who communicated with whom. What might we find? One of the major questions we would like to answer would no doubt be about the relationship between the patterns of communication within the group and the patterns of affection we found earlier. Naturally we would wish to find the differences, if any, between the patterns in our group and those in other groups. Why might such differences exist? In order to get some idea of what the answer to this last question might be, let us look at one of the more famous studies of communication patterns within groups and how they appear to affect other role relations.[3]

The Leavitt experiments were conducted with groups of five individuals, each of whom was given a card with five of six possible symbols marked on it. The patterns of communication (role relationships) within the groups were artificially structured by allowing each individual to communicate only with certain other individuals and only via a written message. The task of each group was to discover the identity of all six symbols. The four basic communication patterns (role relations) in the experiment are represented in Figure 9-2. One of the questions asked of the participants was which of the individuals in their group they felt to be a leader. The numbers within the boxes in patterns I, II, and IV represent the number of times the individual in each position, in repeated trials, was thought to be a leader. The lines between each pair of boxes represent the capacity of the occupants of those positions to communicate.

In groups with the first type of communication pattern, there was little agreement on who the leader was. However, in each of the other groups there was rather strong agreement as to who fit the leader role. Since leadership is a variable of great interest to political scientists, it would be a good exercise to look at patterns II and IV and try to explain in terms of possible communications, why the results shown in the figure were obtained. The leadership choices in the pattern III groups

FIGURE 9–2

Four Types of Experimental Communication Patterns

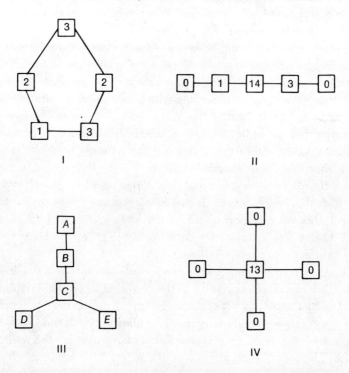

Source: Based on H. J. Leavitt, "Some Effects of Certain Communication Patterns on Group Performance," *Journal of Abnormal and Social Psychology* 46 (1951). Copyright 1951 by the American Psychological Association. Used by permission.

have deliberately not been reported. As a test, which position do you think was most often associated with leadership?

What would happen if we treated the hypothetical data on affection discussed above as if they were data on communication patterns? Judging by Figure 9-1, who do you think would be considered the leader of the group? Member *C* perhaps? Why? What about member *E*? Or *G*? Experiments with this pattern of communication showed that *C* was felt to be the leader in almost every case. (The actual results in this case were $A=0$, $B=1$, $C=17$, $D=1$, $E=1$.) What inferences would you draw from these experimental results?

Another role relation of special interest to students of political behavior is that of *power*, or *influence*. For purposes of discussion, let us assume that we can define power in the following way: An individual, *X*, has power over another individual, *Y*, if *X* can get *Y* to behave in a way that *X* wants him to, whether *Y* wants to or not. Let us now go back to the hypothetical nine-member group of our original experiment. How can we get data on whether any individual has power over any other individual? Actual measurements of power relationships are very difficult to obtain. We could ask each member of the group who they felt had power over each of the other members. Or we might ask each member who had power over them. Or we could ask each member whom they felt they had power over. But such questions would tell us only about *perceived* power relationships. Perceived power relations within a group are an important aspect of group structure, but they are not necessarily the same as the actual power relations within a group. There is no reason, however, why we cannot study perceived power in its own right.

Let us say that we have obtained the data in Table 9-3. From these data we can draw a map, or "graph," of the power relations within the group, as in Figure 9-3.[4]

TABLE 9–3

Hypothetical Data on Power
Relations Within a Group

Group Member	Persons Member "Has Power Over"		
A	D		
B			
C	A	B	E
D	B		
E	F		
F	I	H	
G	C		
H	I		
I			

Compare this map of power relations with the graphs of affection and communication patterns in Figures 9-1 and 9-2. How are they similar? Is the power relationship in Figure 9-3 symmetrical? Would

FIGURE 9–3

Patterns of Power in a Hypothetical Group

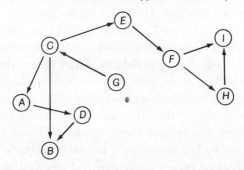

you expect it to be? Why or why not? Are the power relations transitive? Are power and affection related? Who is the most powerful individual in the group? What do the experimental findings discussed above tell you? Are the various role relations different in any significant way?

We have tried to show, through these examples, that the role relations within a group can be multidimensional and interconnected. It is possible, for example, and rather likely, that patterns of affection determine patterns of communication, and that communication is necessary for a power relationship to exist. Empirical data on such relations cannot, of course, be obtained by hypothetical experiments such as we have performed here. We can only hope that the interested student will try to perform his or her own research in this area and learn something, in this way, of the role of the political behaviorist.

Role Conflict

In the previous section we began by speaking of role relations as contingent behavioral expectations. Furthermore, we pointed out that if human interactions are to proceed smoothly, if meanings or inter-pretations of behavior are to be clearly communicated, then the role expectations of each party must be in some sense mutually consistent. When expectations are not consistent, role conflict is the result. In this section, we will discuss the sources of such conflict and some of the possible means for its resolution.

It should be obvious that, as complex as role relations are, the

286

potential for role conflict is enormous. There are at least three fundamental sources of role conflict. The first is a situation in which an
individual has different roles in a single group—roles associated with
incompatible expectations. In the long run this situation is not very
common; for a group, if it is to exist for any period of time, must share
expectations about the behavior of its members. Without such shared
expectations, role conflict is likely to generate intragroup conflict, fac-
tionalism, and the like. For example, this kind of role conflict may occur
within a family group if a woman is married to a man who, because of his
traditional upbringing, expects his wife to be a fastidious housekeeper
but who also, because of his educational experience, expects his wife to
be highly career oriented. The incompatibility of these role expectations
is obvious, and one likely result is divorce.

A more common source of role conflict is the attempt to fill different
roles in different groups whose expectations differ. Mitchell has argued
that elected public officials in the United States are especially prone to
this sort of role conflict. [5] The role of the elected public official, according
to dogma of the democratic political formula, [6] is that of a public servant.
But the elected official is also an ordinary human being who has many
private roles to play, such as that of family provider. In his public role he
must evaluate things in terms of the good of his constituents or in terms
of the public good, depending upon which theory of representation he
accepts. In his private role as breadwinner, he must evaluate situations
in terms of the consequences for his family's financial position. The
potential for conflict here can be very great.

Another example of this kind of role conflict was hinted at earlier in
the discussion of expectations with respect to a member of the House
Appropriations Committee. Like any elected official, a member of this
committee is expected to perform both an administrative and a partisan
role. It is clear from Fenno's research that the members of the committee in general expect their colleagues to function efficiently in an administrative role and to maintain an attitude of affective neutrality.
However, as an *elected* public official, a member of a congressional
committee is expected to play a partisan role. His colleagues on the
committee may be interested chiefly in the committee, but his colleagues in the party are more likely to care about the success of their own
programs and expect affective involvement. The potential for conflict is
clear if we assume that the legislator wishes both to perform adequately

287

as a committee member and to assure himself of party support for his reelection.

A third source of role conflict is ambiguous or highly complex role expectations. For example, an individual moving to a new school, traveling in a foreign country or an ethnic ghetto, or simply meeting someone he knows absolutely nothing about, has no clear idea of what is expected of him in any given situation. He is uncertain which role to adopt. Some would argue that in our society women in particular are surrounded by ambiguous role expectations.

The general result of role conflict (ignoring, for the moment, the psychological effects on the individual) is to make meaningful interaction between persons difficult or impossible. In some cases, the ultimate result may be violence. In any case, where role conflict exists, we tend to look for ways of resolving it by manipulating expectations: by isolating or insulating the role or roles with conflicting expectations or by attempting to change the contradictory expectations themselves.

An example of the first way of resolving role conflict is the way in which university educators attempt to insulate (and, some would argue, to isolate) the teacher and the classroom from the pressures of the local community, trustees, state legislators, university administrators, and even other faculty members. This mode of resolution is predicated on the idea that the individual faculty member and his students are dedicated to "the search for truth." This assumption constitutes one source of role expectations within the educational process. Other expectations, based perhaps on a perception of the teacher's role as one of disseminating particular "truths" or inculcating accepted values, may come from outside the classroom. If the university is committed to fulfilling the first set of expectations and some faculty member wishes to teach what he believes to be true, rather than what the public feels is necessary for the students as members of a particular community to learn, then keeping the classroom insulated from outside pressures is one way of minimizing potential conflict.

Another way of minimizing role conflict can be illustrated by looking again at the role of a member of the House Appropriations Committee. Often, when the occupant of a position is expected to serve as a liaison between groups with conflicting demands, the two groups exhibit what is called *pluralistic ignorance*. Pluralistic ignorance can take two forms. The group members may assume that their expectations are not shared by any other individual or group, even though they are. Or, the members of the two groups may be unaware that their expectations are contradictory. One way to minimize the potential conflict for an individual who, like the representative described earlier, is "in the middle," is to sensitize one or both of the groups to their conflicting expectations about his behavior and thereby change them.

In our example, the House committee member was expected to support subcommittee reports. However, if the report on a particular bill conflicted with the interests or preferences of his constituency, he might inform the other members of the subcommittee of the conflict. In this way, he might change their expectations to include violation of the norm of unity in this one case. This, of course, would be possible only because of the committee's shared expectation that reelection was important.

A Simple Theory of Behavior

Up to this point we have examined the concept of a role as a set of behavioral expectations that define the rights and duties associated with specific positions within a group. Very little has been said about the individuals who occupy these positions and play these roles. It should be obvious that the occupant of a social or political position is not motivated by the expectations of others alone. On the contrary, individuals bring to the positions they occupy behavioral expectations of their own, as the previous chapter on attitudes showed. As scientists we are interested in generalizations about behavior, and role theory is a means of moving beyond descriptions of idiosyncratic role performance. However, this does not mean that we are uninterested in the relation of personality or psycho-logic to behavior (i.e., role performance). Apparently, both belief systems and role expectations are factors in role performance. Both attitude theory and role theory, therefore, are functional in the sense described in Chapter 7. Both explain behavioral phenomena. In order to formulate a more general theory of behavior, however, it is necessary to make some hypotheses about the relationship between attitudes and expectations. In this section, we shall outline a simple

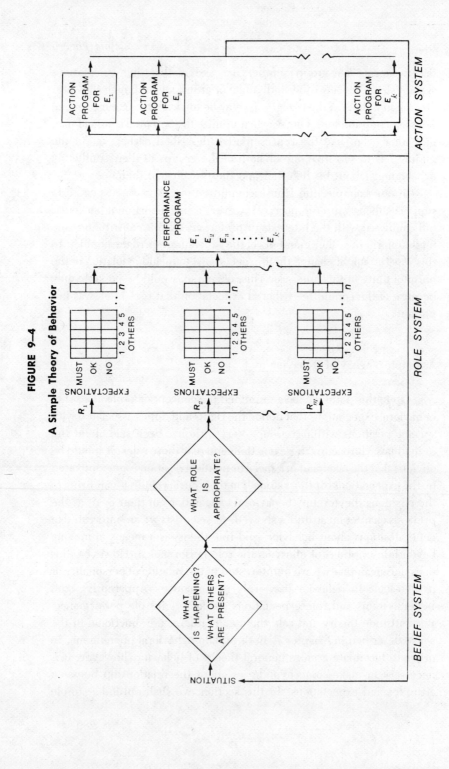

FIGURE 9–4

A Simple Theory of Behavior

theory of behavior that does just this. It is a highly abstract theory that should not be taken as anything more than speculation, but it does tie up some loose ends.

The fundamental system in this theory is a behavioral, or *action, system.* The basic units of this system are learned motor responses. It is extremely complex, containing, in effect, all the physiological "programs" for behavior. These programs organize elemental motor responses (such as contracting a bicep) into significant actions (such as waving a hand). The system also includes all the "automatic" mechanisms that allow an individual to perform complex behavior without exerting any conscious effort.

The action system is guided by a *role system*, a set of "master programs" used to determine what role is required in a given situation and which specific action programs, in which sequences, will be performed. The role system's data bank contains all the patterns of expectations (all the prescribed, permitted, and prohibited actions) that go with each role in the individual's repertoire.

Complementing the role system is a *belief system*, which operates in conjunction with the cognitive and perceptual apparatus of the individual to inform the role system what is happening in a given situation—what others are present, what behaviors they are exhibiting, and what the significance of these behaviors is.

A highly simplified representation of these three systems in action is presented in Figure 9-4. The belief system enables the individual to define the situation by interpreting what is happening. The role system then selects the "general" pattern of behavior required (R) and the set of expectations associated with the significant others in the situation. This set of expectations governs how the role chosen will be performed and thereby determines which set of action programs will be used.

In the diagram, there is a path leading back to the situation at the point where the belief system couples with the role system. This is because, once an individual perceives what others are significant in a situation and what is going on, his attitudes toward these people and their actions, as well as his perception of them, become an integral part of the situation. In a sense, then, each new perception creates a new situation. This may seem rather complicated, but the basic idea is not. Suppose you walk into a strange room in which there are several other people. As you identify these people and observe what they are doing, you associate them and their actions with other idea elements in your belief system. In this way, you define the situation. In defining the situation, however, you must also take into account the effect of your own perceptions and attitudes. By entering the situation and defining it in your own way, you have, in effect, altered it.

There is also a path leading back to the situation at the point where the role system couples with the action system. Earlier in the chapter, we noted the capacity of an individual to rehearse his behavior mentally and anticipate the reactions of significant others to it. This *covert rehearsal process* that occurs once you have selected what you feel is an appropriate performance program is predicated on expectations about the behavior of others in the situation. But just as your beliefs about a situation become part of it, so too do your expectations. If these expectations make the performance program originally selected seem inappropriate, a new one can be selected, creating another new situation, and so on.

The path that leads back to the situation from the end of the diagram represents yet another factor input—the behavior you actually exhibit. This too becomes a part of the situation and changes it. This creates yet another new situation, which, too, will be defined and redefined as new beliefs, expectations, and behavior are generated. Naturally, all the other individuals in the situation are going through the same sort of process—evaluating what is happening, creating expectations, rehearsing and revising behavior, and so on. Each, by his actions, perceptions, and reactions, is constantly altering the situation. Though human social interaction may appear relatively simple on the surface, the processes of interaction are complex almost beyond belief. Even this general theory is wide open to the charge that it is an extremely oversimplified representation of human behavior.

Conclusion

In this chapter, as in the last, we have discussed a theoretical construct that many political scientists have found useful in studying political behavior. The notion of a role as a set of potential behaviors which are available to the individual in a specific situation goes a long way toward explaining similarities in the behavior of individuals in certain political positions. Yet the concept of roles, like the concept of attitudes, is simply a construct that helps to summarize the ways in which socialization structures behavior. The basic principles of role theory are quite simple. Unfortunately, the reports of behavioral scientists who use role theory tend to be very technical and laden with jargon. Hopefully, the student will be able to use the rather simple and basic concepts developed here to see through the jargon to the way in which role theory provides a significant perspective on human behavior.[7]

Notes

1. Richard Fenno, *The Power of the Purse: Appropriations Politics in Congress* (Boston: Little, Brown, 1966), pp. 160-167.
2. See Theodore Newcomb, Ralph Turner, and Philip E. Converse, *Social Psychology* (New York: Holt, Rinehart & Winston, 1965). Chapter 11 contains an extensive treatment of this topic from the social psychologist's point of view.
3. H. J. Leavitt, "Some Effects of Certain Communication Patterns on Group Performance," *Journal of Abnormal and Social Psychology*, Vol. 46 (1951), 38-50.
4. Extensive discussions of the application of this technique in analyzing role relations, or structures, can be found in Oscar A. Oeser and Frank Harary, "A Mathematical Model for Structural Role Theory, I," *Human Relations*, Vol. 15 (1962), 89-109;

Frank Harary and R. Z. Norman, *Graph Theory as a Mathematical Model in Social Science*, (Ann Arbor, Mich.: Institute for Social Research, 1953); Frank Harary, R. Z. Norman, and D. Cartwright, *Structural Models: An Introduction to the Theory of Directed Graphs* (New York: Wiley, 1965).
5. William C. Mitchell, "Occupational Role Strains: The American Elective Public Official," *Administrative Science Quarterly* (September 1958), 219-228.
6. This topic is discussed more extensively in Chapter 11.
7. The classic applications of role theory in political science can be found in John Wahlke *et al.*, *The Legislative System* (New York: Wiley, 1962); and James David Barber, *The Lawmakers* (New Haven, Conn.: Yale University Press, 1963).

10

Choice,
Conflict, and
Coalition:
Decision-Making
and
Political
Behavior

Choice is a fundamental characteristic of political behavior. Some choices are *individual*, as when a citizen votes for a candidate or a referendum, a candidate selects an election strategy, a prime minister implements wage and price controls, a legislator flips a switch on the floor of the U.S. House of Representatives, or a bureaucrat passes on a budget request to a superior. Other choices are *collective*, as when a popular majority elects a candidate, parliament approves legislation, a study group makes recommendations, or the U.S. Supreme Court hands down a decision. In this chapter we will focus on *choice behavior* or *decision-making*. We will use, for the most part, the perspective of the *theory of games* as our primary means of analysis.[1]

The Nature of Choice

Whenever a decision is made, a choice is made among *alternatives*. A *decision is a process in which a single alternative or a number of alternatives are selected from some set, or class, of alternatives*. The kinds of alternatives relevant to the study of political behavior are potential courses of action for an individual or a group. These potential courses of action are tentative (that is, they have not as yet been selected), and they are possible (that is, if selected they can be effected). For example, a man on a window ledge may make a decision by choosing between the alternatives of jumping or not jumping. However, if he jumps, it is absurd to say that he may choose between falling up and falling down. In such a situation there can be no decision and no choice because there are no alternatives; that is, no effective alternatives.

Theories of decision-making are directed toward the analysis of behavior with respect to choices. In some ways the theories in this area of political behaviorism are unique. They are perhaps the most highly developed, mathematically, of any theories in behavioral science. They are also, in many cases, explicitly normative. The theory of games, which underlies many specific theories of decision-making, is concerned not so much with describing the process by which individuals or collectivities make choices, but with creating a logical framework that will enable a decision-maker, under certain conditions, to make the "best possible" selection from among the alternatives open to him. It is a normative theory in that its goal is to inform the decision-maker what he *should* do when faced with particular alternatives. Of course, it makes no claim to provide the best absolute solution to a problem. It is, rather, an *instrument* that enables the theorist to say "under these conditions, if you wish to accomplish this objective, you should select that alternative course of action."

The basic variables in decision theory include the number of alternatives, the consequences of those alternatives, and the relation between the selection of an alternative and its consequences. Implicit in the notion of an *alternative* is the notion of an outcome or a set of outcomes. An alternative (jumping off a building) is chosen because of its consequences, or the expected outcome (leaving this mortal coil). The *expectation* of an outcome is possible because of the laws that govern behavior. (Jumping off a building is, the law of gravity tells us, a fairly

295

effective method of suicide.) Implicit in the act of *choosing an alternative* is the notion that certain outcomes are preferable to others. It is assumed, in decision theory, that individuals have *preferences* concerning specific states of affairs or possible outcomes. It is also assumed that the amount of information available about these outcomes has an important effect on the character of a decision.

Decision Environments

Decisions are affected by the *information environment* in which they occur. This means, simply, that the amount of information a decision-maker has about the number of alternatives in a situation, the number of outcomes, the expected relation between the alternatives and outcomes, and the order in which the outcomes are preferred has an important effect on the kind of decision that is possible. In an information environment of *certainty*, all the possible alternatives are known to the decision-maker and each alternative is known to lead, invariably, to a specific outcome. Thus the decision-maker can select the alternative that he expects, with certainty, will lead to the most preferable outcome. In an information environment of *risk*, all the possible alternatives are again known, but each alternative can lead to any one of a number of outcomes, each of whose probability is known. In this case, as we shall see, the best the decision-maker can do is to select the alternative that is most likely to lead to a preferred outcome. In an information environment of *uncertainty*, each of the possible alternatives may again lead to any one of a number of possible outcomes, but the probabilities of these outcomes are unknown. The decision-maker must therefore make some a priori assumptions about the "state of nature" (that is, what will "really" happen) and select an alternative that will, if his assumptions are correct, have a greater possibility of achieving a preferred outcome than one that is distinctly not preferred. In an information environment of *deficiency*, these problems also exist. In addition, either the complete set of possible alternatives or the complete set of possible outcomes, or both, are unknown. Under these conditions a decision-maker can only examine as many alternatives and possible outcomes as he can within a given time and select the alternative which appears, at that time, to have the best chance of leading to an acceptable outcome.

Basically, decision theory attempts to relate alternative courses of action to preferred outcomes given different amounts of information. In the sections that follow, we will examine decision-making under the various conditions described above in some detail.

Making Decisions Under Conditions of Certainty

When a decision-maker is aware of all the possible courses of action he may take and knows that each alternative will surely result in a specific outcome, the information environment for his decision is said to be one of certainty. Essentially, this means that he can be certain about the result of his decision, no matter which course of action he selects. For example, suppose that a committee has ten members, including the chairman. Suppose, also, that the rules of the committee specify that the chairman is to vote only in the case of a tie. Say that the committee is electing a secretary; three members have been nominated, and each has received three votes. In this situation the chairman must vote; that is, he must make a decision. Moreover, he must choose between three alternatives (the three candidates) and no others. Whichever choice he makes will obviously determine the outcome of the election in the sense that it will determine which of the members will become the committee's secretary. Because the chairman knows all the possible alternatives, knows all the possible outcomes, and is assumed to have an order of preference with respect to the candidates, we can say that his decision takes place in an environment of certainty.

Using Utility as a Measure of Preference

A fundamental problem in decision theory and the theory of games is how to describe and account for the preferences of the decision-maker. Decision theory assumes that when an individual selects a particular course of action under conditions of certainty, he does so because it will result in a preferred outcome. Theories of decision-making under conditions of certainty are designed to allow the individual to choose the alternative that best suits his own preferences.

We need, first, to be able to describe preferences in a way that

297

allows us to discuss decisions no matter who the specific decision-maker might be, and no matter what his preferences are. As we pointed out in Chapter 2, it is often useful to be able to assign numbers to certain kinds of events, or "variables," so that we can use the rules of arithmetic or the language of statistics to test hypotheses. This is essentially what we are interested in doing here. An individual's preferences (his likes and dislikes) are variables, and it is possible for us to assign useful numbers to them.

For example, consider a survey of a voting population intended to predict the outcome of an election two years in advance, or to serve as a beginning for a study of changes in voter preferences during the period preceding the election. We do not know which candidates will actually be running at the time of the election. (Some, after all, may drop out or die, and others may announce their availability at a later date.) We can, however, ask the individuals in our sample to choose between pairs of candidates taken from a list of all conceivable contestants. To make the example very simple, let us say that there are only four possible candidates: Gray, Black, White, and Claghorn. We begin by pairing these candidates in every possible way. We then present our list of pairs to the individuals being surveyed and ask them which of each pair they prefer. Finally, we use these pairwise preferences to assign numerical values to each candidate (each alternative) that represent each individual's preferences.

Say the results for two survey respondents, *A* and *B*, are as described in Table 10-1. What numbers can we assign to their preferences? Since there are four people running for office, it seems only logical to

TABLE 10–1

Pairwise Preferences

| Possible Two-Man Races | PREFERENCES | |
	Individual A	Individual B
Black/White	White	White
Black/Gray	Gray	Gray
Black/Claghorn	Black	Claghorn
White/Gray	White	Gray
White/Claghorn	White	Claghorn
Gray/Claghorn	Gray	Gray

give a "4" to the candidate preferred most often, a "3" to the candidate preferred slightly less often, and so on down the line. Thus, for respondent *A*, White is assigned a value of 4, Gray is assigned a value of 3, Black is assigned a value of 2, and Claghorn is assigned a value of 1; for respondent *B*, Gray is assigned a value of 4, Claghorn a value of 3, White a value of 2, and Black a value of 1. These numbers, which reflect the pairwise preferences of *A* and *B*, are said to indicate the *utility* of each candidate (each alternative) for *A* and *B*. *Utility*, in decision theory, is a measure of the order in which alternatives are preferred. It is an *ordinal measure* of individual preferences.

Two key things should be observed here: (1) the assignment of numbers to preferences is a direct result of the choices made by individuals, and (2) each individual is assumed to choose the candidate that has, in his view, the maximum utility. The significance of the first point will be discussed in the next section. The significance of the second point, which seems a trivial observation here, is more evident in analyses of more complex kinds of decisions. We will discuss one such decision here to show what we mean.

To see how useful the concept of utility can be, let us look at a slightly more complicated situation. Say a friend has come to you, as an expert in decision-making, complaining that he finds it very difficult to make up his mind how to vote in a coming election for city commissioner, in which the four candidates mentioned above are running. He has no clear overall preference for any one of the candidates; he likes White's personality and his general political image, but he also likes Black's stands on the issues and is a relatively loyal member of Gray's political party. In order to help him make up his mind, you ask him if these three variables are the only ones he feels are important. He says that this is the case, but that the candidates' stands on the issues are at least twice as important to him as any of the other variables.

Armed with this information, you proceed by pairing the candidates in every possible way, as before, and asking your friend to choose which member of each pair he prefers on the basis of personality alone, which he prefers on the basis of stands on issues alone, and which he prefers on the basis of partisan affiliations. Let us say that he makes the choices listed in Table 10-2.

This information and your knowledge of how your friend feels about the relative importance of the variables enable you to set up a *utility*

TABLE 10–2

Pairwise Preferences Based on Three Variables

	PREFERENCES		
Possible Pairs of Candidates	Based on Personality	Based on Issues	Based on Party
Black/White	W	B	W
Black/Gray	G	B	G
Black/Claghorn	B	B	C
White/Gray	W	W	G
White/Claghorn	W	W	C
Gray/Claghorn	G	G	G

function (simply, a rule which allows us to assign numbers to preferences in some logically consistent way) relevant to the decision at hand. You have three measures of utility: personality, stands on issues, and partisan affiliations. These three measures of utility, in the order mentioned, make up a *utility vector* for each candidate. (A *vector* is simply a set of numbers in some meaningful order.) The utility vectors in this case are as follows:

$$\text{White: } (4, 3, 2)$$
$$\text{Gray: } (3, 2, 4)$$
$$\text{Black: } (2, 4, 1)$$
$$\text{Claghorn: } (1, 1, 3)$$

Your next step is to devise a utility function that assigns a unique value to each candidate. You do this by finding the *expected utility* over the range of the utility vector in each case. You take each individual utility value, weight it by its relative importance (in this case issue stands were felt to be twice as important as the other two variables), add the values, and divide the total by the sum of the weights. This gives you a utility value that is a weighted arithmetic average:

$$U_{\text{White}} = \frac{1(4) + 2(3) + 1(2)}{4} = \frac{4 + 6 + 2}{4} = \frac{12}{4}$$

$$U_{\text{Gray}} = \frac{1(3) + 2(2) + 1(4)}{4} = \frac{3 + 4 + 4}{4} = \frac{11}{4}$$

300

$$U_{\text{Black}} = \frac{1(2) + 2(4) + 1(1)}{4} = \frac{2 + 8 + 1}{4} = \frac{11}{4}$$

$$U_{\text{Claghorn}} = \frac{1(1) + 2(1) + 1(3)}{4} = \frac{1 + 2 + 3}{4} = \frac{6}{4}$$

You can now advise your friend to choose the candidate that has the highest expected utility, based on the preferences he expressed. This candidate is White.

Rationality and Decision Theory

In the previous section we mentioned that the utility assigned to alternatives is a direct result of the preferences expressed by the decision-maker, that is, of his own *behavior*. If an individual expresses preferences among outcomes, and these preferences are consistent, or *transitive* (that is, if whenever he prefers A to B and B to C he prefers A to C), then decision theory (or, more generally, the theory of games) allows us to re-express those preferences as a quantitative utility function. A decision, or choice, is said to be *rational* when it is made *by maximizing a utility function over the range of preferences*—that is, when the alternative chosen is one that guarantees the decision-maker the highest possible utility in terms of outcomes. Since decision theory predicts which behavioral alternative will produce the maximum utility, it does, in a sense, predict rational behavior. However, what constitutes rational behavior is a consequence of our definition of utility.

It is often argued that alternative A is preferred to alternative B *because* A has a greater utility than B. This implies that utility is the reason we have preferences. *This is not the case*. It is because an individual does in fact prefer alternative A to alternative B that we can assign utility to these courses of action. Utility is a result, or measure, of preference and does not cause it.

The lack of evidence that individuals always behave rationally is often felt to be a major stumbling block to the application of decision theory and the theory of games to the real world. This is, indeed, a very real problem; but its dimensions are limited by our definition of rationality. Decision theory defines rationality as behaving in a way that maximizes expected utility. This in itself causes no problem in applying the

301

theory; there is nothing illegitimate about such a definition. But decision theory is, in the first place, designed as an aid for the person whose preferences are consistent or transitive. If a person behaves in a consistent manner, that is, if his preferences are transitive and he acts on them, then his choices will in fact maximize expected utility. This is a deduction from our definition of consistent behavior. It can be proven mathematically, but it is descriptive of the real world only if individuals have consistent preferences. What the theory says, in effect, is that if a person wishes to behave consistently then he must maximize expected utility. If he does not wish to behave consistently, then the theory has nothing to say about what choices should be made.

For decision theory to work, all that is required of the individual is that he make consistent choices, not that he be rational in the ordinary sense of having preferences which are in some sense in his best interest.[2] Here we assume that individual decision-makers know what is in their best interest, and this knowledge is reflected in the preferences they express.

Making Decisions Under Conditions of Risk

When the decision-maker's information environment is one of *risk*, he knows all the courses of action open to him, all the outcomes that may occur, and which outcomes he prefers. The difference between an information environment of certainty and one of risk is that, in the latter, there is not necessarily a unique outcome attached to each choice. A choice may have a number of possible outcomes. However, we assume that the decision-maker knows the precise possibility of a particular outcome, given a specific choice.

The most obvious application of decision theory under conditions of risk is in gambling. However, simple examples of decisions under conditions of risk can be found in everyday life. Say you are taking a class in which the teacher regularly gives pop quizzes. You know from his past behavior that he gives about ten quizzes a semester. You also know, since each semester consists of about 40 class periods, that on any specific day there is one chance in four of a quiz. Let us assume that this has been a bad week for you; you have a mild cold, and you have taken tests in three other courses. As a result, you have not been able to read the material for this week for this particular class as thoroughly as you should. Let us also assume that a friend has told you that he will be seeing someone whom you have been very anxious to meet at the very time that this class meets and that if you can join them an introduction can be arranged. Since your teacher has a rather severe policy with respect to missed quizzes (you fail the quiz if you miss it), you are faced with a difficult decision.

This decision can be characterized as follows: You can either go to class or not go. If you go, and there is a quiz, you will probably get a low grade, because you haven't been able to study, but still a passing one. If there is no quiz, you will probably learn something; and that is reasonably valuable to you as a student, if for no other reason than that it may help you pass the final examination. If you do not go and a quiz is given, you will receive a failing grade on the quiz, a result you consider totally unacceptable; but at least you will have been able to meet the person you are interested in and perhaps establish a basis for a future relationship. If you do not go and a quiz is not given, little harm will have been done to your education and you will have met the person you want to meet.

Given these particular preferences, we can devise a utility function that represents your preferences among the various outcomes numerically. Not going to class and missing a quiz is the situation you prefer least of all. Going to class, being given a quiz, and getting a low grade is preferable to failing, but not to attending a class in which no quiz is given. Of course the most preferable situation is keeping the date with your friend and "lucking out" with respect to the quiz. This decision situation is summarized in Table 10-3. The utilities assigned to each outcome are in parenthesis.

Failing the quiz, the most repugnant outcome, has a utility of zero. The differences among the utilities of the other possible outcomes are roughly equal. The expected utility of each alternative is the sum of the utilities assigned to the outcomes associated with that alternative, each of which is weighted by the possibility it will occur. If you attend class, there is one chance in four that you will get a quiz and receive a low grade, whereas there are three chances in four that you will learn something. Thus, the expected utility for attending class in this situation is:

$$(1/4)(2.0) + (3/4)(2.5) = \frac{2 + 7.5}{4} = 2.37$$

The expected utility for not attending class is

$$(1/4)(0) + (3/4)(3) = \frac{0 + 9}{4} = 2.22$$

Therefore, if you wish to maximize your expected utility (i.e., behave consistently with respect to your stated preferences), you will choose to attend class.

As we noted at the outset, when decisions are made in an information environment of risk, all possible courses of action are known, and all possible consequences of these actions are known. Moreover, the decision-maker's preferences with respect to the outcomes are consistent, and we know the laws that govern the relationship of the alternatives to the outcomes. Bearing these facts in mind, you might try to work out the example above using different people and different utility functions. Or you might try to see how different relationships between alternatives and outcomes affect the decision. For example, if there was only one chance in six that a quiz would be given, you would probably decide not to go to class, if all other aspects of the problem were the same. Finally, you might try this sort of analysis on a completely different problem, as long as you had the same kind of information.

TABLE 10–3

Alternatives and Outcomes in an
Information Environment of Risk

	OUTCOMES	
Alternatives	Quiz	No Quiz
Attend class	Low grade (2.0)	Learn something (2.5)
Not attend	Fail (0.0)	Keep date (3.0)

Making Decisions Under Conditions of Uncertainty

An information environment of uncertainty occurs when the decision-maker does not know the laws that govern the relationships between possible alternatives and outcomes. He or she is assumed to know all the possible alternatives, and all the consequences that may occur, but not which outcomes are more or less likely once a particular alternative has been selected.

To make the discussion a bit less abstract, let us tie it to a specific example. Let us assume that the decision-maker is an advance man for someone who is running for political office. The advance man's job is to set up speeches to various groups and make all the necessary preparations—advertising the speech, picking a location, setting up public address equipment, and so on. He is new at his job, having just been hired to replace another man who, the candidate had found, had actually been working for the opposition. This man had often misinformed the candidate about the nature of the group he would be addressing and in other ways undermined the campaign. In one instance, his "advance information" had resulted in the candidate's making several jokes about the women's liberation movement to a group of professional social workers, many of whom were strong supporters of the movement.

The situation now is this: The candidate is scheduled to address a group, in one-half hour, in a city the advance man cannot possibly get to. The candidate has just had three new speeches written, which he has read over only once, and will have to use a teleprompter. It is up to our decision-maker, his new advance man, to tell the technicians which speech to set up for the address: a pro-labor speech, a conservative speech with many anti-big labor comments and a few women's lib jokes, and a speech on the moral problems of the nation. The former advance man, before he left, informed the candidate that the group was the local retail clerks' union. Because his predecessor had misinformed the candidate before, the new man has no idea whether his employer will actually be addressing that group or one of the other groups the local newspaper has listed as meeting in the same building on that night: the local chapter of the John Birch Society and a Methodist Church group. The problem, of course, is that some of the candidate's speeches are very inappropriate for certain of these groups.

The major problem in decision-making under conditions of uncertainty is that the outcome of the decision depends upon the actual "state of nature." In our example, there are three possible states of nature, depending on which group the candidate is actually scheduled to address. It is necessary to formulate some sort of criterion for deciding which speech (i.e., which alternative) should be chosen. The first thing to do, once again, is to devise a utility function that will allow us to assign values to each of the possible outcomes.

A summary of this decision problem is given in Table 10-4. The entries in the table indicate the utility of each state of nature for the candidate. The candidate is a Democrat who depends to a great extent on the support of organized labor, and it would be very helpful to his cause to deliver the pro-labor speech to the labor union local. Giving the conservative speech to the labor union group would be a relatively bad mistake, even though some labor union members are rather conservative and see many bad aspects of huge labor unions. It would be preferable to give the conservative speech to the Birch Society meeting and the morals speech to the church group; but since such speeches would probably be expected by the groups, the "payoff" (the utility actually received) would not be terribly high. Giving the pro-labor speech to the Birch Society would be a very bad move, and giving it to the church group might alienate some of the more conservative members of the audience. The morals speech would probably not be offen-

TABLE 10–4

The Utility of Various Alternatives and Outcomes (States of Nature) in an Information Environment of Uncertainty

	STATES OF NATURE		
Alternatives	S_1 Union Group Scheduled	S_2 Birch Society Scheduled	S_3 Church Group Scheduled
A_1 Pro-labor speech	8	−3	−1
A_2 Conservative speech	−2	3	1
A_3 Morals speech	0	2	3

sive to any of the groups, but it would probably be considered irrelevant by the labor union group.

In deciding which course of action to take in the environment of uncertainty, we face one fundamental problem we did not face in the other situations discussed above. In this instance, we have no idea what probabilities to assign to each possible outcome, and hence no way to calculate their expected utility. In order to make a decision, we must make some further assumptions about the situation.

THE PRINCIPLE OF INSUFFICIENT REASON

One possible assumption is that each of the states of nature in our example is equally likely. The advance man might make this assumption if there was no more reason to believe that the candidate had been scheduled to address the John Birch Society than that he had been scheduled to address the church group or the union local. Given this assumption, he might calculate the expected utility of each state of nature in the following way:

$$U_L = (1/3)(8) + (1/3)(-3) + (1/3)(-1) = 4/3$$
$$U_C = (1/3)(-2) + (1/3)(3) + (1/3)(1) = 2/3$$
$$U_M = (1/3)(0) + (1/3)(2) + (1/3)(3) = 5/3$$

Thus, using this particular decision criterion (that is, making the assumption that each state of nature is equally likely), our decision-maker would maximize his expected utility by choosing the morals speech.

THE MAXIMIN CRITERION

It is not necessary, in making decisions under conditions of uncertainty, to always assume that particular states of nature are equally likely. In some cases, we may wish to make very conservative assumptions about the state of nature. If we are of a pessimistic turn of mind, we may assume that nature operates according to Murphy's Law—"If it can happen, it will, and to me." If we expect the worst from nature, we may wish to use a decision criterion that allows us to emerge from a situation with the minimum possible loss. The *maximin criterion*, which tells us to select the alternative with the maximum minimum utility, does exactly this. It lets us be as sure as we can that we will get hurt as little as possible.[3]

The maximin criterion is not nearly as bizarre as it may initially appear. One way to look at decision-making under conditions of uncertainty is as a kind of game we play with Mother Nature. In our example, the decision-maker has three possible "moves" (selecting one of three possible speeches). Mother Nature also has three possible moves (since there are three possible states of nature). The maximin criterion for making a decision, or, to stay with the analogy, making a move, tells the decision-maker to play the game as if Mother Nature knew exactly what he was going to do and would, in turn, make the move that would do him the most damage. Thus this criterion would have the decision-maker assume that if he chose to set up the pro-labor speech, Mother Nature would most assuredly give the candidate the John Birch Society to address; if he chose the conservative speech or the morals speech, the candidate would certainly wind up speaking before the union group. The maximin criterion, then, suggests that the rational decision is to select the speech that will produce the highest possible utility, given the worst possible state of nature.

Another way of looking at the maximin criterion is to argue that, if the advance man does not know which state of nature will prevail, he should select the speech with the greatest minimum utility. That is, he should select the alternative that has the highest (i.e., maximum) minimum payoff compared to all the other alternatives. As Table 10-4 shows, the alternative with the highest minimum payoff is A_3, the morals speech. At *worst*, this alternative will have no utility. If the advance man chooses either of the other two speeches, he risks an outcome with negative utility (a loss).

THE MINIMAX REGRET CRITERION

Some people argue that the maximin criterion is unnecessarily pessimistic about the probable state of nature and that the resulting decision does not take into account the regrets the decision-maker will have for not capitalizing on the possibility of a more fortunate state of nature. In our example there is relatively little to be gained from making the morals speech, but a good deal might be gained by making the pro-labor speech if it happened that the meeting to be addressed was indeed the union's. That is, if the advance man chose the morals speech and it turned out that the candidate was to address the union group, he would regret his choice.

The *minimax regret criterion* for making choices under conditions of uncertainty is an attempt to take these considerations into account. It suggests that the decision-maker create, from the original decision table, a new, "regrets" decision table. The utilities in the new table are obtained by adding to the original utility entries in each column the amount necessary to make them equal to the maximum utility in the column. This is an attempt to quantify the regrets the decision-maker would have, *given* that a particular state of nature occurred. For example, if the decision-maker selected the morals speech, and the candidate talked to the union group, we might argue that the advance man would have at least eight units of regret that he did not choose the pro-labor speech.

Table 10-5 shows the regret associated with each outcome in the example. To satisfy the minimax regret criterion, the advance man would have to select the alternative that would minimize the maximum amount of regret possible. Thus he would choose the pro-labor speech,

TABLE 10–5

Units of Regret Associated with Various Alternatives and Outcomes (States of Nature) in an Information Environment of Uncertainty

	STATES OF NATURE		
Alternatives	S_1 Union Group Scheduled	S_2 Birch Society Scheduled	S_3 Church Group Scheduled
A_1 Pro-labor speech	0	6	4
A_2 Conservative speech	10	0	2
A_3 Morals speech	8	1	0

which would result, at most, in six units of regret if the candidate had to address the Birch Society.

These are not the only possible criteria for making decisions in an uncertain information environment, and they are all extremely conservative ones. It might be instructive for a student to see what would happen if he or she assumed the best possible motives on the part of nature, or constructed some kind of sliding scale of optimism that would affect the relative weights given the distribution of utilities. At this stage, however, it is not important to learn how to calculate expected utilities for all possible criteria. It is enough to realize that differing assumptions yield different rational decisions and to understand the general effects of the kinds of assumptions one might make.

Making Decisions Under Conditions of Deficiency

In all the decision-making environments discussed up to this point, we have been concerned with providing guides for achieving the maximum possible payoff when all possible alternatives and all possible outcomes are known to the decision-maker at the time the decision is to be made. In an information environment that is deficient, we need different kinds of guidelines for decision-making, ones that can be used when we do not know all the alternatives open to us and all the outcomes associated with them. To find these guidelines we shall examine some decision theories that not only reject the enterprise of explicitly trying to maximize expected utility but are less normative and more descriptive of the actual decision-making processes of individuals or groups.

SATISFICING

One way of approaching decision-making in a deficient information environment is to modify the notion of rationality as making decisions that maximize expected utility. We might, for example, adopt a more general definition of rationality such as the selection of alternatives that serve the general goals the decision-maker has in making the decision. We assume, in this event, that the goals of the decision-maker are

310

already given and that he can formulate criteria for deciding whether a particular course of action is satisfactory in serving those goals relative to any other alternatives which may be considered. These *satisficing criteria* may be quantitative or comparative utility measures, or much more informal guidelines such as "informed and experienced intuition."

The key to understanding satisficing criteria for making decisions is to think of decision-making as a process of *searching* for possible alternatives.[4] It is taken for granted, in applying these criteria, that the decision-maker cannot possibly discover all the alternatives in a situation and analyze them completely because his resources, including his time and energy, are limited. He therefore makes a sequential search for alternatives that can be compared, one by one, with the criteria he has formulated for a satisfactory selection. He stops when he comes upon the first alternative that meets his minimum satisficing criteria.

To see how satisficing operates, let us pretend that we are omniscient observers of a particular decision situation; that is, we know all the alternatives and their outcomes. We also know precisely how much each course of action would contribute to satisfying a particular goal. Our knowledge is represented graphically in Figure 10-1.

The decision-maker in this hypothetical example does not have this information, so he decides to evaluate each alternative as he comes upon it in light of some particular satisficing criterion he has chosen. Let us say that he selects as a satisficing criterion a degree of satisfaction equivalent to 60 on the scale in Figure 10-1. Let us also assume that he discovers various alternatives in the following order: 17, 18, 3, 2, 19, 1, 6. The process of discovery is represented graphically in Figure 10-2. The broken line in the figure represents the satisficing criterion chosen by the decision-maker. The first alternative he comes upon in his search which exceeds that criterion is alternative 6. Therefore, alternative 6 will be selected, even though it is less satisfactory than alternative 9—the solution that would have been predicted by decision theory had the information environment been one of certainty.

Another kind of satisficing criterion would be some kind of time limit on the search procedure. At the end of a certain time, the decision-maker would select that alternative which provided the maximum satisfaction of all the alternatives examined up to that time. If the decision-maker in the example above had allowed himself only enough

311

FIGURE 10–1

**A Universe of Alternatives and the Degrees of Satisfaction
Associated with Them**

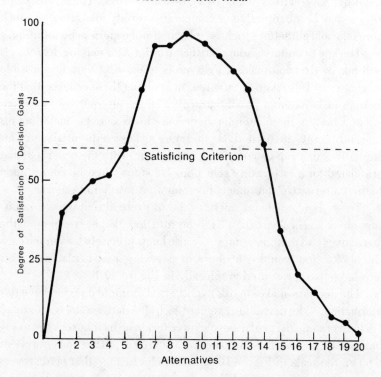

time to examine six alternatives, and they presented themselves in the
same order as above, he would have selected alternative 3. Of the first
six alternatives examined, it would provide the highest degree of satisfaction.

INCREMENTALISM

Another approach to decision-making in a deficient information
environment, which is very much related to the concept of satisficing, is
to view the decision process as one of making small incremental changes
over time from some previous state.[5] This approach to the process of
decision-making emphasizes the very real problem of diffuse and rather
ill-defined goals. The decision criteria discussed above all entailed

312

FIGURE 10–2

A Subset of Alternatives and the Degrees of Satisfaction Associated with Them

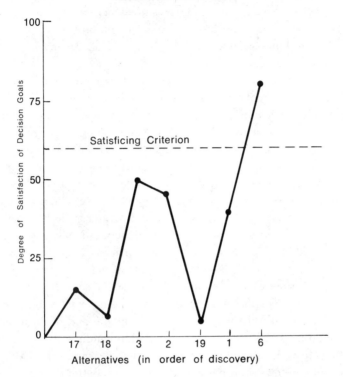

rather specific assumptions about the decision-maker's goals. It was his goals (or values, or preferences) which allowed us to assign quantitative values (utilities) to alternatives. If the decision-maker's goals are not well defined, it is not possible to assign values to alternatives as a basis for rational decisions.

Some theorists argue that in situations where specific preferences are not known, generally those kinds of situations in which the problems are very complex and the number of alternatives and outcomes is seemingly infinite, the decision-maker takes what he is given—that is, the status quo—as a preliminary definition of the goals he ought to be serving. Such situations are typical in politics, where decisions often have very wide-ranging effects over long periods of time, and where there is not likely to be a firm consensus on goals. Under such conditions

313

it is felt that the status quo, which is viewed as a composite of decisions which have already been made, is a reasonable initial statement of goals, and that a current decision should attempt only to effect some sort of marginal change in a past decision. This small incremental, or marginal, change can then be evaluated, and information on the consequences (the new status quo) used to assist the decision-maker in making further incremental decisions.

For a simple, everyday example of such incremental decision-making, consider a situation in which an individual decides to take up photography as a hobby. In making this decision, he may commit himself completely to taking the best possible photographs, read several books on photography, analyze carefully the merits of all the equipment he will need—cameras, lenses, processing equipment, an enlarger, and so on, then go out and buy the best available equipment and begin his search for the perfect photograph. This, of course, could be a very expensive decision. After a few months his interest in photography might wane. If it does, he will have several thousand dollars invested in equipment that is worthless to him, and worth much less than what he paid for it to someone else. Another person may decide to take up photography somewhat differently. He may spend some time talking to others interested in photography, do some reading on the subject, buy a rather simple and relatively inexpensive camera, and begin trying to take pictures. As he becomes more skilled in handling the equipment and finds that his interest is not flagging, he may invest in some processing equipment. Later, perhaps, he may buy a better quality camera. In other words, he may build up his investment in or commitment to the goals underlying his decision over a period of time, periodically reviewing his commitment and giving himself an opportunity of changing his goals without losing a great deal. The underlying assumption, of course, is that the longer he maintains his interest, the longer he can expect it to continue.

In this type of decision-making, we proceed by eliminating alternatives that are not similar to (i.e., only marginally different from) a given status quo. We attempt to successively approximate goal satisfaction in long-run decisions through incremental rather than radical, and possibly misguided, changes.

Other examples of incremental decision-making are more directly political. For example, some students of the budgetary process argue that decisions about what governmental agencies ask for and what legislative bodies finally allocate for public policies and programs are incremental.[6] Because social security or national defense policies are such complex issues, students of the budgetary process argue that, when budgetary decisions must be made each year or two, as is typically the case in American governmental structures, it is impossible (and, some argue, unnecessary) for whole programs to be reviewed from top to bottom each time. Rather, it is felt, budget-makers try to decide what marginal program or policy changes can be made given the kind of marginal change in funding expected on the basis of handling of similar programs in the past. Further, legislators decide what kind of marginal changes are acceptable in view of policy decisions already made. Also, some students of the judicial process argue that certain aspects of legal decision-making can be viewed from an incremental perspective. Because of the reliance on precedent in many kinds of case and administrative law, lawyers are willing to ask for only minimal changes, and judges are willing to grant only minimal changes, in existing legal interpretation.[7]

It must be realized that this kind of decision-making, which depends heavily on the status quo, is politically conservative. It is not very conducive to widespread reforms of existing programs or to radically new policies. To the extent that this way of looking at decision-making under conditions of deficiency is descriptive of actual decision-making behavior, this is not terribly important. However, to the extent that the theory is a normative one (i.e., to the extent that it provides guidelines for making decisions), it is necessary to understand and be able to defend its conservativeness and all the possible unpleasant consequences. Some argue that, rather than providing an opportunity for changing goals with a minimum of sunk costs (investments that would be lost if the goals in a situation were changed), incremental decisions lead the decision-maker by the nose to ever-growing commitments, even though preferences and evaluations of program effectiveness may change. Incremental decisions, it is argued, are commitments to be guided by the dead hand of the past rather than by contemporary preferences and needs. But, perhaps, when we are not sure of our goals, and knowledge is severely limited, we may be able to do no better.[8]

315

Game Strategies for Competitive Decisions

One kind of decision theory, which appears to deserve considerable study by political scientists, applies to situations in which there is more than one decision-maker and there is competition among them to determine the outcome of the decision. A small taste of this kind of decision-making was given in the section on decision-making in uncertain information environments. We suggested there that one could reasonably view such decisions as games played with nature; and we argued that under some conditions it was useful to assume that nature knew exactly what you were going to do and would make, from your point of view, the worst possible move. This assumption is not necessarily true in general game theory, where one simply assumes that one's opponents are intelligent and that each player is ignorant of the moves the other players will make.

The "game" of making decisions under conditions of uncertainty may at first appear different from many familiar games in that for each play there is only one move. Most familiar games have a set of rules that define sequences of moves available to each player in a given situation. For example, in chess, the first move is to "randomly" assign the white pieces to one player (and therefore start the actual play). That player then has twenty possible moves. After he has selected one, it is his opponent's turn to move. As the game continues, each player continues to move in turn, and each turn leaves open only certain legal moves.

Since chess is an extremely complicated game, we shall abandon our analogy at this point in favor of a simpler one. Suppose we make up a hypothetical game using six ordinary playing cards, the two through seven of a single suit. The first move of the game is a chance one; that is, the cards are shuffled and three dealt to each of two players. The players then simultaneously turn over a card. The winner of the trick is the player of the highest card. Two more tricks are played, and the winner of the hand is the player who has won the most tricks. There are only four possible outcomes to the game: either player *A* wins all three tricks (and player *B* wins none), or he wins two (and *B* wins one), or he wins one, or none. There are, however, 720 ways in which one of these outcomes could be reached; that is, there are 720 possible plays in even this simple game. The 720 possible plays come about in the following way. There are twenty possible ways in which the cards could be dealt. For each of these deals, there are nine distinct possible alternatives for the first trick. (That is, player *A* could choose any one of three cards, and player *B* could choose any of his three.) After the first trick, each player can play one of two possible cards; thus the second trick can be played in any of four different ways. Given the first two tricks, the third can be played in only one way (since each player has only one card left). Thus there is one chance move that yields twenty possible alternatives, and there are thirty-six possible ways in which each of these hands might be played.

For example, let us say that player *A* was dealt the two, the four, and the six and chose to play the four on the first move. From that point, the game could be completely described by the *game tree* in Figure 10-3.

FIGURE 10–3

A Partial Game Tree

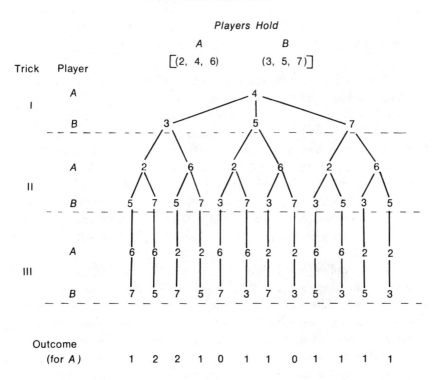

The important thing to notice about this game tree is that, given the deal of the cards and the first move by player A, all possible plays and all possible outcomes can be determined in advance. Moreover, since it would be quite possible to construct a game tree which described all the possible plays for each deal of the cards, the players could, if they wished, plan a complete *strategy* of play before the game actually started. In fact, each player could select a complete (or *pure*) strategy which detailed the moves he would make at each stage of the game and give that strategy to an umpire. The umpire could then use the strategies to move along a single path through the game tree, and, on the basis of the strategies selected, assign the payoff for that particular play. In this way, all games in which there are a finite number of possible moves for each player and a finite number of possible plays can be reduced to a single move for each player—the selection of one of a number of possible strategies. Understanding this concept of strategies allows us to take a slightly more sophisticated approach to game theory.

TWO-PERSON, ZERO-SUM GAMES

The simplest games are those which have only two competing players and in which the winnings of one player will equal the losses of the other. Such a game is called a *two-person, zero-sum game* (since the sum of the payoffs to each player equals zero). Suppose, for example, that we have two players, R and C, both of whom have three possible strategies open to them. Table 10-6 describes the information available to them. Each player knows what strategies are possible both for himself and his opponent, and what payoffs will occur given specific strategic choices. For example, R knows that if he selects strategy r_2 and C selects strategy c_2, then he (R) will "receive" a payoff of -2 and C will receive a payoff of 2.

The problem in the theory of games is to formulate some sort of criterion for the players of the game that will allow them to select a strategy consistent with their preferences. As before, the problem is to select a strategy that will maximize the expected utility of the outcome. Since this is a *strictly competitive* game, in that one player's winnings equal the other's losses, there is no point in cooperation between the players. Player R might select strategy r_1 because this would yield the

TABLE 10–6

Strategies and Payoffs for a Simple Two-Person, Zero-Sum Game

R's STRATEGY	c_1	c_2	c_3	Row Minima
		C's STRATEGY		
r_1	8	−4	−10	−10
r_2	2	−2	6	−2
r_3	5	−1	7	−1
Column Maxima	8	−1	7	

maximum payoff of 8 units *if* C chose strategy c_1. In game theory, however, we assume that *all* players are utility maximizers. R would know that C could select alternative c_3, which would give R his maximum possible loss (and, therefore, C his maximum gain). Thus R would be well advised to choose a different strategy. Is there a strategy available to *each* of the players which will be a stable one—that is, one which they will see no advantage in changing? We can easily see such a strategy for player R. If he selects r_3, player C can select no strategy that will force R to lose more than 1 unit. In general, game theory suggests that R's strategy should be a *maximin* strategy; that is, one which maximizes the row minima. Player C, if he selected strategy c_2, would be using the *minimax* strategy; that is, he would be selecting the minimum of the column maxima.

The interesting thing about this particular type of game is that it is what the game theorist calls *strictly determined*. If R assumes that C is a utility maximizer, then he would be advised to select his strategy so that C's maximum payoff was a minimum for that game. This maximin strategy would establish a *security level* of −1 for R. The game is strictly determined because, upon examination, C's minimax strategy establishes a security level for C of −1. Because neither player can guarantee himself a greater security level by selecting a different strategy, the game is said to be in *equilibrium*.

Are the maximin and minimax strategies always in equilibrium? That is, are all games strictly determined? Before answering the question, let us look at another game with which most of us are familiar

319

—matching pennies. In this game player R may choose to display a head or a tail on his penny. The same is true for player C. If the pennies match, player R receives one utility unit (usually C's penny). If they do not match, player R loses one utility unit. (That is, he gives up his penny to C.) The game matrix appears in Table 10-7.

TABLE 10–7

Matching Pennies

R's PENNY	C's PENNY		
	H	T	Row Minima
H	1	−1	−1
T	−1	1	−1
Column Maxima	1	1	

Obviously, the maximin and minimax criteria do not allow a player to distinguish between strategies. This does not necessarily mean, however, that the game is not strictly determined. Anyone who has actually played at matching coins knows that it does indeed make a difference which strategy is used. A person would not be well advised to choose the same strategy each time—that is, to play only heads or only tails in repeated trials. If he did, his opponent would quickly learn his strategy and choose a competing strategy that would do the most damage. To keep this from happening, the players let "chance" decide their strategy. They flip their coins and play them the way they come up. A game theorist would call this a *mixed strategy*, that is, a choice of strategies according to specific probabilities. By flipping the coin, each player is selecting a strategy with a probability of 1/2. This serves two functions: It keeps his opponent from second-guessing his play correctly and using the information against him, and it allows each player to achieve a security level, in the long run, of zero units. In the long run, there is no advantage to either player. It is an important theorem of game theory that every two-person, zero-sum game is strictly determined if mixed strategies are allowed. This theorem is important to decision theory, because it tells us that there is a "rational" way of making a decision under these competitive conditions.

TWO-PERSON, NON-ZERO-SUM GAMES

For the most part, two-person, zero-sum games are of most interest to mathematicians. They do not have many direct applications in the real world. Other games, which make different assumptions, are more realistic; but they are also not as easily solvable within the framework of game theory. For example, let us look at a two-person game that is not a zero-sum game; that is, we have two players, but the winnings of one do not necessarily equal the losses of the other. This game is sometimes called "the prisoners' dilemma."

The prisoners' dilemma assumes that two men have been captured by the police and are accused of committing a crime together. When they are questioned (separately), each is told that if he confesses he will get off and his partner will get a ten-year sentence. If neither confesses, they can each be convicted only on minor charges and will get a two-year sentence each. However, if they both confess, both will be convicted on major charges and each will receive a nine-year sentence. The entries in the game matrix in Table 10-8 represent the negative utilities associated with each course of action.

TABLE 10–8

The Prisoners' Dilemma

	C's STRATEGY	
R's STRATEGY	Confess	Don't Confess
Confess	(−9, −9)	(0, −10)
Don't confess	(−10, 0)	(−2, −2)

The prisoners' dilemma, of course, is that if they both play to win as much as they can (i.e., the minimum sentence) by "squealing," they will both receive close to the minimum payoff (i.e., the maximum sentence). The game is not strictly competitive. Therefore, by *cooperating*, the players could easily achieve the mutually satisfying payoff of −2, −2. The important aspect of this game, from our point of view, is that, through cooperative or collective rationality, game theory provides a solution.

N-PERSON GAMES

The theory of games becomes even more realistic when we allow more than two players. However, n-person games create more theoretical difficulties. One major problem is that whereas in two-person games it was possible to find a stable solution (i.e., one pure, mixed, or cooperative strategy), this is not the case in the n-person game.

In n-person theory some new concepts are necessary. The most important is the concept of the *coalition*. [9] Many times, when more than two players are involved in a game, a greater payoff can be achieved if some of the players cooperate than if they act on their own. For example, in a three-person game where the players as a group decide who gets what payoff, two players can decide to act together, divide equally the total value of the game between them, and assign the total loss to the third player. Say, for example, the point of the game is to divide $100 among the players by majority rule. Two players may get together and decide that the distribution will be $50 to each of them and nothing to the third player. Because the two players constitute a majority, they are a *winning coalition* and can receive a higher payoff by acting together than by acting separately. (Acting separately, they would probably get only $33 apiece.)

The major theoretical problem here is what coalition will form —that is, what the solution to the game will be. Will players A, B, and C form a coalition of the whole? Will we find A and B siding against C, or A and C against B, or B and C against A? And how will the winnings be distributed among the players in the winning coalition?

This simple three-person game illustrates some of the problems associated with n-person theory. There are, first of all, a large number of possible *imputations* for this game; that is, there are a great number of ways in which the total payoff can be distributed among the players. For example, one possible imputation would be $90 for A, $5 for B, and $5 for C. But is this likely to be the actual outcome? Or, looking at things another way, is this an outcome that should be recommended? To prevent this particular solution, B could offer C a payoff of $40 to enter into a coalition with him that would result in an imputation of ($0, $60, $40). But this too is not a likely solution, for A could then offer C $50 to join him in a coalition against B that would result in an imputation of ($50, $0, $50). Would such a coalition hold up? A game theorist would argue this solution is stable because, under the rules of the game, any other possible distribution will not get a majority vote. This imputation is therefore said to form part of the *core* of the game. The core of a game constitutes all those imputations which would win, or *dominate,* if pitted against any other imputation outside the core. The core for this game would also include imputations of ($50, $50, $0) and ($0, $50, $50). There is no way in game theory to predict which of these outcomes will in fact occur.

The idea that, in the example above, the imputation ($50, $50, $0) dominates the imputation ($33, $33, $33) leads us to one of the more important principles of *n*-person theory: the *size principle.* To illustrate this principle, let us say that we have a committee of ten people. We will assume this is a political group capable of allocating tangible and intangible rewards (patronage, deference, etc.) to its members. We will further assume that the decisions of the committee are made by majority rule. What coalitions are likely to form? Any coalition, in order to push through a decision, must have at least six voting members. However, we could also have effective (winning) coalitions of seven, eight, nine, or even ten members. The size principle states that coalitions of seven, eight, nine, or ten members are not likely to occur and that in general coalitions tend to include the minimal number of persons needed to achieve a desired goal.

Intuitively, it is easy to see why this might be so. If the amount of the payoff to the committee is fixed, a large winning coalition means that each member will receive a relatively small share. For example, if the total payoff to the committee could be said to have a money value, say, of $100, a winning coalition of seven members would receive (given the simplest possible imputation) about $14 apiece. If the winning coalition had six members, each could receive over $16. There is therefore a motive for a seven-member coalition to expel one of its members. William Riker uses this basic size principle to explain why, for example, political parties who win overwhelming majorities in one election appear to search for ideological purity by cutting themselves off from conservative or liberal wings of the party.[10]

Making Collective Decisions

Thus far we have reviewed some aspects of theories of individual decision-making and decision-making in situations in which there are various degrees of competition and cooperation. Another important type of decision-making for students of political behavior is collective, or social, decision-making. In theories of collective decision-making, the object is to analyze how societies allocate their resources among individual members. In effect, this is what we do when we study the institutions of government, public policy formation, output analysis, and impact analysis.

An important problem that is related to this topic and is very much connected with the theoretical discussion in this chapter is whether it is possible to make social decisions which will, in some sense, satisfy individual values and preferences. Theorists have asked if it is possible to define a rule for formulating social decisions based on and reflective of the preferences of the individual members of a society. Such a rule would be a *social welfare function*.

In order to see how such a function might be used, let us look at a hypothetical political decision in a society of three members. Let us assume that there are three basic tasks this society must perform and, further, that some of these tasks are more important than others. Let the three tasks be hunting (*H*), the preparation of food (*P*), and general care of the living site (*C*). Let us also assume that the first member of the society thinks that hunting is more important than food preparation and food preparation is more important than caring for the campsite. The second member, however, feels that the greatest amount of social resources should be devoted to food preparation, fewer social resources should be devoted to care of the living quarters, and still fewer resources' should be devoted to hunting. The third individual argues that hunting is the group's most important task, care of the living site is the second most important job, and food preparation is the least important chore. We can represent this problem by the following matrix:

	INDIVIDUALS		
Preferences	I	II	III
1	H	P	H
2	P	C	C
3	C	H	P

To make things as simple as possible, let us assume that the decision rule (i.e., the social welfare function) for this society is majority rule. Our task is to use the individual preferences described above to resolve a social preference ordering. We see from the matrix that hunting is felt to be more important than food preparation by members I and III. We can say, therefore, that the society, since it operates by majority rule, prefers more resources allocated to hunting than to food preparation. The matrix also shows that food preparation is felt to be more important than care of the campsite by individuals I and II. The majority, and therefore the society, prefers that more resources be allocated to food preparation than to campsite care. Finally, as we would logically expect, hunting is thought to be more important than care of the campsite. The social preference ordering derived from the individual preferences by the social welfare function majority rule is, therefore,

$$H \quad P \quad C$$

The question the student should ask now is whether majority rule is, in general, an adequate social welfare function. If we assume that a social decision rule must resolve a social preference ordering from *any* set of individual preferences, majority rule will not serve us well. Let us assume that the individual preferences of our little group change, as follows:

I	II	III
H	P	C
P	C	H
C	H	P

Individual III now feels that care of the living quarters is more important than hunting, which is, in turn, more important than food preparation. How does this affect the order of social preferences? Majority rule says that more resources should be allocated to hunting than to food preparation, and more to food preparation than to care of the living quarters. It is logical, therefore, to assume that more resources should be allocated to hunting than to care of the living quarters; but a majority of the society feels that care of the living quarters is more important than hunting. Given these particular individual values, the order of social preferences yielded by a majority rule is inconsistent.

This particular phenomenon is generally called the *Arrow paradox* (or the paradox of voting) after Kenneth Arrow, a theorist interested in collective decisions who argued that a satisfactory democratic decision rule ought to satisfy certain specific assumptions. First, he argued, a social welfare function ought to be able to assign a consistent preference ordering based on all possible individual preference orderings. Second, if the social ordering resulted in, say, apples being preferred to oranges, then they should still be preferred to oranges in a social ordering that included pears.[11] Third, there should be a positive association between the social order of preferences and the individual order. If an individual decides to reorder his preferences in favor of some particular alternative and no one else in the society changes preferences, that alternative should *not* be lower down in the new social ordering than it was in the old one.

Surprisingly, Arrow was able to prove conclusively that any social welfare function which was consistent with these assumptions about the necessary character of democratic decisions would have to be dictatorial or imposed from outside the society. The implication of this finding is that democratic decision-making processes will not, in general, yield rational (i.e., consistent) social decisions.

However, this does *not* mean that rational democracy is mathematically impossible, only that consistent democratic decision-making cannot rest on the normative assumptions Arrow cites. Some theorists have argued that these assumptions are not empirically compatible with democratic decision-making. They have pointed out, for example, that, in effect, evaluating apples and oranges when the universe holds only apples and oranges is quite different from evaluating apples, oranges, and pears when all three are available. To take a more pragmatic example, it is quite possible that a member of the electorate who preferred Humphrey to Nixon would, in a three-man race between Humphrey, Nixon, and Wallace, vote for Nixon.

Another issue in decision theory is whether it is necessary to admit all possible individual preference orders into the social welfare function. It may well be that individual preferences which create inconsistencies in the social preference ordering, though mathematically possible, are not likely from an empirical point of view. It has been shown that, if a particular society has reasonably well defined or culturally common standards for judgment, Arrow's paradox will never occur.[12]

Summary and Conclusions

What we have tried to do in this chapter is present the basic concepts needed to understand one of the major theoretical approaches in the behavioral sciences. The theory of games is a complex and, for the most part, rigorous body of knowledge. We have, however, tried wherever possible to communicate an intuitive understanding of its fundamental principles that will equip the reader who wishes to do so to graduate to a more sophisticated treatment of the subject.

It is important to recognize that, though the theory of games is based on individual decision-making processes, it is in no sense a psychological theory of decisions. There are psychological variables, such as preferences, in the theory, but it does not attempt in any way to explain or account for various individual preference structures. Thus there is a great difference between it and the behavioral theories expounded in Chapters 8 and 9.

The interested reader may see, even in this rather basic treatment of game theory, some opportunities for further theorizing. For example, if, having noted the psychological limitations of the theory of games as described, we are interested in making it less normative and more descriptive, we might argue that game theorists should incorporate more sophisticated psychological assumptions into their work. The more realistic game theory is from a psychological point of view, the more useful it will be to political theorists who are interested in explaining the allocation of values in real societies.

Notes

1. The basic work on which this chapter is based is R. Duncan Luce and Howard Raiffa's *Games and Decisions: Introduction and Critical Survey* (New York: Wiley, 1957). The classic work in this field is John Von Neumann and Oskar Morgenstern's *Theory of Games and Economic Behavior* (Princeton, N.J.: Princeton University Press, 1954). The Luce and Raiffa book is more useful for beginning students, but both books have the virtue of

being essentially self-contained and can be comprehended with a little effort and only elementary mathematical training. A simpler book, written from a different perspective, is Irwin D. J. Bross's *Design for Decision: An Introduction to Statistical Decision-Making* (New York: Macmillan, 1953).

2. Other approaches to rational decision-making emphasizing specific means and ends can be found in James G. March and Herbert Simon's *Organizations* (New York: Wiley, 1958) and Robert A. Dahl and Charles E. Lindblom's *Politics, Economics and Welfare: Planning and Politico-Economic Systems Resolved into Basic Social Processes* (New York: Harper & Row, 1953).

3. This is referred to as the *minimax principle* if "disutilities" rather than utilities are considered. Our goal then would be to assure ourselves of the minimum possible maximum loss. Sometimes, as we will see in the discussion of game theory, the minimax and the maximin "points" or "strategies" are the same.

4. See Herbert Simon, *Models of Man: Mathematical Essays on Rational Human Behavior in a Social Setting* (New York: Wiley, 1957), especially Chapter 14.

5. See Charles E. Lindblom, "The Science of 'Muddling Through,' " *Public Administration Review*, Vol. 19 (Spring 1959), 79-88. See also Ira Sharkansky, "Agency Requests, Gubernatorial Support, and Budget Success in State Legislatures," *American Political Science Review*, Vol. 62 (December 1968); John P. Crecine, *Governmental Problem-Solving* (Chicago: Rand McNally, 1969); O. A. Davis, M. A. H. Dempster, and Aaron Wildavsky, "On the Process of Budgeting: An Empirical Study of Congressional Appropriation," in Gordon Tullock (ed.), *Papers on Non-Market Decision-Making*, (Charlottesville, Va.: Thomas Jefferson Center of Political Economy, 1966); Davis, Dempster, and Wildavsky, "A Theory of the Budgetary Process," *American Political Science Review*, Vol. 60 (September 1966); and John Wanat, "Bases of Budgetary Incrementalism," *American Political Science Review* (forthcoming, December 1974).

6. Davis, Dempster, and Wildavsky, both articles cited above; and Wanat, *op. cit.*

7. See, for example, Martin Shapiro, "Stability and Change in Judicial Decision-Making: Incrementalism or Stare Decisis?" *Law in Transition Quarterly*, Vol. 2 (Summer 1965), 134-157.

8. Another approach to decision-making in a deficient information environment can be found in Lawrence V. Grant, "Specialization as a Strategy for Legislative Decision-making," *American Journal of Political Science*, Vol. 17 (February 1973), 123-147.

9. Applications can be found in Sven Groennings, E. W. Kelley, and Michael Leiserson (eds.), *The Study of Coalition Behavior: Theoretical Perspectives and Cases from Four Continents* (New York: Holt, Rinehart & Winston, 1970).

10. William Riker, *The Theory of Political Coalitions* (New Haven, Conn.: Yale University Press, 1962).

11. You can think of it in this way: If you should ask someone if he prefers apples to oranges and he replies "apples," you would not expect him to respond "oranges" if you asked whether he preferred apples, oranges, or pears.

12. See Clyde Coombs, *A Theory of Data* (New York: Wiley, 1964), Chapter 18.

11

Communication
and
Control

In the last chapter we pointed out that choice is a fundamental aspect of political behavior. Choice also plays an important part in the discussion of what we rather loosely call communications theory. In this chapter we will discuss the basic concepts of communications theory: the components of communications systems, the fundamentals of information theory, and the implications of these ideas for political communication.

The Nature of Communication

Communication can be defined as any procedure by which one mind affects another mind. Any behavioral act, as such, has some potential for communication. Speech, writing, painting, dancing, gestures—all are examples of behavior that may result in communication. In fact, we might go so far as to say that any significant behavioral act is an act of communication.

It may seem ironic that, once again, a theory which is supposed to be of use in understanding behavior finds its core in the mind. Yet the history of behaviorism includes a strong tradition of reaction to theories based on mental constructs. In the discussion of attitudes and roles (Chapters 8 and 9) we argued that certain theoretical constructs which are inherently mental are useful in understanding human behavior. If it is argued that it is necessary to understand predispositions to behave, and if it is further argued that an individual's behavior is contingent not only on his own dispositions but on the dispositions of others (i.e., role expectations), it is clearly necessary for the behavioral theorist to attempt to account for the process by which one individual's dispositions affect another's; that is, how mind affects mind. Within the framework of role theory, interactions are processes by which the expectations of the self and others are communicated. Especially if our concern is *political* behavior, it is necessary to consider more general phenomena than the behavior of single individuals. Politics occurs only when individuals interact. Communications theory provides a perspective from which behavioral theorists can view the processes of interaction.

The Essentials of a Communications System

In analyzing the process of communication, theorists have developed the notion of a communications system. Any communications system has the following components: a *source* of messages, a *semantic encoder*, a *transmitter*, a *communications channel*, a *receiver*, a *semantic decoder*, and a *destination* for the message. (See Figure 11-1.)

The source of messages is, in effect, a repository for, or a collection of, ideas, any number of which may be selected for transmission. The semantic encoder is a device by which an idea is encoded into an actual message using specific *signs*. The transmitter is capable of processing the signs in such a way that a signal can be sent across some sort of medium—the communications channel. It is the function of the com-

FIGURE 11–1

Essential Components of a Communications System

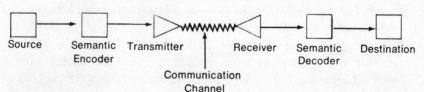

Source   Semantic Encoder   Transmitter   Receiver   Semantic Decoder   Destination

Communication Channel

munications channel to "carry" the signal to the receiver, which in turn provides the transmitted signs to the semantic decoder. The semantic decoder then processes the signs into ideas (that is, into a meaningful message) for the destination. In sum, a communications system is a system for encoding a message from a source into a form that can be transmitted to a destination in such a way that the message becomes a part of the total amount of information available to the destination.

For example, suppose an individual wishes to communicate to another individual the sound a duck makes. The first individual is the source of the message (i.e., the sound a duck makes), and he or she may semantically encode the message into the word "quack." The person may then transmit the message by writing this word on a piece of paper (the communications channel) and physically pass the paper to the other person. The recipient decodes the written message into the word "quack" which refers to the sound of a duck.

The communications process, as outlined here, is rather straight-forward. However, in all real communications systems there is another factor that must be taken into account. This factor is *noise*. The term *noise* is used in communications theory to refer to any event that impedes the accurate flow of information from the source to the destination. There are two primary kinds of noise: engineering and semantic. As we shall see, one of the major problems in communications research is finding a means of communicating effectively in the face of noise.

Engineering noise is primarily a "hardware" problem. It occurs because the mechanisms that serve as transmitters, communications channels, and receivers (speech, writing, hearing, telephone "connections," etc.) are imperfect. For example, if the person who initiated the communication in the example above had illegible handwriting, or if the person at whom the communication was directed had faulty eyesight, the message "quack" might have been received as "quick." Because of an imperfection in the components of the system the message might have been distorted.

Semantic noise is not due to the physical technology of communications systems. Semantics relates to the meaning (or "referents") of specific signs. Semantic noise is introduced into a communications system when the meaning attributed to a sign by a source is at variance with the meaning attributed to it by a destination. This problem can occur even when a communications channel is free of engineering noise.

331

A major source of semantic noise is the ambiguity of language. For example, even if the source transmits "the sound a duck makes" by a communications channel that is completely noiseless (in an engineering sense), the message may still be distorted if the semantic decoder takes the sign "quack" to mean "an incompetent physician."

Associated with these two types of noise in communications systems are specific problems of information transmission. The "technical problem" centers on eliminating engineering noise—on sending accurate messages from transmitters to receivers. It should be obvious that unless signals can be transmitted accurately (that is, unless the signal received is the same as the signal sent) communication is impossible.[1] The "semantic problem" centers on the accurate transmission of meaning from the source to the destination. The major difficulty here is devising a language, or a "code," with a minimum of ambiguity. To eliminate semantic noise, we need to create a set of signs, each of which has a single, unambiguous referent. In addition to these two problems, there is a "control," or "effectiveness," problem in any communications system. Given that signals are accurately received and translated, we must still determine whether the message has the effect on the destination intended by the source.

If we think carefully about this "control problem," we should be able to see why it is of significance, particularly to the study of political behavior. It has been argued many times that the essence of politics is *power*—the capacity of individuals and groups to control the behavior of others. The problem of control in a communications system is also a fundamental problem of politics. However, in order to adequately discuss how these concepts may be applied to understanding political behavior, it is necessary to discuss some basic constructs of *information theory*.

Information Theory

From the perspective of communications theory, the source affects the destination (a mind affects a mind) through the transmission of information. As we pointed out above, a source is a repository of messages that may be transmitted to a destination. According to information theory, the amount of information in any given message is related to our *uncertainty* as to which of the possible messages from a source will actually be transmitted. If we are completely certain which message will actually be sent by a source, we receive no information from the message (i.e., the message "contains" no information) when it is actually sent. For example, if a source has only one message to send and it is certain that the message will be sent, the message will contain no information. Suppose a candidate for office travels from town to town giving the same speech. To the newsmen who have followed him, his speech is essentially a single message; and because they are certain that it will be given in every area they visit, no information is transmitted when it is. In more everyday language, we would say that the speech contains no *new information* for the newsmen.

On the other hand, if a source can send any one of a number of possible messages, we are uncertain which one will actually be sent. Therefore, when a message is actually sent, we receive information (according to the theory) because our uncertainty about the message is reduced. In information theory the amount of information conveyed by a message is not related to its "content," but to the number of messages it is possible for the source to send and the possibility that a particular message will be chosen. For example, let us suppose that we have a message source which can communicate only the result of a one-trial coin-flipping experiment; that is, it can send only the messages "heads" or "tails." There would be information in the message from this source because we would be uncertain which message would be transmitted until it was sent. Another message source might be able to transmit the results of a two-trial coin-flipping experiment. Thus it could send any one of four possible messages—"heads-heads," "heads-tails," "tails-heads," or "tails-tails." Intuitively, it should be clear that a message from this second source would have more information associated with it than a message from the first source.

From the perspective of information theory, a message from the second source "contains" more information than one from the first source because we (i.e., the destination) are *more uncertain* which message will actually be sent. The important point here is, as we noted above, that the amount of information transmitted by a message does not depend on the content of the message; it depends, rather, on our

333

freedom to choose a specific message from a set. Thus, even if the two messages that could be sent by the first source in the example above had been, respectively, "heads" and the entire contents of the *Summa Theologica*, a message from the source with four alternatives would "contain" more information.

The quantity of information in a source or destination is called *entropy*. Entropy is thus a measure of information. Entropy depends on the relative number of possible messages a source may send (or a destination may receive) and the structure of, or relations among, the various messages. The notion of structure is important. We know that for any interesting message source the probability that any given message will be sent depends, for example, on the messages that have been sent before. In the English language, for instance, we know that the letter "t" is very often followed by the letter "h" and that the word "the" is always followed by a noun. In political speeches, we know that words and phrases such as "America" and "our great purpose" are used with great regularity. Because the collection of ideas in a message source (and in a destination) is structured, the communicative behavior of such sources displays patterns, or regularities.

One of the important problems in information theory, and one that has significant implications for the study of human interaction, is the rate at which information may be transmitted from a source to a destination. Information theorists tell us that the rate of transmission of information depends upon the entropy in the source, the entropy in the destination, and their joint entropy, or the entropy they have in common. In human interactions, what is important is the general relationship between the rate of information transmission and common structure of the source and the destination. This relationship is described graphically in Figure 11-2.

We can see from Figure 11-2 that when the source and the destination are in complete agreement in the sense that it is certain which message the source will send and also which message the destination will receive, the rate of transmission is at a minimum. It is also at a minimum when, for example, the information in the destination is in no way dependent upon the structure of information in the source. In human interactions, this may occur when the attitudes and beliefs of the source are so divergent from those of the destination that the messages received by the destination are so totally foreign from his own attitudes

334

FIGURE 11–2

**The Rate of Information Transmission and the Degree of Agreement
Between the Source and the Destination**

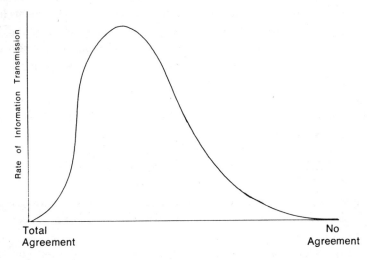

Source: John H. Kessel, George F. Cole, and Robert G. Seddig, *Micropolitics: Individual and Group Level Concepts* (New York: Holt, Rinehart & Winston, 1970), p. 461. Copyright © 1970 by Holt, Rinehart & Winston, Inc. Reprinted by permission of Holt, Rinehart & Winston, Inc.

and beliefs that they are interpreted as essentially random noises. The rate of transmission is at a maximum when the information in the source and destination is divergent enough so that the information sent is "new" to the destination, but not so divergent as to make communication impossible.

Information Theory and Human Behavior

In applying information theory to the analysis of human behavior, we assume that individual actors can be treated as message sources whose behavior has the effect of transmitting messages and whose senses have the effect of receiving messages. The point of this assumption is to see if the relationships postulated by information theory can lead us to a new and significant perspective on human behavior. Perhaps, by using information theory as a *model* for a theory of human behavior, we can perceive human behavior in a new and clearer light.

335

In general we will regard the individual as a source of messages and any behavior on the part of the individual as communicative behavior. We will regard speech, writing, gestures, and other acts as messages chosen by the individual according to the psycho-logic that governs his or her beliefs and the process of perceiving the behavior of an "other" as one of receiving the message that the other's behavior symbolizes. In short, we shall regard all human interaction as a process in which meanings are transmitted by behavior.

As the chapters on attitudes and roles suggest, the set of messages any given source contains is structured by the beliefs he or she holds and the roles he or she has learned. Thus we can expect certain kinds of messages (behavior) from individuals who hold certain beliefs, and not others. Because the destination of a message is also structured (i.e., that individual also holds certain beliefs), the meaning of any behavior that is observed is likely to be restructured to be more or less compatible with the belief structure of the destination. This complicates the process of interaction.

This theoretical perspective gives rise to two major questions: (1) Why does a source select a given message? (2) Why does a destination attribute a specific meaning to any given message? Our approach to these questions should help us comprehend the processes of human interaction.

To try to explain why a source selects a given message is to attempt to account for behavior in general. The perspective of information theory serves at this point only to structure the question. That is, it enables us to view the source as selecting a particular message from some collection of messages, and behavior as a symbolic means of transmitting messages. There are at least two basic approaches to understanding why a given source transmits a given message. The first is the approach taken in the chapter on role theory. From this point of view, behavior (i.e., sending messages) is primarily a reaction, or a response, by individuals to the situations in which they find themselves. Thus a particular message is selected because the source has learned that it is appropriate to the situation at hand. Learning is essentially a process of acquiring a set of potential messages and a structure that determines which message is appropriate to which situation.

The second approach to explaining why a given source transmits a given message focuses on the individual's motivations, or purposes.

Although, clearly, behavior can transmit unintended information, messages that are intended to serve one of several possible purposes of the source are more important to a student of human interaction. In general the purpose of an intentioned message is to change the structure of the set of messages at the source or the destination. Thus some messages are designed to obtain information for the source. For example, by asking a question, the source informs the destination of a discrepancy in their respective sets of messages for the purpose of reducing that discrepancy. Other messages are intended to provide information to the destination. In this case the source assumes that the destination lacks some kind of information and is willing to provide it.

The motives which underlie the sending of messages are assumed to be self-expressive or self-defensive. *Self-expressive messages* are those whose purpose is to provide a destination with information about the structure of the source. They may inform the destination about the source's attitudes or beliefs, his goals, or his possession or nonpossession of certain kinds of information. *Self-defensive messages* are those whose purpose is to disguise or otherwise protect the actual structure of the source. A message of this kind may be expressive of a belief that is not actually characteristic of the source's cognitive structure, or of a belief that the source feels will be supportive of some future self-expressive message. Self-defensive messages may also be intended to give the destination the impression that the source has certain information which he in fact does not, or that certain information is lacking when it is not. These sorts of messages may also be seen as *future oriented,* in that they are likely to be motivated by a desire to obtain more information about some other individual.

Even though what we have said so far does seem to make some intuitive sense, we have not really answered the question of why a source of messages transmits the message actually sent. We assume that communicative behavior, like behavior in general, is dependent upon the specific situation and the cognitive structure (the quantity of information, beliefs, motives, etc.) of the source. Thus we assume that messages sent are consistent with (expressive or defensive of) the source's cognitive structure. However, these assumptions have not been *tested.* Our information about cognitive structure is based on communicative behavior. Because we *assume* that communicative behavior is dependent upon certain types of attitudes and beliefs, we use

337

the resulting behavior to make inferences about cognitive structure. But if our only knowledge of cognitive structure is based upon observations of behavior, we cannot use that same behavior to test these assumptions directly.

Because of this problem, the second major question raised earlier is scientifically more interesting than the first. The question, again, was "Why does a destination attribute a specific meaning to a given message?" The first thing to understand is that individuals who serve as destinations for messages are not passive receivers, accepting messages as "wax receiving the imprint of a seal."[2] The meaning a destination imparts to any given message will depend on how he or she perceives the source, how he or she perceives the message, and the information he or she already possesses. In general, receiving a message is a perceptual process; thus the characteristics of the object of perception (the message and its source) and the predispositions of the receiver are important determinants of meaning. However, the general psychology of perception is far beyond the scope of this book, and we will restrict ourselves to the discussion of this question from the viewpoint of communications theory, taking some minimal understanding of the psychology of perception for granted.

As an object of perception, a message can be very complex. It is likely to contain many *referents*, to have many aspects or characteristics that the receiver may perceive as significant. Referents are, simply, the "things" the message says something about. Which referents are taken to be significant by the destination affects the meaning of the message for the destination. Imputations of significance depend in part on the destination's prior information on a subject or his cognitive structure. For example, take a speech made by a candidate for public office which charges that former members of the present administration who, during their tenure as public officials, negotiated the sale of certain public lands for private development are now working for the developer who purchased the land. A supporter of the candidate might take as the most salient referent in this message "members of the present administration." On the other hand, a member of the Sierra Club might see "the sale of certain public lands for private development" as the most significant referent. A supporter of the present administration might well view the candidate himself as the primary referent in the message. These reactions would illustrate the general principle that "the greater the receiver's motivation to decrease his uncertainty about any possible referent in a message, the more likely he is to select it as a major referent."[3]

Given that the destination has selected a primary referent in a message, the "meaning" attributed to that referent, and thereby to the message as a whole, is dependent upon the structure of information relevant to that referent which the destination already has. The principle here is that the meaning attributed to the message will to a large extent come from, and therefore be consistent with, the existing cognitive structure. Thus in our example the supporter of the candidate would take the message as indicating just another example of the deplorable way in which the present administration was betraying the public trust and as even more reason to support the candidate. The member of the Sierra Club might take the message to mean that the political system as a whole was perverting the public interest for the benefit of a few and at the expense of the environment. A supporter of the present administration, however, would be more likely to take the message to mean that the candidate was resorting to scurrilous and unfounded attacks on the government in his insatiable quest for power.

It should not be thought, however, that the destination of a message will necessarily manufacture a meaning only in the interest of cognitive consistency. Though it is true that most individuals are resistant to "new information" about matters which are highly central to their belief systems, we do know that attitudes can change, that new beliefs can be created, and that messages can affect behavior. The effect of political campaigning on the attitudes of individuals is, naturally, of some importance to political scientists. A point of considerable significance concerning communicative behavior can be made by considering the hypothetical relationship between the exposure of individuals to information during a campaign and the probability that attitudinal changes will take place. It can reasonably be argued that if an individual is exposed to no new information during the course of a political campaign, the probability of a change in his attitudes toward the candidates is zero. It can also be reasonably argued that an individual who is constantly exposed to new information is likely to have a good deal of interest in, and perhaps commitment to, the campaign of one or the other candidate. Such a person is likely to have a good deal of informational support for his attitudes and beliefs, to have a relatively constrained belief system, and to be relatively resistant to attitudinal change. On the other hand, the individual who is only slightly exposed to campaign information is likely to have relatively unorganized beliefs and relatively little informational support for his attitudes. Thus the probability that his attitudes will change is high.[4]

These relationships between attitudinal change (the effects of information), cognitive organization, and exposure to information are very relevant indeed to a discussion of human interaction. Consider, for example, the similarity of the graph in Figure 11-2 and that in Figure 11-3, which shows the relation between exposure to campaigning and the probability of attitudinal change. The shape of these two relations

FIGURE 11-3

The Hypothetical Relation Between Exposure to Campaigning and the Probability of Attitudinal Change

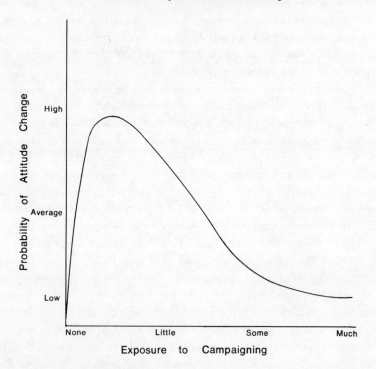

Source: Theodore Newcomb, Ralph Turner, and Philip E. Converse, *Social Psychology* (New York: Holt, Rinehart & Winston, 1965), p. 81. Copyright 1950 © 1965 by Holt, Rinehart & Winston, Inc.

suggests what we might expect about the importance of cognitive organization in human interaction (i.e., communication). Any message sent by an information source has an intended meaning that is determined by the source's cognitive structure. The meaning of the message which the destination receives is at least partially determined by the destination's cognitive structure; that is, by how the destination *perceives* the intended meaning of the message. Therefore, the similarity of the cognitive structure of the source and the destination is an important variable in the transmission of information.

There are some experimental findings which support this conclusion. One particular piece of research started with the same basic idea expressed in this chapter: The meaning of a message to an individual depends on how that message "fits into" the individual's cognitive structure.[5] The specific hypothesis to be tested stated that the performance of students in a class was related to the cognitive similarity or compatibility of the student and his or her teacher.

Each student in seven sections of an introductory psychology class was asked to express agreement or disagreement with the following five statements:

(1) The conditions of living in the United States tend to narrow the range of things we are able to do, think about, etc.
(2) People who have a firm moral code are in general better adjusted than those who have not.
(3) The biggest weakness of present day psychology is that it is too theoretical.
(4) Individuals could be changed in practically any way one might wish if the environment could be appropriately controlled.
(5) The strongest influence in shaping a person into the kind of person he becomes is his mother.[6]

The teachers of each of these sections were also asked to respond to the statements. The responses of both teachers and students were used as simple indicators of their cognitive structures. Those students whose responses were internally inconsistent (i.e., whose preferences with respect to the items were intransitive) were excluded from the experiment on the assumption that they were so uncertain about their preferences with respect to these items that they could not be said to have any meaningful cognitive structure for the purposes of the experiment. The remaining students were divided into two groups: those whose cognitive structures were similar to that of their instructor and those whose cognitive structures differed from that of their instructor. The grades of each student were then converted into a number that took into account possible variations in the distribution of grades from instructor to instructor, thus allowing a comparison across classes. These numbers are called *standard scores* and have a mean of 0.0. The hypothesis that the students who had cognitive structures similar to their instructors' would achieve higher grades, on the average, than those whose cognitive structures were dissimilar was then tested. The results are given in Table 11-1.

TABLE 11-1

Standard Scores for Students with Cognitive Structures Similar and Dissimilar to Their Instructors' Cognitive Structures

Cognitive Structure	STANDARD SCORES		
	N	Mean	Range
Similar to instructor's	17	0.60	−1.16 to 2.77
Dissimilar to instructor's	19	−0.25	−2.56 to 1.74

Source: Clyde Coombs, *A Theory of Data* (New York: Wiley, 1964), p. 128.

The probability that such a difference in scores is due to chance is less than one in twenty. This experiment, then, is reasonably clear evidence that cognitive structure does, indeed, affect the transmission of meaning. The political implications of these findings are the subject of the following section.

Communication and Control:
The Use of Symbols in Politics

The nature of the effectiveness problem—that is, the problem of control—in communications systems should be apparent from the example in the preceding section. It is clear that it is necessary for the source and the destination to have some sort of common cognitive structure if meanings are to be transmitted. It is also clear that unless meanings can be transmitted effectively, it is impossible for a source to control the behavior of a destination. If we go beyond the interactions of just a few individuals, the problem of control becomes even more complex. Nevertheless communications theory provides an interesting perspective on politics in any society. In this section we wish to expand the focus of our analysis somewhat and to use communications theory (and the perspective it provides on a body of theory having to do with what is called "symbolic interaction") to take a more general approach to political interaction.

Definitions of politics generally seem to focus on concepts such as authority, power, and control.[7] For our purposes here, it is useful to regard politics as the various means by which societies control the behavior of their members. It has long been known that language is a most pervasive instrument of social control, and the use of language in this way in politics is an important focus for study. In talking about political communication, language may be defined as the human use of verbal or nonverbal *symbols* to produce certain desired effects in other individuals.

A *symbol* is anything that has meaning, or significance. Basically, symbols are things that refer to other things. For example, the word "flags" refers to a particular class of objects and is therefore a symbol of that class. A particular flag is also a symbol, perhaps of some particular event (a white flag, for example, has long been a symbol of surrender) or some particular group of people (a nation). Other symbols, called "sentiment symbols," not only refer to a particular object or class of objects but also to an emotion (feeling, sentiment) attached to the referent. In general, symbols express perspectives on social objects or values.

One of the most important aspects of any social order is its values (or goals, or things valued) and value patterns (the distribution of values). Related to these value patterns is the influence—the position or potential position—of each individual or group. It is the patterns of influence within a social order which make up the social structure. According to political scientist Harold Lasswell, a description of a social structure is a description of "who gets what, when and how."

343

According to Lasswell and Kaplan in their classic work *Power and Society* (on which the remainder of this chapter relies heavily), one of the most important values affecting a social structure is power. In essence, power is the relative ability to influence things or goals someone else values. It is also, itself, a thing of value. An important value pattern in any society, then, is the power structure. One might describe a *power structure* as a relative distribution among individuals (or aggregates of individuals) of the ability to make decisions that affect the values of others. The study of politics can be thought of as the study of social structures, and particularly the power structures that describe the distribution of values within social structures. In sum, the organization of a society revolves around certain things which are valued, and politics is the process through which these values are distributed among its members.

Within this context, a political symbol is one that has particular relevance to the political process and therefore to the relationships and practice of power. *Political symbols* are defined, specifically, as symbols which "function directly in the power process, serving to set up, alter, or maintain power practices."[8] Thus, political symbols both provide perspectives on a society's power structure (that is, ways of looking at the power structure) and form a part of the "instrumentalities" of power. Political symbols include such things as treaties, constitutions, party platforms and slogans, and even political theories. They also include flags, songs, uniforms, stories, monuments, and memorial days. The principle function of the political symbol as one of the instrumentalities of a power structure is that of legitimizing social relationships. The specific nature of this function can be seen in a discussion of two topics, political myths and propaganda (or political language).

POLITICAL MYTHS

A political myth is a pattern of basic political symbols. It comprises the "fundamental assumptions" members of a society make about political affairs, and consists of symbols which not only explain but justify specific power practices.[9] There are two basic parts to a political myth—a political doctrine and a political formula.

A political doctrine is made up of the basic expectations of, and demands on, the power structure. It contains both a *credenda* (a set of beliefs about the power structure) and a *miranda* (a set of things to be admired). The credenda is found in constitutions, in charters, and frequently in political theories. It constitutes the basic philosophy of the state or government.

The miranda in political doctrines includes all the legends, heroes, flags, and ceremonies—all the symbols of sentiment toward, and identification with, the state found in the political myth. It is that set of symbols "whose function is to arouse admiration and enthusiasm, setting forth and strengthening faiths and loyalties. [These symbols] not only arouse emotions indulgent to the social structure, but also heighten awareness of the sharing of these emotions by others, thereby promoting mutual identification and providing a basis for solidarity."[10]

It is important to understand that a political myth does not necessarily provide only those basic assumptions of a political doctrine which support the power structure within which the myth develops. Political doctrines do arise which involve changing the social structure. The difference between these doctrines and those supportive of the status quo is the difference between an ideology and a utopia. According to Lasswell and Kaplan, an *ideology* consists of symbols which function to maintain and preserve the power structure. A *utopia* is based on a pattern of political symbols which function to induce fundamental changes in the power structure.

Another part of political myths is the *political formula*. A political formula is made up of those symbols of the political myth which describe and prescribe in detail the social structure; it is, then, the fundamental public law of a society. A political formula outlines the formal power patterns of a political doctrine. It is essentially prescriptive, since it does induce conformity to its specifications, and it provides the symbols invoked in the detailed justification or crimination of particular power practices. However, a political formula is also descriptive "in the degree to which there is in fact conformity to its requirements, and purportedly in that the formula is widely accepted as correctly describing power patterns and practices."[11]

As we implied earlier, a social structure can be defined as a pattern of shaping, distribution, and enjoyment of social values. It is made up of aggregates of people who engage in practices which give them a similar relation to the shaping, distribution, and enjoyment of one or more

345

specific values. These aggregates are classes. If we accept this view, we can analyze the social structure in terms of relationships among classes. Of course, classes are aggregates of individuals, and many of the ideas developed here have implications for interactions among individuals.

It is essential to understanding the notion of class introduced here to distinguish it from the traditional Marxian notion of class. First of all, classes, as defined here, are not necessarily groups; they are more accurately conceived of as aggregates, since there need not be any concrete interaction among the members of a class. Therefore, a class structure that is based on economic values and necessitates a "class consciousness" is not required. Moreover, Marxian analysis purely in terms of "self conscious" economic classes is useful only where the major social values are in fact economic, and this is not necessarily the case for all societies.

Given this point of view, what is the function of political symbols? A major part of the symbols of a political doctrine are symbols of morality—theories of what is good, or right, or proper; they are social norms. John Stuart Mill once observed that wherever there exists an ascendent class (that is, a class whose influence or power is dominant —an elite), "a large proportion of the morality of the country emanates from its class interests, and its feeling of class superiority."[12] Moreover, morality does not only emanate from the social structure; "it may serve also to formulate fundamental justifications for that structure."[13] Thus it is possible to view a political myth not only as a major support of the power position of an elite, but also as largely generated by that elite. Once a myth is established, however, the elite must adhere to the political doctrine it embodies; otherwise it will probably have to rely on simple violence to maintain the social order (that is, to maintain its position of power). Political theorists have long recognized the impossibility of the latter option. As Hobbes puts it, "Even the tyrant must sleep." It is this belief which accounts for the proposition that the main function of political symbols is to legitimize the power structure that exists in a given social structure. In Lasswell's words, a political myth attempts to effect the "transformation from might to right."[14] It attempts to transform power into authority, the legitimate possession of power. In sum, then, the fundamental function of political symbols is to assign the symbols and relationships of authority to the symbols and relationships of power. For this reason, the symbols of a society with a stable social structure will be a matter of consensus, and not opinion; they will not be controversial.

POLITICAL PROPAGANDA

Political rhetoric, or propaganda, is defined as the manipulation of the symbols which constitute a social ideology or utopia (i.e., a political myth) in order to control public opinion. The political symbols themselves are not propaganda, but their manipulation is if the intended effect is to change public opinion on matters about which there is disagreement. Propaganda cannot create opinions (consensuses) out of whole cloth. They must be supported by and supportive of the society's political myth. Thus propaganda can only alter the power structure in ways the members of that structure are already disposed to allow; and where a power elite (which is naturally interested in maintaining its own position of power) exists, the intended effect of the manipulation of political symbols is most likely to be to preserve the existing power and social structures.

The immediate implication of all this in terms of communications theory is that a political myth forms the basis for a good deal of the cognitive similarity necessary in a political community for political communication; that is, for the transmission of meaning. If this is so, it is possible that political communication uses language not for the purpose of reasoned argument, but for the manipulation of symbols which, as Edelman argues, provide "Pavlovian cues" for the interpretation of meaning.[15] In other words, it is possible that meaning is transmitted in political language not by structured or logical political arguments, but by psycho-logical sequences of symbols which are interpreted from the perspective of a given individual's belief system and the dominant political myth which organizes them into meaningful relationships. Thus, Edelman suggests that political argument, "when it is effective, that is, when it is a communication which does provide control, calls the attention of a group with shared interests to those aspects of their situation which make an argued-for line of action seem consistent with the furthering of their interests."[16]

If we look at the Kennedy-Nixon debates in 1960 from this perspective, it is clear that their effectiveness is not measurable in terms of

347

changed opinions due to the reasoned arguments of the candidates.[17] The debates, if they had any effect at all, simply made it possible for many people to create an image of, or attach a "meaning" to, the candidates on the basis of their (the viewers') own predispositions. The debates provided cues (clearly founded on the symbols which make up the American political myth) to which observers could respond in ways compatible with their structure of beliefs. They gave Kennedy a good deal of exposure and allowed observers to see that his image was compatible with traditional Democratic and American symbols important to many viewers. They allowed Kennedy to present himself, symbolically, in such a way that those predisposed to sympathize with these symbols could create an image of him compatible with their own views.

The points made here are important ones. Exercising control through the manipulation of political symbols is not simply a process of leading the masses by the nose. Elites or individuals cannot simply lead masses of people or other individuals in any direction they choose, no matter how whimsical. Political or individual control through communications processes has definite limits. These limits are defined by the existing political myth, by the extent to which this myth is shared by the members of the society, and by the cognitive structure or belief systems of particular individuals. It is for this reason that political scientists argue that leadership is a process of generating a willingness of followers to follow or, more simply, perhaps, of finding out where it is prospective followers wish to go and attempting to get there first.

Conclusion

Although in this chapter we have not gone into great detail concerning the nature of information theory or the social psychology or politics of communication, we have provided some important ideas which may lead to a broader theory of political behavior. Taking the fundamental problem of politics to be one of control, we can easily see that control depends largely upon the communications processes within a given society. Communication, as we have seen, is dependent upon cognitive structure (the kinds of beliefs, attitudes, and roles that individuals have learned). Decisions, of course, are forms of behavior and can therefore be viewed as depending upon the cognitive structures of an individual.

Also, decisions are an important form of political behavior, for one way of defining power, an essential aspect of politics, is the participation in decision-making.[18]

Another significant point raised in this chapter is the possible effect of social structure on individual cognitive structure. We argued that an important aspect of a social structure is the set of symbols (the political myth) associated with that structure, and that the political myth plays an important role in structuring individual attitudes, beliefs, and roles with respect to a particular political system. Thus, politics and power practices depend upon decisions; decisions depend upon processes of communication; communication depends upon cognitive structure; and cognitive structures relevant to political decision-making are influenced by political and social structures. In other words, each of the separate theoretical perspectives discussed in Part 3 is intimately related to an overall perspective on political behavior. Although we have presented these perspectives as distinct, it would be useful for the reader to think about how they could be combined in a coherent whole. In actuality, the student of political behavior must choose from among various perspectives. Ideally, however, it would be significant if all these perspectives could be linked together in a single, overarching theory which would help us to understand better the human behavior we call politics.

Notes

1. Harold Guetzkow, "Communication in Organizations," in James G. March (ed.), *Handbook of Organizations* (Chicago: Rand McNally, 1965), pp. 550-569.
2. Theodore Newcomb, Ralph Turner, and Philip E. Converse, *Social Psychology* (New York: Holt, Rinehart & Winston, 1965), p. 204.
3. *Ibid.*, p. 206.
4. John H. Kessel *et al.*, *Micropolitics: Individual and Group Level Concepts* (New York: Holt, Rinehart & Winston, 1970), p. 461.
5. See Clyde Coombs, *A Theory of Data* (New York: Wiley, 1964), pp. 122-129.
6. *Ibid.*, p. 125.

7. See, for example, David Easton, *A Framework for Political Analysis* (Englewood Cliffs, N.J.: Prentice-Hall, 1965); Harold Lasswell and Abraham Kaplan, *Power and Society* (New Haven, Conn.: Yale University Press, 1950); and G. E. G. Catlin, *Systematic Politics* (Toronto: University of Toronto Press, 1962).
8. Lasswell and Kaplan, *op. cit.*, p. 103.
9. *Ibid.*, p. 117.
10. *Ibid.*, p. 119.
11. *Ibid.*, p. 126.
12. *Ibid.*, p. 119.
13. *Ibid.*
14. *Ibid.*, p. 121.
15. Murray Edelman, *The Symbolic Uses*

349

of Politics (Urbana: University of Illinois Press, 1964).

16. *Ibid.*, p. 123.

17. See Kurt Lang and Gladys E. Lang, "Ordeal by Debate: Viewer Reactions," *Public Opinion Quarterly* (Summer 1961), 277-288.

18. Lasswell and Kaplan, *op. cit.*, p. 75.

PART IV

Conclusion

12

The Limitations
of
This Book

We hope that readers will at this point feel a certain discontent, a sense of unfulfillment. We, as authors, had much the same feeling upon completing this book. But this does not mean that we are unhappy with the outcome of our efforts. Indeed, one of our chief purposes was to create such feelings of inadequacy. We hope that we have dealt adequately with the task of providing a straightforward, understandable introduction to the systematic, empirical study of political behavior. But even achieving that goal would leave us with a sense of incomplete accomplishment. Ideally, of course, all introductory efforts should leave the reader with a sense of unfulfillment—not just because they are necessarily relatively simple in approach and incomplete in scope, but because, in addition, they create the feeling that there is much more of an exciting and interesting world waiting to be explored. Thus the limitations one may sense in an introduction may not represent a liability; instead they may be evidence of a great virtue, nothing less than the excitation of intellectual curiosity.

Nonetheless, we feel that we should discuss some of the limitations of this book. The student should be shown how he can broaden the understanding of political behavior he has garnered from this introduction.

353

Philosophical and Conceptual Limitations

We have attempted to be very straightforward in this book, focusing on basic "first principles." It is our view that a straightforward approach is most conducive to the basic learning which must underlie an understanding of subtle complexities. Many of the points we have made, though we think them sound and meaningful, are capable of considerable elaboration and refinement. The choices we have discussed may in practice appear far more ambiguous, or they may prove to rest on the resolution of previous problems which we have not discussed. For example, our discussion of facts and values suggests that the two can be easily distinguished. In fact, this may not always be the case. Philosophers tell us that what we consider to be facts and what we consider to be values are dependent on the particular philosophic position, or *epistemology*, we happen to hold. A widely accepted epistemology in modern Western culture, and the one that underlies our remarks in Chapter 1, stresses the validity of scientific inquiry. But the choice of such a world view is in some sense arbitrary. It is well to keep this in mind. We do not advance our epistemology as the necessary one or the best one. We do, however, suggest that it is a useful one. A truly curious individual may well want to examine in some detail the kinds of assumptions that underlie our choice. Such a study is one way in which he could advance his understanding of political behavior.

The discussion of explanation and description treats causation and explanation as identities. There are, however, problems with the notion of causation. In a strict philosophic sense (and indeed, as we have seen, often in a statistical sense as well), one cannot equate association with causation. This has led some scholars to avoid the use of the term *cause* altogether and has led others, as we have seen, to develop rigorous techniques of "causal analysis." In any event, we should be aware that we are not using the word *cause* in the strictest sense in the first chapters of this book. All that we are saying is that when certain phenomena are observed, the probability that certain others will also be observed increases (or decreases). Though it is speaking loosely to say that this relationship between phenomena is a causal one, knowledge of it is certainly useful and valuable.

Similarly—and in part it follows from the remarks just made—our characterization of what the political behaviorist does and how he is differentiated from other political scientists may not enable us to neatly categorize real, live people and what they are doing. In point of fact, a person may choose to spend some of his time as a political engineer and some as a behaviorist. Also, some projects undertaken by political scientists represent a mix of the types of studies we have noted. The motivations and choices of scholars, like those of people in general, are often mixed. A "pure" type may be a relatively rare animal. Also, as we have suggested at several points in this book, scholars may do work of one kind of political science because it is in some way preparatory to work of another kind. Political behavior research may provide the data for some good political engineering. Political history or political anecdotes may supply the inspiration for important generalizations generally thought to be the province of the behaviorist.

The point is that the concepts we have developed are useful in thinking about the notion of political behavior. If we treat these ideas as helpful devices and not somehow as part of the real world, their inadequacies become less important.

Procedural Limitations

Behaviorists follow certain procedures, and our discussion of these procedures suffers from two characteristics that are typical of introductory presentations. We do not discuss procedures in complete detail, and many kinds of procedures are not treated at all. Although we do comment on the survey and direct observation, we only partly discuss the problems inherent in these kinds of research. We mention experimentation only briefly, and we devote no attention whatever to, for example, formal modeling and computer simulations of organizations or international affairs. It is impossible to treat all the relevant procedures or to treat them thoroughly. We hope that we have communicated to the reader the realization that our presentations are incomplete and that there is much more to be learned. Our selections were made with an eye to providing some good examples of research, not to restricting the reader's horizons.

As far as our treatment of analytical techniques is concerned, the same two qualifications hold. We have touched on a few techniques such as cross-tabulation, correlational analysis, and testing differences in means. But we have not plumbed all the problems of these analytical approaches, nor have we fully explored their possibilities. In particular, we have seldom discussed control procedures in detail. Some techniques, such as multiple regression analysis and smallest space analysis, are mentioned in passing or not at all. Some forms of notation, mathematical, algebraic, and statistical, are not discussed.

On the other hand, the procedures we do discuss are in wide use in the professional literature, and we have drawn examples from that literature to illustrate our points. The basic techniques we present do indeed allow one to understand a large part of what behaviorists are saying and writing. In addition, we think that, by emphasizing what these techniques are for, we are laying the groundwork for an appreciation of more sophisticated techniques. If a student understands what can be accomplished with these basic tools, he can more easily gain insight into how to deal with more complicated problems. Techniques are to be used for solving problems, after all, not merely to be learned for their own sake.

Substantive Limitations

As we pointed out in Chapter 1, the political behavior approach is applicable to virtually any area of political inquiry. For simple reasons of space, however, we have discussed research in only a few substantive areas. Although the areas we have touched upon are quite important, there is nothing particularly sacred about them. Persons who have a particular interest in, for example, international law, organizations, or public administration, will find few references to their concerns. But the political behavior approach can be and is employed to further understanding in these areas. We have merely chosen certain examples of how this approach may be used. Perhaps our selection was somewhat arbitrary, but we were guided by topical and historical considerations. Similarly, some persons may not find the classification of factors affecting individual behavior (group, personal, and political) particularly congenial; this is only one of several systems that could reasonably be used. But it serves as a useful vehicle for expressing some basic ideas.

However, given the range of substantive problems we do discuss

356

(which is wide) and the significance of these problems (which is great), a truly curious reader should be able to use his imagination and conceptualize the operation of the political behavior approach in a broad variety of important areas.

Theoretical Limitations

We have made absolutely no attempt to be comprehensive in our treatment of theory. The four examples of theories we chose to present are typical of those that should have applications in political science, but many others could perhaps have been chosen with equal logic. The curious reader will search out other theories relevant to his own interests and needs. A more serious problem, however, results from the fact that a great deal of the empirical conceptual thinking that occurs in political science does not really correspond to what we have described as theory. Often, a few plausible ideas are all that constitutes the theory underlying research. Of course, this should be clear from Chapter 7, which indicates that theory is a very strange and amorphous thing indeed. Many people may articulate theories that are quite informal and not describable in terms of the standard social science notions of how the world is put together.

We should also keep in mind that theories of a slightly different type are sometimes made to relate to empirical phenomena. One may deduce propositions from the canons of probability, mathematics, or logic rather than from synthetic conceptions of what the world is like. Thus, the basic theoretical underpinning of a piece of research may be nothing more than a few assertions that somehow fit together, a logical postulate, or a mathematical expression. Though this type of theory may not look too much like the material discussed in Chapters 8-11, it is designed to have the same function.

As we have stressed before, the features of theory render it difficult to appreciate and deal with in a truly precise way. Its value comes to be appreciated more the more one works with data. Thus, our treatment of theory is perhaps more limited than any other part of this book. Indeed, it must be so. Yet if we have communicated some appreciation for theory, we have accomplished our goal.

A Final Note

Not only is the treatment of political behavior in this book in a sense inadequate, but the political behavior approach is itself in a sense inadequate. No single book, especially an introduction, can provide a truly comprehensive treatment of the systematic, empirical study of politics. Nor can the systematic, empirical study of politics provide a comprehensive answer to all the questions human beings may have about politics. Choosing to search for *some* kinds of knowledge means renouncing the search for *other* kinds of knowledge. Thus, we have, at this point, a partial treatment of an approach which offers partial answers. Such a situation might be viewed as cause for discouragement, but it should not be. In this world there are few cosmic, all-encompassing answers. No single formula, and no single science, is likely to solve all our problems in one simple operation. The world is a complex place and we can hope to unravel its mysteries only slowly and on a piecemeal basis. It is difficult to imagine that the job will ever be completed. Human ingenuity always seems to be able to devise new questions to ask. We suggest that one device that aids in understanding such a world is the study of political behavior. We further suggest that a good way of starting to come to grips with this device is to read this book. It offers no final answers to political behavior problems and political behaviorism offers no cosmic solutions. But in this kind of world, it's a start.

INDEX